Real-Time UML

Second Edition

The Addison-Wesley Object Technology Series

Grady Booch, Ivar Jacobson, and James Rumbaugh, Series Editors

For more information check out the series web site [http://www.awl.com /cseng/otseries/] as well as the pages on each book [http://www.awl.com/cseng/I-S-B-N/] (I-S-B-N represents the actual ISBN, including dashes).

David Bellin and Susan Suchman Simone, *The CRC Card Book*, ISBN 0-201-89535-8

Robert V. Binder, *Testing Object-Oriented Systems: Models, Patterns, and Tools*, ISBN 0-201-80938-9

Bob Blakley, *CORBA Security: An Introduction to Safe Computing with Objects*, ISBN 0-201-32565-9

Grady Booch, *Object Solutions: Managing the Object-Oriented Project*, ISBN 0-8053-0594-7

Grady Booch, *Object-Oriented Analysis and Design with Applications, Second Edition*, ISBN 0-8053-5340-2

Grady Booch, James Rumbaugh, and Ivar Jacobson, *The Unified Modeling Language User Guide*, ISBN 0-201-57168-4

Don Box, *Essential COM*, ISBN 0-201-63446-5

Don Box, Keith Brown, Tim Ewald, and Chris Sells, *Effective COM: 50 Ways to Improve Your COM and MTS-based Applications*, ISBN 0-201-37968-6

Alistair Cockburn, *Surviving Object-Oriented Projects: A Manager's Guide*, ISBN 0-201-49834-0

Dave Collins, *Designing Object-Oriented User Interfaces*, ISBN 0-8053-5350-X

Jim Conallen, *Building Web Applications with UML*, ISBN 0-201-61577-0

Bruce Powel Douglass, *Doing Hard Time: Designing and Implementing Embedded Systems with UML*, ISBN 0-201-49837-5

Bruce Powel Douglass, *Real-Time UML, Second Edition: Developing Efficient Objects for Embedded Systems*, ISBN 0-201-65784-8

Desmond F. D'Souza and Alan Cameron Wills, *Objects, Components, and Frameworks with UML: The Catalysis Approach*, ISBN 0-201-31012-0

Martin Fowler, *Analysis Patterns: Reusable Object Models*, ISBN 0-201-89542-0

Martin Fowler, *Refactoring: Improving the Design of Existing Code*, ISBN 0-201-48567-2

Martin Fowler with Kendall Scott, *UML Distilled, Second Edition: Applying the Standard Object Modeling Language*, ISBN 0-201-65783-X

Peter Heinckiens, *Building Scalable Database Applications: Object-Oriented Design, Architectures, and Implementations*, ISBN 0-201-31013-9

Christine Hofmeister, Robert Nord, Soni Dilip, *Applied Software Architecture*, ISBN 0-201-32571-3

Ivar Jacobson, Grady Booch, and James Rumbaugh, *The Unified Software Development Process*, ISBN 0-201-57169-2

Ivar Jacobson, Magnus Christerson, Patrik Jonsson, and Gunnar Overgaard, *Object-Oriented Software Engineering: A Use Case Driven Approach*, ISBN 0-201-54435-0

Ivar Jacobson, Maria Ericsson, and Agneta Jacobson, *The Object Advantage: Business Process Reengineering with Object Technology*, ISBN 0-201-42289-1

Ivar Jacobson, Martin Griss, and Patrik Jonsson, *Software Reuse: Architecture, Process and Organization for Business Success*, ISBN 0-201-92476-5

David Jordan, *C++ Object Databases: Programming with the ODMG Standard*, ISBN 0-201-63488-0

Philippe Kruchten, *The Rational Unified Process: An Introduction*, ISBN 0-201-60459-0

Wilf LaLonde, *Discovering Smalltalk*, ISBN 0-8053-2720-7

Dean Leffingwell and Don Widrig, *Managing Software Requirements: A Unified Approach*, ISBN 0-201-61593-2

Chris Marshall, *Enterprise Modeling with UML: Designing Successful Software through Business Analysis*, ISBN 0-201-43313-3

Lockheed Martin Advanced Concepts Center and Rational Software Corporation, *Succeeding with the Booch and OMT Methods: A Practical Approach*, ISBN 0-8053-2279-5

Thomas Mowbray and William Ruh, *Inside CORBA: Distributed Object Standards and Applications*, ISBN 0-201-89540-4

Bernd Oestereich, *Developing Software with UML: Object-Oriented Analysis and Design in Practice*, ISBN 0-201-39826-5

Meiler Page-Jones, *Fundamentals of Object-Oriented Design in UML*, ISBN 0-201-69946-X

Ira Pohl, *Object-Oriented Programming Using C++, Second Edition*, ISBN 0-201-89550-1

Rob Pooley and Perdita Stevens, *Using UML: Software Engineering with Objects and Components*, ISBN 0-201-36067-5

Terry Quatrani, *Visual Modeling with Rational Rose 2000 and UML*, ISBN 0-201-69961-3

Brent E. Rector and Chris Sells, *ATL Internals*, ISBN 0-201-69589-8

Paul R. Reed, Jr., *Developing Applications with Visual Basic and UML*, ISBN 0-201-61579-7

Doug Rosenberg with Kendall Scott, *Use Case Driven Object Modeling with UML: A Practical Approach*, ISBN 0-201-43289-7

Walker Royce, *Software Project Management: A Unified Framework*, ISBN 0-201-30958-0

William Ruh, Thomas Herron, and Paul Klinker, *IIOP Complete: Middleware Interoperability and Distributed Object Standards*, ISBN 0-201-37925-2

James Rumbaugh, Ivar Jacobson, and Grady Booch, *The Unified Modeling Language Reference Manual*, ISBN 0-201-30998-X

Geri Schneider and Jason P. Winters, *Applying Use Cases: A Practical Guide*, ISBN 0-201-30981-5

Yen-Ping Shan and Ralph H. Earle, *Enterprise Computing with Objects: From Client/Server Environments to the Internet*, ISBN 0-201-32566-7

David N. Smith, *IBM Smalltalk: The Language*, ISBN 0-8053-0908-X

Daniel Tkach, Walter Fang, and Andrew So, *Visual Modeling Technique: Object Technology Using Visual Programming*, ISBN 0-8053-2574-3

Daniel Tkach and Richard Puttick, *Object Technology in Application Development, Second Edition*, ISBN 0-201-49833-2

Jos Warmer and Anneke Kleppe, *The Object Constraint Language: Precise Modeling with UML*, ISBN 0-201-37940-6

Real-Time UML
Second Edition

Developing Efficient Objects for Embedded Systems

Bruce Powel Douglass

ADDISON–WESLEY

An Imprint of Addison Wesley Longman, Inc.

Reading, Massachusetts • Harlow, England • Menlo Park, California
Berkeley, California • Don Mills, Ontario • Sydney
Bonn • Amsterdam • Tokyo • Mexico City

Many of the designations used by manufacturers and sellers to distinguish their products are claimed as trademarks. Where those desginations appear in this book and Addison Wesley Longman, Inc., was aware of a trademark claim, the designations have been printed in initial capital letters or in all capitals.

The author and publisher have taken care in the preparation of this book, but make no expressed or implied warranty of any kind and assume no responsibility for errors or omissions. No liability is assumed for incidental or consequential damages in connnection with or arising out of the use of the information or programs contained herein.

The publisher offers discounts on this book when ordered in quantity for special sales. For more information, please contact:

AWL Direct Sales
Addison Wesley Longman, Inc.
One Jacob Way
Reading, Massachusetts 01867
(718) 994-3700

Visit AW on the Web: www.awl.com/cseng/

Library of Congress Cataloging-in-Publication Data

Douglass, Bruce Powel.
    Real-time UML : developing efficient objects for embedded systems / Bruce Powel Douglass.—2nd ed.
       p. cm.—(The Addison-Wesley object technology series)
    Includes bibliographical references (p.   ).
    ISBN 0-201-65784-8
     1. Embedded computer systems—Programming.   2. Real-time data processing.
   3. Object-oriented methods (Computer science)   I. Title.   II. Series.

QA76.6.D66   1999
005.1'17 21—dc21   99-044872

Executive Editor: J. Carter Shanklin
Editorial Assistant: Kristin Erickson
Production Manager: John Fuller
Cover Design: Simone R. Payment
Compositor: Stratford Publishing Services, Inc.
Copyeditor: Jill E. Hobbs

ISBN 0-201-65784-8
Text printed on recycled and acid-free paper.
1 2 3 4 5 6 7 8 9 10—MA—0302010099
First printing, October 1999

This book is dedicated to my two boys—Scott Powel Douglass and Blake William Douglass—who, despite their few years, have more to teach me than I have to teach them.

Contents

Figure List

Additional figures appear in Appendix A.

About the Author

Bruce was raised by wolves in the Oregon wilderness. He taught himself to read at age 3 and calculus before age 12. He dropped out of school when he was 14 and traveled around the US for a few years before entering the University of Oregon as a mathematics major. He eventually received his M.S. in exercise physiology from the University of Oregon and his Ph.D. in neurophysiology from the USD Medical School, where he developed a branch of mathematics called autocorrelative factor analysis for studying information processing in multicellular biological neural systems.

Bruce has worked as a software developer in real-time systems for almost 20 years and is a well-known speaker and author in the area of real-time embedded systems. He is on the Advisory Board of the *Embedded Systems* and *UML World* conferences, where he has taught courses in software estimation and scheduling, project management, object-oriented analysis and design, communications protocols, finite state machines, design patterns, and safety-critical systems design. He has developed and taught courses in real-time, object-oriented analysis and design for many years. He has authored articles for a number of journals and periodicals in the real-time domain.

Bruce is currently the Chief Evangelist[1] for i-Logix, a leading producer of tools for real-time systems development, and has worked with Rational and the other UML partners on the specification of the UML.

---

[1] Being a Chief Evangelist is much like being a Chief Scientist, except for the burning bushes.

He is one of the co-chairs of the Object Management Group's Real-Time Analysis and Design Working Group, which is currently examining the UML for possible future real-time extensions. He also consults, trains, and mentors a number of companies building large-scale, real-time, safety-critical systems. He is the author of four other books on software, including *Doing Hard Time: Developing Real-Time Systems with UML, Objects, Frameworks, and Patterns* (Addison-Wesley, 1999) as well as a short textbook on table tennis.

Bruce enjoys classical music and has played classical guitar professionally. He has competed in several sports, including table tennis, bicycle racing, running, and full-contact Tae Kwon Do, although he currently only fights inanimate objects that don't hit back. He and his two sons contemplate epistemology in the frozen north. He can be reached at *bpd@ilogix.com*.

Foreword

Embedded computerized systems are here to stay. Reactive and real-time systems likewise. As this book aptly points out, one can see embedded systems everywhere; there are more computers hidden in the guts of things than there are conventional desktops or laptops.

Wherever there are computers and computerized systems, there has to be software to drive them. And software doesn't grow on trees. People have to write it; people have to understand and analyze it; people have to use it; and people have to maintain and update it for change in future versions. It is this human aspect of programming that calls for modeling complex systems on levels of abstraction that are higher than that of "normal" programming languages. From this also comes the need for methodologies to guide software engineers and programmers in coping with the modeling process itself.

There is broad agreement that one of the things to strive for in devising a high-level modeling approach is good diagrammatics. All other things being equal, pictures are usually better understood than text or symbols. But we are not interested just in pictures or diagrams, since constructing complex software is not an exclusively human activity. We are interested in *languages* of diagrams, and these languages require computerized support for validation and analysis. Just as high-level programming languages require not only editors and version-control utilities, but also—and predominantly!—compilers and debugging tools, so do modeling languages require not only pretty graphics, document generation utilities, and project management aids, but also means for executing models, for synthesizing code, and for true verification.

This means that we need *visual formalisms* that come complete with a syntax to determine what is allowed and semantics to determine what the allowed things mean. Such formalisms should be as visual as possible (obviously, some things do not lend themselves to natural visualization) with the main emphasis placed on topological relationships between diagrammatic entities, and then, as next-best options, also geometry and metrics, and perhaps iconics, too.

Over the years, the main approaches to high-level modeling have been *structured analysis* (SA), and *object orientation* (OO). The two are about a decade apart in initial conception and evolution. SA, started in the late 1970s by DeMarco, Yourdon, and others, is based on "lifting" classical, procedural programming concepts up to the modeling level and doing it graphically. The result calls for modeling system structure by functional decomposition and flow of information, depicted by (hierarchical) data-flow diagrams. As to system behavior, the early and mid-1980s saw several methodology teams (such as Ward/Mellor, Hatley/Pirbhai, and the STATEMATE team from I-Logix) making detailed recommendations that enriched the basic SA model with means for capturing behavior based on state diagrams or the richer language of statecharts. Carefully defined behavioral modeling, we should add, is especially crucial for embedded, reactive, and real-time systems.

OO modeling (often under the name of *OO analysis and design,* or OOAD) started in the late 1980s, and, in a way, its history is very similar. The basic idea for system structure was to "lift" concepts from object-oriented programming up to the modeling level, and to do so graphically. Thus, the basic structural model for objects in Booch's method, in the OMT and ROOM methods, and in many others, deals with classes and instances, relationships and roles, operations and events, and aggregation and inheritance. Visuality is achieved by basing this model on an embellished and enriched form of entity-relationship diagrams. As to system behavior, most OO modeling approaches adopted the statecharts language for this (a decision that the undersigned cannot claim to be too upset about). A statechart is associated with each class, and its role is to describe the behavior of the instance objects. The subtle and complicated connections between structure and behavior—that is, between object models and statecharts—were treated by OO methodologists in a broad spectrum of degrees of detail, from vastly insufficient to adequate. The test, of course, is whether the languages for structure and behavior and their interlinks are defined sufficiently to allow the "interpretation" and "compilation" of high-level models—that is, full model execution and code synthesis, and eventually—and hopefully—also full formal verification against requirements. This was achieved only in a couple of cases, namely, in the ObjecTime tool (based on the ROOM method of Selic, Gullekson, and Ward), and the Rhapsody tool (from i-Logix, based on work of Gery and the undersigned on Executable Object Modeling).

In a remarkable departure from the similarity in evolution between the SA and OO paradigms for system modeling, the last four to five years have seen OO methodologists working together. They have compared notes, debated the issues, and finally cooperated in formulating a general Unified Modeling Language, or UML for short, in the hope of bringing together the best of the various OO modeling approaches. This sweeping effort, which in its teamwork is reminiscent of the Algol60 and Ada efforts, is taking place under the auspices of the Object Management Group, and was led by by Grady Booch (of the Booch method), Jim Rumbaugh (codeveloper of the OMT method), and Ivar Jacobson (czar of use-cases). Version 0.8 of the UML was released in 1996 and was rather open-ended, vague, and not nearly as well-defined as one might have expected. For about a year, the UML team went into overdrive, with a lot of help from methodologists and language designers from various companies, and version 1.0, whose defining documents were released in early 1997, was much tighter and more solid. Since then there have been a number of revisions. In 1997 the UML was adopted as a standard by the Object Management Group (OMG), and with more work there is a good chance that it will become not just an officially approved, if somewhat dryly documented, standard, but the main modeling mechanism of choice for the software that is constructed according to the object-oriented doctrine. And this is no small matter, as more and more software engineers are now claiming that more kinds of software are best developed in an OO fashion.

For capturing system structure, the UML indeed adopts a diagrammatic language for classes and objects that is based on the entity-relationship approach. For early-stage behavioral analysis, it recommends use cases and utilizes sequence diagrams (often called message sequence charts or MSCs), and for the full constructive specification of behavior it adopts statecharts, as modified in the aforementioned executable object modeling work.

Bruce Douglass' book does an excellent job of dishing out engineering wisdom to people who have to construct complex software—especially real-time, embedded, reactive software. Moreover, he does this using UML as the main underlying vehicle, a fact which, given the recent standardization of the UML and its fast-spreading usage, makes the book valuable to anyone whose daily worry is the expeditious and smooth development of such systems.

Moreover, Bruce's book is clear and very well written, and it gives the reader the confidence boost that stems from the fact that the author is not writing from the ivy-clouded heights of an academic institution or the religiously tainted vantage point of a professional methodologist, but that he has extensive experience in engineering the very kinds of systems the book deals with. This stark difference might be termed "the grand duality of system behavior." We are far from having a good algorithmic understanding of this duality. While statecharts seem adequate for the intraobject specification, sequence diagrams can specify use cases pretty well, but they are far too weak to serve the general role of full interobject specification (for example, they cannot specify "anti-scenarios"—ones that are forbidden). There have been recent proposals to extend sequence diagrams so that they can be used to capture more, but the jury is not in on those yet. Also, we are far from having a good algorithmic understanding of the duality between the two modes of modeling. We don't know yet how to effectively derive one view from the other, or even how to efficiently test whether descriptions presented in the two are mutually consistent.

The recent wave of popularity that the UML is enjoying will bring with it a true flood of books, papers, reports, seminars, and tools, describing, utilizing, and elaborating upon the UML, or purporting to do so. Readers will have to be extra careful in finding the really worthy trees in this messy forest. I have no doubt that Bruce's book will remain one of those.

As to the UML itself, one must remember that right now UML is a little *too* massive. We understand well only parts of it; the definition of other parts has yet to be carried out in sufficient depth to make crystal clear their relationships with the constructive core of UML (the class diagrams and the statecharts). For example, use-cases and their associated sequence and collaboration diagrams are invaluable to users and requirements engineers trying to work out the system's desired behavior in terms of scenarios. In the use-case world, we describe a single scenario (or a single cluster of closely related scenarios) for all relevant objects—*inter-object behavior* we might call it. In contrast, a statechart describes all the behavior for a single object—which is *intra-object behavior.*

Other serious challenges remain, for which only the surface has been scratched. Examples include true formal verification of object-oriented software modeled using the high-level means afforded by the UML, automatic eye-pleasing and structure-enhancing layout of UML diagrams, satisfactory ways of dealing with hybrid systems that involve discrete, as well as continuous, parts, and much more.

As a general means for dealing with complex software, object-orientation is also here to stay. Perhaps this is true of the UML too, although my personal feeling is that in the wake of the initial excitement about a standard for modeling software the UML will have to be made smaller and tighter. Otherwise, it will become too cumbersome and multifaceted to be really useful. I think it will gradually shrink, leaving only three or four types of diagrams that are really needed and are useful. The rest will probably become obsolete and will eventually disapper.

OO is a powerful and wise way to think about systems and to program them, and will for a long time to come be part and parcel of the body of knowledge required by any self-respecting software engineer. This book will greatly help in that. On the other hand, OO doesn't solve *all* problems, and by extension neither does UML. There is still much work to be done. In fact, it is probably no great exaggeration to say that there is a lot more that we don't know and can't do yet in this business than what we do and can. Still, what we have is tremendously more than we would have hoped for just a few years ago, and for this we should be thankful and humble.

Professor David Harel
Dean, Faculty of Mathematics and Computer Science
The Weizmann Institute of Science
Rehovot, Israel
July 1999

Preface to the Second Edition

I have been both pleased and gratified by the success of the first edition of *Real-Time UML: Developing Efficient Objects for Embedded Systems.* I think the popularity of the first edition is due to both its timeliness and the appropriateness of object technology (in general) and the UML (in particular) to the development of real-time and embedded systems. At the time of the publication of the first edition, it was clear that the UML would be a major force in the development of object-oriented systems. However, even its strongest supporters have been surprised by the rapidity and near totality of its acceptance by developers. As one methodologist supporting a different modeling approach expressed to me, "I ignored the UML and then got hit with a freight train." The UML is wildly successful in the Darwinian sense of the term, as well in its technical superiority, and has become the most dominant life form in the object ecosphere.

As embedded systems gain in complexity, the old hack-and-ship approaches fail utterly and completely and, occasionally, spectacularly. The complexity of today's systems is driving developers to construct models of the system from different viewpoints in order to understand and plan the various system aspects. These views include the physical, or deployment, view, and the logical, or essential, view. Both views must support structural and behavioral aspects. This is what the UML is about, and this is why it has been so successful.

Audience

The book is oriented toward the practicing professional software developer and the computer science major in the junior or senior year. This book could also serve as an undergraduate- or graduate-level text, but the focus is on practical development rather than a theoretical introduction. Very few equations will be found in this book, but more theoretical and mathematical approaches are referenced where appropriate. The book assumes a reasonable proficiency in at least one programming language and at least a cursory exposure to the fundamental concepts of both object orientation and real-time systems.

Goals

The goals for the first edition remain goals for this edition, as well. This book is still meant to be an easy-to-read introduction to the UML and the application of its notation and semantics to the development of real-time and embedded systems. At the time of this writing, it is one of two books on the UML and real-time systems. I am also the author of the other, *Doing Hard Time: Developing Real-Time Systems with UML, Objects, Frameworks, and Patterns* (Addison-Wesley, 1999). *Doing Hard Time* is a more in-depth look at the fundamentals and vagaries of real-time systems, with emphasis on analysis of object schedulability, the use of behavioral patterns in the construction of statechart models, and how to use real-time frameworks effectively. It is a deeper exploration of real-time systems, which happens to use the UML to express these concepts. In contrast, *Real-Time UML* is primarily about the UML and secondarily about capturing the requirements, structure, and behavior of real-time systems using the UML.

In addition to these original goals for the first edition, the second edition adds two more: (1) to bring the book in conformance with the recent changes in the UML standard, and (2) to enhance the book's effectiveness based on feedback from the first edition.

The UML has undergone a couple of revisions since its original acceptance by the OMG. The first revision, 1.2, is almost exclusively editorial, with no significant modification. The UML revision 1.3, on the other hand, is a significant improvement in a variety of ways. For example, the «uses» stereotype of generalization of use cases has now been replaced with the «includes» stereotype of dependency, which makes a great deal more sense.

Similarly, the notion of an action in UML 1.1 relied heavily on the use of "uninterpreted text" to capture its details. The UML 1.3 has elaborated the metamodel to encompass a number of different kinds of actions, making behavioral modeling more complete. The action semantics metamodel and how it relates to object messaging, is discussed in Chapters 2 and 4.

There have been a number of changes to the statechart model in the 1.3 revision, as well. The first edition of *Real-Time UML* devoted a lot of space to statecharts, and this second edition expends even more effort in the coverage of behavioral modeling with statecharts. Much of this space is used for the new features of statecharts—synch pseudostates, stub states, and so on. This resulted in a significant rewrite of Chapter 4, which deals with object behavioral modeling.

Recent consulting experience in fields ranging from advanced medical imaging to the next generation of intelligent, autonomous spacecraft, in addition to reader feedback from the first edition, is reflected in this second edition. For example, numerous consulting efforts have convinced me that many developers have a great deal of difficulty understanding and applying use cases to capture requirements for real-time and embedded systems. To address this need, I developed a one-day course called *Effective Use Cases*, which I have given at NASA and elsewhere. Principles that have proven their effectiveness in the field are captured here, in Chapter 2. Similarly, the techniques and strategies that have worked well for capturing object models or state behavior, have wound up expressed in this book, as well.

Another change in this book is the elaboration of an effective process for using the UML in product development. I call this process Rapid Object-Oriented Process for Embedded Systems (ROPES). The most common questions I have been asked since publication of the first book have been about the successful deployment of the UML in project teams developing real-time and embedded systems. Thus, Chapter 1 explains this process and identifies the work activities and artifacts produced during different parts of the iterative lifecycle. In fact, the

ROPES process forms the basis for the organization of the book itself, from Chapter 2 through 7.[2]

Despite the goals of the UML in terms of providing a standard, there has been some fractionalization as vendors try to differentiate themselves in the marketplace. While progress will naturally involve vendors providing new and potentially valuable model constructs above and beyond those provided by the UML, several vendors have claimed that their new features will be part of some new yet-to-be-announced UML for Real-Time. Interestingly, some of these vendors don't even participate in the OMG, while others provide mutually incompatible "enhancements." By spreading this FUD (fear, uncertainty, and doubt) among the developer community, I feel these vendors have done a great disservice to their constituency. Developers should understand both the benefits *and* risks of using single-source modeling concepts. These features may make the system easier to model (although, in many cases, these so-called enhancements fail in that regard), but they also lock the product development to a single vendor's tool. Another risk is the inability to use model interchange between tools when the models no longer adhere to the UML standard. This can greatly decrease the benefits to the developer of using the UML. In an effort to dispel some of the FUD, I've added Appendix B to outline what it means to make changes to the standard, why *no* single vendor can claim it owns the UML standard (it is, after all, owned by the OMG), and what changes are likely to be made to the UML over the next several years.

Finally, I would suggest that interested readers visit the I-Logix Web site, *www.ilogix.com.* There you will find a number of papers on related topics, written by myself and others, as well as the UML specifications, tool descriptions, and links to relevant sites.

Bruce Powel Douglass, Ph.D.
Spring, 1999

---

[2] More information on the ROPES process can be had from the I-Logix web site, *www.ilogix.com*, as well in another book, *Doing Hard Time: Developing Real-Time Systems with UML, Objects, Frameworks, and Patterns* (Addison-Wesley, 1999).

Preface to the First Edition

Goals

Real-Time UML: Developing Efficient Objects for Embedded Systems is an introduction to object-oriented analysis and design for hard real-time systems using the Unified Modified Language (UML). UML is a third-generation modeling language that rigorously defines the semantics of the object metamodel and provides a notation for capturing and communicating object structure and behavior. Many methodologists—including Grady Booch (Booch Method), Jim Rumbaugh (Object Modeling Technique [OMT]), Ivar Jacobson (Object-Oriented Software Engineering [OOSE]), and David Harel (Statecharts)—collaborated to achieve UML. Many more participated, myself included, in the specification of the UML, and we believe that it is the leading edge in modeling for complex systems.

There are very few books on the use of objects in real-time systems and even fewer on UML. Virtually all object-oriented books focus primarily on business or database application domains and do not mention real-time aspects at all. On the other hand, texts on real-time systems have largely ignored object-oriented methods. For the most part, they fall into two primary camps: those that bypass methodological considerations altogether and focus solely on "bare metal" programming, and those that are highly theoretical, with little advice for actually implementing workable systems. *Real-Time UML: Developing Efficient Objects for Embedded Systems* is meant to be a concise and timely bridge for these technologies, presenting the development of deployable real-time systems using the object semantics and notation of the

UML. This has many advantages, including focusing the development process of real-time systems into logical, concrete steps that progress in an orderly fashion, with a standardized notation.

Audience

The book is oriented toward the practicing professional software developer and the computer science major in the junior or senior year. This book could also serve as an undergraduate- or graduate-level text, but the focus is on practical development rather than a theoretical introduction. Very few equations will be found in this book, but more theoretical and mathematical approaches are referenced where appropriate. The book assumes a reasonable proficiency in at least one programming language and at least a cursory exposure to the fundamental concepts of both object orientation and real-time systems.

Organization

The book follows the normal analysis → design → implementation approach followed by most development projects. The first chapter identifies the fundamental concepts of objects and real-time systems. The next two discuss analysis—the identification and specification of the problem to be solved. Analysis is divided into two portions: black-box requirements analysis using context diagrams, use cases, and scenarios (Chapter 2), and capturing the key concepts and their relationships from the problem domain (Chapter 3).

Design follows analysis and adds details as to how the analysis model should be implemented. Design is broken up into three parts, each taken up in a separate chapter—architectural, mechanistic, and detailed design. The parts differ in the scope of their concerns. Architectural design deals with very broad scope strategic decisions, such as tasking models and inter-processor design. Mechanistic design focuses on how groups of objects collaborate to achieve common purposes. Both architectural and mechanistic design chapters include a number of patterns that have been found generally applicable in real-time systems. Finally, detailed design specifies the internal structure and function of individual objects.

Throughout the book, UML notation is introduced where and as needed. However, a notational summary is provided in the appendix so that this book can continue to serve as a reference guide as your projects evolve.

Examples

Two different approaches to examples are used in different texts. Some authors (and readers) prefer a single example taken throughout the book to illustrate the various concepts. The other approach is to use many different examples, with the idea that it is more useful to see the concepts used in a wide variety of applications. This book uses a compromise approach. A variety of real-time examples illustrate the concepts and notation of UML in the several real-time application domains, but they reappear in different chapters of the book. This approach reinforces the concepts by showing how they apply in various situations. Special care has been taken to select real-time examples with rich behavioral semantics; however, examples that are not strictly real-time are used where appropriate.

Bruce Powel Douglass, Ph.D.
Summer, 1997

Acknowledgments

I wish to express thanks to my reviewers, who tried hard to keep me honest and on topic, and who, I think, more or less succeeded:

Jack Carter, Senior Consultant/Instructor, ObjectSpace, Inc.
Therese M. Douglass
Doug Locke, Lockheed Martin Corp.
Larry McAlister

I would also like to thank Jerri Pries and Gene Robinson of i-Logix for their support and for allowing me to spend so much effort on this book; Sylvia Pacheco, also of i-Logix, for her input; and the editorial and production teams at Addison-Wesley, including Carter Shanklin, Kristin Erickson, John Fuller, Kathy Glidden at Stratford Publishing Services, and others.

I would like to add a special thanks to Catherine Joy, who assisted me by providing emotional, as well as editorial, support during the development and editing process.

—Bruce Powel Douglass

Chapter 1

Introduction to Real-Time Systems and Objects

Real-time applications vary in size and scope from wristwatches and microwave ovens to factory automation and nuclear power plant control systems. Applying a general development methodology to the development of real-time systems means that it must meet the tight performance and size constraints of small 4-bit and 8-bit controllers, yet scale up to networked arrays of powerful processors coordinating their activities to achieve a common purpose. Object-oriented methodologies are no silver bullet, but they offer significant improvements over traditional structured methodologies for the development of real-time systems.

Real-time systems are ones in which timeliness is essential to correctness. Object-oriented modeling is a natural fit for capturing the various characteristics and requirements of systems that have hard deadlines on performance.

Notation and Concepts Discussed

What is special about real-time systems

Dealing with time

Real-time operating systems

Advantages of objects

Objects and the UML

UML notation

1.1 What Is Special About Real-Time Systems?

If you read the popular computer press, you would come away with the impression that most computers sit on a desktop (or lap) and run Windows. In terms of the number of deployed systems, embedded real-time systems are orders of magnitude more common than their more-visible desktop cousins. A tour of the average affluent American home might find one or even two standard desktop computers, but literally dozens of smart consumer devices, each containing one or more processors. From the washing machine and microwave oven to the telephone, stereo, television, and automobile, embedded computers are everywhere. They help us to toast our muffins and to identify mothers-in-law calling on the phone. Embedded computers are even more prevalent in industry. Trains, switching systems, aircraft, chemical process control, and nuclear power plants all use computers to safely and conveniently improve our productivity and quality of life (not to mention, they also keep a significant number of us gainfully employed).

The software for these embedded computers is more difficult to construct than it is for the desktop. Real-time systems have all the problems of desktop applications plus many more. Non-real-time systems do not concern themselves with timelines, robustness, or safety—at least not to the same extent as real-time systems. Real-time systems often do not have a conventional computer display or keyboard, but lie at the heart of some apparently non-computerized device. The user of these devices may never be aware of the CPU embedded within, making decisions about how and when the system should act. The user is not intimately involved with such a device as a computer *per se*, but rather as an electrical or mechanical appliance that provides services. Such systems must often operate for days or even years, in the most hostile environments, without stopping. The services and controls provided must be autonomous and timely. Frequently, these devices have the potential to do great harm if they fail unsafely.

Real-time systems encompass all devices with performance constraints. *Hard deadlines* are performance requirements that absolutely must be met. A missed deadline constitutes an erroneous computation and a system failure. In these systems, *late* data is *bad* data. *Soft* real-time systems are characterized by time constraints that can be a) missed occasionally, b) missed by small time deviations, or c) occasionally skipped altogether. Another common definition for soft real-time systems is that they are constrained only by average time constraints (examples include online databases and flight reservation systems), although such constraints actually refer to throughput requirements rather than the timeliness of specific actions. In soft real-time systems, *late* data may still be *good* data. The methods presented in this text may be applied to the development of all performance-constrained systems, hard and soft. When we use the term *real-time* alone, we are specifically referring to hard real-time systems. In actuality, most real-time systems are a mixture of hard and soft real-time constraints, together with some requirements that have no timeliness requirements whatsoever. It is common to treat these different aspects separately, although when present, the hard real-time constraints tend to dominate the design.

An *embedded system* contains a computer as part of a larger system; it does not exist primarily to provide standard computing services to a user. A desktop PC is not an embedded system unless it is within a tomographical imaging scanner or some other device. A computerized microwave oven or VCR is an embedded system because it does no "standard computing." In both cases, the embedded computer is part of a larger system that provides some noncomputing feature to the user, such as popping corn or showing Schwarzenegger ripping telephone booths from the floor.[1]

Most real-time systems interact directly with electrical devices and indirectly with mechanical ones. Frequently, custom software, written specifically for the application, must control the device. This is why real-time programmers have the reputation of being "bare-metal code pounders." You cannot buy a standard device driver or Windows VxD

---

[1] (*Commando*, a heart-warming tale if there ever was one).

to talk to custom hardware components. Programming these device drivers requires very low-level manipulation and intimate knowledge of the electrical properties and timing characteristics of the actual devices.

Virtually all real-time systems either monitor or control hardware, or both. Sensors provide information to the system about the state of its external environment. Medical monitoring devices, such as electro-cardiography (ECG) machines, use sensors to monitor patient and machine status. Air speed, engine thrust, attitude, and altitude sensors provide aircraft information for proper execution of flight-control plans. Linear and angular position sensors sense a robot's arm position and adjust it via DC or stepper motors.

Many real-time systems use actuators to control their external environment or guide some external processes. Flight-control computers command engine thrust and wing and tail control surface orientation so that the aircraft follows the intended flight path. Chemical process-control systems control when, what kind, and the amounts of reagents added to mixing vats. Pacemakers make the heart beat at appropriate intervals, with electrical leads attached to the walls inside the (right-side) heart chambers.

Naturally, most systems containing actuators also contain sensors. While there are some open-loop control systems,[2] the majority of control systems use environmental feedback to ensure that the control loop is acting properly.

Standard computing systems react almost entirely to the user and nothing else.[3] Real-time systems, on the other hand, may interact with the user but have more concern for interactions with their sensors and actuators.

One problem that arises with environmental interaction is that the universe has an annoying habit of disregarding our opinions of how and when it ought to behave. External events are frequently not predictable. The system must react to events when they occur rather than

---

[2] An *open loop system* is one in which feedback about the performed action is not used to control the action. A *closed loop system* is one in which the action is monitored and that sensory data is used to modify the action.

[3] It is true that behind the scenes even desktop computers must interface with printers, mice, keyboards, and networks. The point is that they do this only to facilitate the user's whim.

when it might be convenient. To be of value, an ECG monitor must alarm quickly following the cessation of cardiac activity. The system cannot delay alarm processing until later that evening, when the processor load is less. Many hard real-time systems are *reactive* in nature, and their responses to external events must be tightly bounded in time. Control loops, as we shall see later, are very sensitive to time delays. Delayed actuations destabilize control loops.

Most real-time systems do one or a small set of high-level tasks. The actual execution of those high-level tasks requires many simultaneous lower-level activities. This is called *concurrency*. Since single-processor systems can do only one thing at a time, they implement a *scheduling policy* that controls when tasks execute. In multiple-processor systems, true concurrency is achievable because the processors execute asynchronously. Individual processors within such systems schedule many threads pseudoconcurrently (only a single thread may execute at any given time, but the active thread changes according to some scheduling policy), as well.

Embedded systems are usually constructed with the least expensive (and, therefore, less powerful) computers that can meet the functional and performance requirements. Real-time systems ship the hardware along with the software, as part of a complete system package. As many products are extremely cost sensitive, marketing and sales concerns push for using smaller processors and less memory. Providing smaller CPUs with less memory lowers the manufacturing cost. This per-shipped-item cost is called *recurring cost*; it recurs as each device is manufactured. Software has no significant recurring cost—all the costs are bound up in development, maintenance, and support activities, making it appear to be free.[4] This means that choices are most often made to decrease hardware costs while increasing software development costs.

Under UNIX, a developer needing a big array might just allocate space for 1,000,000 floats with little thought of the consequences. If the program doesn't use all that space, who cares? The workstation has dozens of megabytes of RAM and gigabytes of virtual memory in the form of hard disk storage. The embedded-systems developer cannot make these simplifying assumptions. He or she must do more with less, which often results in convoluted algorithms and extensive

---

[4] Unfortunately, many companies opt for decreasing (primarily hardware) recurring costs without considering all the development cost ramifications.

performance optimization. Naturally, this makes the real-time software more complex and expensive to develop and maintain.

Real-time developers often use tools hosted on PCs and workstations but targeted to smaller, less-capable computer platforms. This means they must use cross-compiler tools, which are often more temperamental than the more widely used desktop tools. In addition, the hardware facilities available on the target platform, such as timers, A/D converters, and sensors, cannot be easily simulated on a workstation. The discrepancy between the development and the target environments adds time and effort for the developer wanting to execute and test his or her code. The lack of sophisticated debugging tools on most small targets complicates testing, as well. Small embedded targets often do not even have a display on which to view error and diagnostic messages.

Frequently, the real-time developer must design and write software for hardware that does not yet exist. This creates very real challenges because the developer cannot validate his or her understanding of how the hardware functions. Integration and validation testing become more difficult and lengthy.

Embedded real-time systems must often run continuously for long periods of time. It would be awkward to have to reset your flight-control computer because of a GPF[5] while you're in the air above Newark. The same applies to cardiac pacemakers, which last up to 10 years after implantation. Unmanned space probes must function properly for years on nuclear or solar power supplies. This is different from desktop computers that may be frequently reset. It may be acceptable to reboot your desktop PC when you discover one of those hidden Excel "features," but it is much less acceptable for a life support ventilator or the control avionics of a commercial passenger jet.

Embedded system environments are often computer-hostile. In surgical operating rooms, electrosurgical units create electrical arcs to cauterize incisions. These produce extremely high EMI (electromagnetic interference) and can physically damage unprotected computer electronics. Even if the damage is not permanent, it is possible to corrupt memory storage, degrading performance or inducing a systems failure.

Apart from increased reliability concerns, software is finding its way ever more frequently into safety systems. Medical devices are

---

[5] *General Protection Fault,* a term that was introduced to tens of millions of people with Microsoft's release of Windows 3.1.

perhaps the most obvious safety-related computing devices, but computers control many kinds of vehicles, such as aircraft, spacecraft, trains, and even automobiles. Software controls weapons systems and ensures the safety of nuclear power and chemical plants. There is compelling evidence that the scope of industrial and transportation accidents is increasing [1,2].[6]

For all the reasons mentioned above, developing for real-time software is generally much more difficult than for non-real-time software. The development environments have fewer tools, and the ones that exist are often less capable than those for desktop environments or for Big Iron mainframes. Embedded targets are slower and have less memory, yet must still perform within tight deadlines. These additional concerns translate into more complexity for the developer, which means more time, more effort, and (unless we're careful, indeed) more defects than standard desktop software of the same size.

1.2 Dealing with Time

A critical aspect of real-time systems is how time itself is handled. The design of a real-time system must identify the timing requirements of the system and ensure that the system performance is both correct *and* timely.

Most developers concerned with timeliness of behavior express it in terms of actual execution time relative to a fixed budget, called a *time constraint*. In the most extreme case, the constraint is specified as a deadline, a single time value (specified from the onset of an initiating stimulus) by which the resulting action must complete. The three types of time constraints commonly used are:

Hard   The correctness of response includes a description of timeliness. A late answer is incorrect and constitutes a system failure. A cardiac pacemaker must pace outside specific periods of time following a contraction, or fibrillation (uncoordinated contraction of random myocardial cells, a *bad thing*) can

---

[6] It is not a question of whether safety-critical software developers are paranoid. The real question is, "Are they paranoid enough?"

occur. The time of pacing is an example of a hard real-time requirement. Deadlines are specified as points in time that occur at a fixed interval following an event.

Soft   Soft timeliness requirements are specified as time constraints that may be violated to some degree, without affecting the correctness of the system's behavior. If a single computation is late, for example, it is not usually significant, although consistently late computation can result in system failure. If an airline reservation system takes a few extra seconds, the data remains valid. Throughput may be specified as an average response time or bandwidth or as a bounded mean-lateness.

Firm   Firm deadlines are a combination of both hard and soft timeliness requirements. The computation has a shorter soft requirement and a longer hard requirement. A patient ventilator must mechanically ventilate the patient a certain amount in the long run. A breath could come a few seconds late without affecting patient safety. However, a several-minute delay in the initiation of a breath is unacceptable.

The basic concepts of timeliness in real-time systems are straightforward. Most time requirements come from bounds on the performance of reactive systems. The system must react in a timely way to external events. The reaction may be a simple digital actuation, such as turning on a light, or a complicated control loop that controls dozens of actuators simultaneously. Typically, many subroutines or tasks must execute between the causative event and the resulting system action. External requirements bound the overall performance of the control path. Each processing activity in the control path is assigned a portion of the overall time budget. The sum of the time budgets for any path must be less than or equal to the overall performance constraint.

Because of the ease of analysis with hard deadlines, most timeliness analysis is done assuming hard deadlines and worst-case scenarios. This can lead to over-design of the hardware at potentially much greater recurring cost than if a more-thoughtful analysis is done.

In the design of real-time systems, several time-related concepts must be identified and tracked. An action may be initiated by an external event. Real-time actions identify a concept of *timely*—usually in terms of a deadline specified in terms of a duration following the initiating event. An action that completes prior to that deadline is said to be timely; one completing after that deadline is said to be late. A *schedulable system* is one that is sufficiently timely. A *hard real-time system* is *schedulable* if all deadlines can be guaranteed to be met under all circumstances. Analysis must take into account various properties of actions in order to determine schedulability.

Actions are ultimately initiated by events associated with the reception of messages arising from objects outside the scope of the system. These messages have various *arrival patterns* that govern how the various instances of the messages arrive over time. The two most common classifications of arrival patterns are *periodic* and *aperiodic* (a.k.a. *episodic*). Periodic messages may vary from their defined pattern in a random way. This is known as *jitter.*

There are a number of means by which the arrival of aperiodic messages may be bounded in time. A common measure is the *minimum interarrival time,* the minimum time between subsequent arrivals of message instances. It is also common to model the interarrival time as arising from a stochastic process, with an average interval duration and standard deviation. A *bursty* message arrival pattern indicates that the messages tend to clump together in time (statistically, there is a positive correlation between the arrival of one message and the near arrival of the next).[7]

Knowing the arrival pattern of the messages leading to the execution of system actions is not enough to calculate schedulability, however. It is also important to know how long the action takes to execute. Here, too, several measures are used in practice. It is very common to use a worst-case execution time in the analysis. The advantage of this approach is that it is possible to make very strong statements about absolute schedulability, but it has disadvantages for the analysis of systems in which occasional lateness is either rare or tolerable. In the analysis of so-called *soft real-time systems,* it is more common to use average execution time to determine a statistic that is called *mean lateness.*

Determining a scheduling strategy is crucial for efficient scheduling of real-time systems. Systems no more loaded than 30% have failed because of poorly chosen scheduling policies.[8] Two competing concepts are *importance* and *urgency.* Importance refers to the value to correct

---

[7] Bursty message arrival patterns are characterized by a Poisson distribution, so they do not have a standard deviation but do have an average interarrival time.

[8] Doug Locke, Lockeheed Martin chief scientist for systems solutions, private communication.

system performance of the completion of a specific action. Certainly, correctly adjusting the control surface in a timely manner is of greater importance than providing flicker-free video display of a cabin VCR display. Urgency of an action refers to the nearness of its deadline. It is possible to have highly important, yet not urgent, actions and highly urgent, but not important, ones mixed freely within a system. Most scheduling executives, however, provide only a single means for scheduling actions—priority. Priority is an implementation-level solution offered to manage both importance and urgency.

Complicating the analysis of schedulability is the fact that many actions are not truly independent. If actions share a resource, one action may be blocked until another completes. The execution times used in the analysis must take into account the blocking time—that is, the length of time an action of a specific priority is blocked from completion by a lower-priority action that owns a required resource.

Actions may be concurrent. Due to the complexity of systems, objects executing actions must send messages to communicate with objects executing other actions. In object terminology, a *message* is an abstraction of the communication between two objects. This may be realized in a variety of ways. *Synchronization patterns* describe how different concurrent actions rendezvous and exchange messages. It is common to identify the following means for synchronizing an action initiated by a message sent between objects.

Synchronous call	Indicates that the caller blocks and waits for the completion of the execution of the action.
Function call	A type of synchronous call in which the called action executes in the same stack frame as the caller.
Blocking call	A type of synchronous call in which the called action executes in a different stack frame or thread as the caller (example: remote procedure call).
Asynchronous call	Indicates that the caller does not wait for the completion of the action.
Balking rendezvous	Indicates that the caller aborts the attempt to send the *Message* if the receiver object cannot immediately accept the *Message*.
Timed wait rendezvous	Indicates that the caller waits for the receiver object to accept the *Message,* but only for a specified duration.

After that duration elapses, the caller aborts the attempt to send the *Message*.

Detailed treatment of these concerns is beyond the scope of this book. The interested reader is referred to [5] for a more-detailed discussion of timeliness and schedulability analysis.

1.3 Model-Based Development

The current state-of-the-art in software development process relies on a small number of important principles.

- Iterative Development
  Targeting development toward the early reduction of risk by "drilling down" both to expose the risk and to mitigate it. To be effective, the rapid prototypes must be production-quality software; be small, focused pieces of the overall application; and address identified or perceived risks.

- Model-Based Development
  Large, complex systems can't be effectively constructed using only source-code-level constructs. Abstract models permit the developers to capture the important characteristics of the application and the ways they interrelate independent from low-level implementation concerns.

- Model-Code Bidirectional Associativity
  For model-based systems, it is absolutely crucial that the code and the diagrams are different views of the same underlying model. If the code is allowed to deviate from the design model, the separate maintenance of the code and model becomes burdensome, and the system eventually becomes totally code-based. As a result, system complexity can no longer be effectively managed.

- Executable Models
  You can test only things that execute, so build primarily executable things, both *early* and *often*. The key to this is model-based translation of designs so that transforming a design into something that executes takes on the order of seconds to minutes, not weeks to months using traditional hand-implementation approaches.

- Debug and Test the Design Level of Abstraction
  Because today's applications are extremely complex, we use abstract design models to help us understand and create them. We also need to debug and test them at the same level. We need to be able to ask, "Should I put the control rod into the reactor core?" rather than merely, "Should I be jumping on C or NZ?"

- Test What You Fly and Fly What You Test
  Simulation has its place, but the purpose of building and testing executable models is to quickly develop defect-free applications that meet all their functional and performance requirements. Using appropriate technology, you can get all the benefits of rapid iterative development and deployment, model-level debugging, and executable models using generated production-level software so that the *testing needs to be done only once.*

Using these six principles, even the most demanding and complex real-time and embedded system can be effectively developed. Most development methodologies in practice today utilize these principles—some more effectively than others, mind you—and the approach I recommend is no different. Using the UML to achieve these goals for development projects, I developed the ROPES methodology. ROPES stands for Rapid Object-Oriented Process for Embedded Systems.

1.3.1 Development Activities of the ROPES Process

Several major activities are used in the ROPES process.

- Analysis
  Analysis defines the essential application properties that must be true of all possible, acceptable solutions, leaving all other characteristics free to vary. Analysis consists of three parts:

- Requirements Analysis
  Requirements analysis identifies in detail the black-box[9] requirements, both functional and performance, of the system, without revealing the internal structure (design).

---

[9] By black-box, I mean that the requirements are visible to objects interacting with the system but do not require knowledge of the system's internal structure.

- System Analysis

  Systems analysis focuses on three activities: determining the optimal breakdown between hardware and software; creating a high-level system architecture; refinement and characterization of complex control algorithims. Systems analysis is usually only performed on large or very complex systems. It is common for small or relatively simple systems to skip this step of analysis.

- Object Analysis

  Object analysis consists of two subphases—object structural analysis and object behavioral analysis:

  - Object Structural Analysis

    Object structural analysis identifies the key abstractions of the application that are required for correctness, as well as the relation that links them together. The black-box functional pieces are realized by collaborations of objects working together.

  - Object Behavioral Analysis

    Object behavioral analysis identifies how the key abstractions behave in response to environmental and internal stimuli, and how they dynamically collaborate to achieve system-level functionality.

- Design

  Design defines a particular solution that optimizes the application in accordance with the project objectives while remaining consistent with the analysis model. Design is *always* about optimization. Design also consists of three parts:

  - Architectural Design

    Architectural design identifies the strategic design decisions that affect most or all of the application, including the mapping to the physical deployment model, the identification of run-time artifacts, and the concurrency model.

  - Mechanistic Design

    Mechanistic design adds to the collaborations to optimize their behavior according to some system optimization criteria.

  - Detailed Design

    Detailed design adds low-level information necessary to optimize the final system.

- Translation
  Translation creates an executable application from a design model. Translation usually includes not only the development of executable code, but also the unit-level (that is, individual object) testing of that translation.

- Testing
  Testing applies correctness criteria against the executable application to either identify defects or to show a minimal level of acceptability. Testing includes, at minimum, integration and validation testing.

These activities may be arranged in many ways. Such an arrangement defines the *development process* used for the project. The iterative development process looks like Figure 1-1.

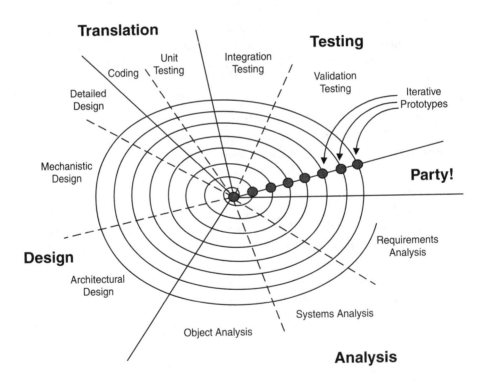

Figure 1-1: *Iterative Rapid Development Process*

The iterative development process model shown in Figure 1-1 is known as ROPES, for *Rapid Object-Oriented Process for Embedded Systems* (see [5] for a more-complete description). Each iteration produces work products, known as *artifacts.* A single iteration pass, along with the generated artifacts, is shown in Figure 1-2. This model is somewhat simplified in that it doesn't show the subphases of analysis and design, but it does capture the important project artifacts and how they are created and used.

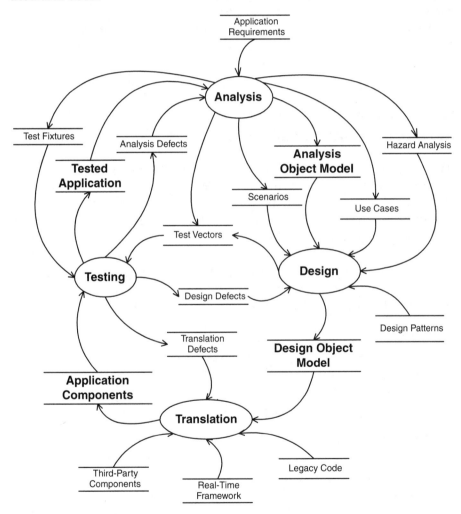

Figure 1-2: *ROPES Process Artifacts*

Rhapsody is an advanced model-creation tool with integrated, product-quality code generation and design-level testing capabilities built in. Rhapsody was developed specifically to aid in the development of real-time and embedded systems and integrates smoothly into the ROPES process model. Fully constructive tools, such as Rhapsody from I-Logix,[10] assist by providing support for all the precepts mentioned at the beginning of this section. Although the UML, in general, and the ROPES process, in particular, can be applied using manual means for translation of models into code and debugging and testing that code, the use of such powerful automated tools greatly enhances their effectiveness. Table 1-1 shows how a fully constructive tool can aid in the generation of development-phase artifacts.

1.4 Advantages of Objects

The previous section was all about the hard luck story that is our profession, developing real-time embedded systems. The good news is that although these issues will never go away, advances in the technology of representing and developing complex systems make them more tractable. It is just as Fred Brooks said, "There is no 'silver bullet' that will magically make software easier," but we can make incremental improvements in the way we think about systems and the way we develop them. This new technology is called object-oriented development, and it has been around for almost two decades now.

The primary advantages are:

- Consistency of model views
- Improved problem-domain abstraction
- Improved stability in the presence of changes
- Improved model facilities for reuse
- Improved scalability
- Better support for reliability and safety concerns
- Inherent support for concurrency

---

[10] See *www.ilogix.com* for more information about the Rhapsody tool. Several white papers on the development of real-time systems are also available on the I-Logix Web site.

Table 1-1: *Phased Artifacts in the ROPES Process*

Activity	Process Step	Generated Artifacts	Tool-Generated Artifacts
Analysis	Requirements analysis	Use case model Use case scenarios	Use case diagrams Use case descriptions Message sequence diagrams Report generation
	Systems analysis	Initial high-level Architectural model Refined control algorithms	Class diagrams represent the subsystem model Deployment diagrams Component diagrams Statecharts Activity diagrams
	Object structural analysis	Structural object model	Class diagrams Object diagrams Reverse engineering creates models from legacy source code Report generation
	Object behavioral analysis	Behavioral object model	Message sequence diagrams Statecharts Report generation
Design	Architectural design	Concurrency model Deployment model	Active objects Orthogonal and-states Component model (file mapping) Framework provides OS-tasking model Use of existing legacy code and components
	Mechanistic design	Collaboration model	Class diagrams Message sequence diagrams Framework provides design patterns Framework provides state execution model

(continued)

Table 1-1: (*cont.*)

		Detailed design	Class details	Browser access to: • Attributes • Operations • User-defined types • Package-wide members Round-trip engineering updates model from modified source code
Translation			Executable application	Fully executable code generated from structural and behavioral models, including: • Object and class diagrams • Sequence diagrams • Statecharts

Testing	Unit testing
	Integration testing
	Validation testing
			Design defects
			Analysis defects
				Design-level debugging and testing on etiher host or remote target, including:
				• Animate multithreaded applications
				• Animated sequence diagrams
				• Animated statecharts
				• Animated attributes in browser
				• Breakpoints on:
				  • operation execution
				  • state entry or exit
				  • transition
				• Event insertion
				• Execution control scripts
				Simultaneous debugging with other design-level tools (such as Rhapsody from I-Logix) and source-level debuggers

The net result is that the object way is *better.* It's not dramatically better in the sense that software will suddenly become easy, but it's better because it enables us to build more-complex systems in less time, with fewer defects. In the coming chapters, it will be clear how developers can realize these benefits.

1.5 Object Orientation with UML

The Unified Modeling Language, or UML, is a language for expressing the constructs and relationships of complex systems. It was begun as a response to the OMG's Request for Proposal (RFP) for a standard object-oriented methodology. Spearheaded by Rational's Grady Booch, Jim Rumbaugh, and Ivar Jacobson, it was submitted to the OMG jointly by some of the major software companies in the world, including I-Logix, Digital, HP, ICON Computing, Microsoft, MCI Systemhouse, Oracle, Texas Instruments, and Unisys. Contributions have been made by many of the top object modelers, such as David Harel, Peter Coad, Jim Odell, and many others. The OMG accepted it as a standard in November 1997. As with all standards adopted by the OMG, work has continued (and continues even now) in the form of a revision task force (RTF) to correct defects and minor omissions in the standard. When the 1.4 version of the UML is completed (expected in 2000), there may be additional RFPs for a 2.x version, although that will probably not occur for a few years. Meanwhile, there are some RFPs scheduled to correct perceived omissions from the standard. The RFPs that are relevant to the real-time and embedded development communities are discussed in Appendix B.

UML is more complete than other methods in its support for modeling complex systems and is particularly suited for including real-time embedded systems. Its major features include:

- Object model
- Use cases and scenarios
- Behavioral modeling with statecharts
- Packaging of various kinds of entities
- Representation of tasking and task synchronization
- Models of physical topology

- Models of source code organization
- Support for object-oriented patterns

Through the course of this book, these features will be described in more detail and their use shown by examples. For now, let's explore the fundamental aspects of the UML object model.

1.5.1 Objects

Structured methods look at a system as a collection of functions decomposed into more-primitive functions. Data is secondary in the structured view, and concurrency isn't dealt with at all. The object perspective is different in that the fundamental decompositional unit is the *object*. So what is an object?

The short form: An object is a cohesive entity that has attributes, behavior, and (optionally) state.

The long form: Objects represent things that have both data and behavior. Objects may represent real-world things, such as airfoil control surfaces, sensors, and engines. They may represent purely conceptual entities, such as bank accounts, trademarks, marriages, and lists. They can·be visual things, such as fonts, letters, ideographs, histograms, polygons, lines, and circles. All these things have various aspects, such as:

- Attributes (data)
- Behavior (operations or methods)
- State (memory)
- Identity
- Responsibilities

For example, a real-world thing might be a sensor, as in Table 1-2, that can detect and report both a linear value and its rate of change.

The sensor object contains two attributes; the monitored sensor value and its computed rate of change (RoC). The behaviors support data acquisition and reporting. They also permit configuration of the sensor. The object state consists of the last acquired/computed values. The identity specifies exactly which object instance is under discussion. The responsibility of the sensor is defined to be how it contributes to the overall system functionality. Its attributes and behaviors must collaborate to help the object achieve its responsibilities.

An airline flight is a conceptual entity, but is nonetheless an important object (see Table 1-3).

Certain of these characteristics (that is, attributes, behaviors, or state) may be more important for some objects than for others. One could envision a sensor class that had no state—whenever you asked it for information, it sampled the data and returned it rather than store it internally. An array of numbers is an object that may have interesting information but no really interesting behaviors.

The key idea of objects is that they combine these properties into a single cohesive entity. The structured approach to software design deals with data and functions as totally separate entities. Data flow diagrams show both data flow and data processes. Data can be decomposed if necessary. Independently, structure charts show the static call

Table 1-2: *Sensor Object*

Attributes	Behavior	State	Identity	Responsibility
• Linear value • Rate of change (RoC)	• Acquire • Report • Reset • Zero • Enable • Disable	• Last value • Last RoC	• Instance for robot-arm joint	• Provide information for the precise location of the end of the robot arm with respect to some reference coordinate frame

Table 1-3: *Airline Flight Object*

Attributes	Behavior	State	Identity	Responsibility
• Flight number • Departure time • Arrival time • Flight plan	• Depart • Arrive • Adjust course	• Current location (x,y,z,t)	• Today's flight NW394 to Minneapolis	• Transfer luggage and passengers to destination • File flight plan • Adhere to flight plan

tree to decompose functions (somewhat loosely related to the data processes). Objects fuse related data and functions together. The *object* is the fundamental unit of decomposition in object-oriented programming (see Figure 1-3).

Abstraction is the process of identifying the key aspects of the entity

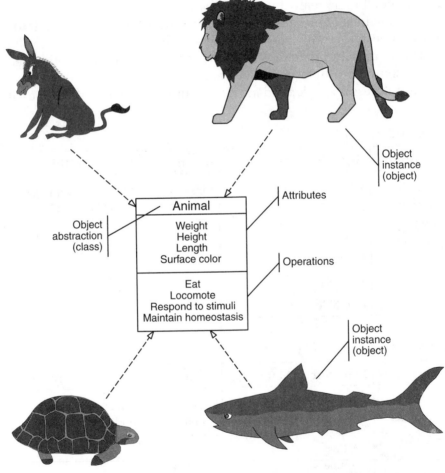

Abstraction uses inductive logic to identify
common characteristics from looking at
many examples

Figure 1-3: *Object Abstraction*

and ignoring the rest. A chair is an abstraction defined as "a piece of furniture with at least one leg, a back, and a flat surface for sitting." That some chairs are made of wood while others may be plastic or metal is inessential to the abstraction of "chair." When we abstract objects, we select only those aspects that are important relative to our point of view. For example, as a runner, my abstraction of dogs is as "high-speed, teeth-delivery systems." The fact that they may have a pancreas or a tail is immaterial to my modeling domain.

The object metaphor is powerful for a couple of reasons. First and foremost, it aligns well with common daily experience. In the "real world," we deal with objects all the time, and each one has all the properties we've assigned to objects above. Rocks may not have interesting behavior, but they do have attributes, such as color, weight, and size. They certainly have responsibilities, such as intimidating hungry pit bulls. Most objects have behavior, as well. Engines turn on or off, deliver torque, guzzle gas, and require maintenance. Object-oriented decomposition allows us to use the hard-won intuition that we've gained by simply living in the world and interacting with it. This is not true of functional decomposition.

In their simplest expression, objects are nothing more than abstract data types (ADTs) bound together with related operators. This is a low-level perspective and doesn't capture all the richness available in the object paradigm. Software developers use such ADTs and operators as low-level mechanisms all the time. Stacks, queues, trees, and all the other basic data structures are nothing more than objects, with specific operations defined. Consider the common ADTs in Table 1-4.

At a low-level of abstraction, these are merely objects that provide these operations intrinsically, rather than ADTs with separate functions to provide the services. Although it may not look like much of an improvement, these ADT objects bind together the data they contain and their associated operations. Because the concept of a stack is meaningless without both the operations and the data, it makes most sense to bind these things tightly together—they are different aspects of a single concept. This is called *strong cohesion,* or the appropriate binding together of inherently tightly coupled properties.

An important advantage of this approach is that it is now possible to bind the pre- and post-conditional invariants (conditions that must be true prior to and following the execution of a behavior) to the data. Think of how you use an array in C, for example.

Table 1-4: *Common ADTs*

Data Structure	Operations
Stack	Push
	Pop
	Full
	Empty
Queue	Insert
	Remove
	Full
	Empty
Linked list	Insert
	Remove
	Next
	Previous
Tree	Insert
	Remove
	Next
	Previous

In C, an array that holds *n* elements has valid indicies between *0* and *n-1*. One of the preconditions for the proper use of the array is that the client index (let's say *j*) is inside that range. The normal C idiom for ensuring this is so is that the client function checks it. This tightly (and pathologically) couples the client of the array with the implementation of the array, since the client *must know* the size of the array. If the array changes, all clients, and potential clients, must be notified. And, of course, all too often, the client does not even bother to check, leading to "interesting" behavior.

In an object-oriented language, such as C++, the array can be subsumed within a class. The class itself can check the preconditions and raise an exception signal should the precondition be violated. This frees the client from even having to know that a linear array is being used while it nevertheless ensures that the preconditions are observed.

System-level capabilities are, as we shall explore later, called *use cases*. Objects are a small unit of decomposition, and only rarely do single objects do anything interesting at the system level. Usually, collaborations of objects work together to realize a use case (see Chapter 2 for more about use cases). Object collaboration is mediated through the sending of messages among objects participating in the collaboration.

Rather than depict one object calling a service of another, the general model is that one object sends a message to the other requesting a service or operation (see Figure 1-4). Messages may be implemented in many ways to achieve different effects. At the modeling stage, message implementation is not an essential detail, therefore, it should not be visible.

1.5.2 Attributes

Attributes, in OO-speak, refer to the data encapsulated within an object. It might be the balance of a bank account, the current picture number in an electronic camera, the color of a font, or the owner of a trademark. Some objects may have just one or a small number of simple attributes. Others may be quite rich. In some object-oriented languages, all instances of data types are objects, from the smallest integer type to the most complex aggregate. In C++, in deference to minimizing the difference between C and C++, variables of the elementary data types, such as *int* and *float,* are not really objects. Programmers may treat them as if they were objects[11] but C++ does not require it.

1.5.3 Behavior

Interesting objects do interesting things. Passive objects supply behaviors for other objects—that is, they provide services that other objects may request. ADTs are typically passive objects. For example, stack objects provide storage for simple data values, provide the means for inserting and removing them from storage, and provide some simple error checking to ensure their integrity. Active objects form the roots for threads and invoke the services (behaviors) of the passive objects.

---

[11] Well, almost, anyway—but that's a programming, rather than a modeling, issue.

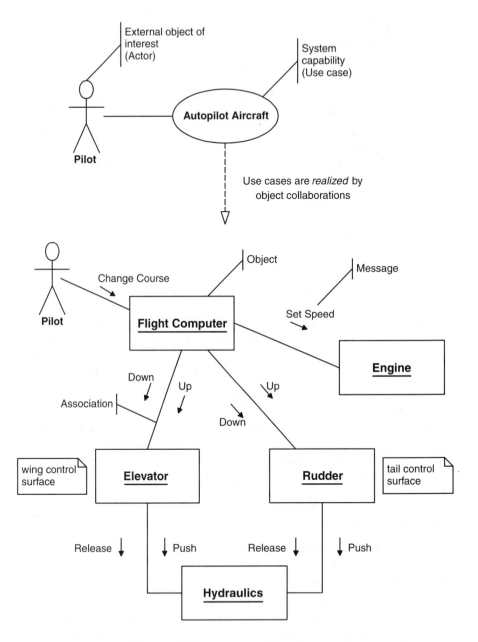

Figure 1-4: *Objects Collaborate to Achieve System Functionality*

The low-level unit of behavior of an object is an operation. In the UML, an *operation* is a specification of a behavior. The actual implementation of an operation is called a *method*. Objects can add constraints on how and under what conditions operations may be invoked. These constraints, along with the primitive behaviors they constrain, are called the *behavioral model* of the object.

Logically, behavior can be modeled as three distinct types: simple, automaton, and continuous. All three are important, although the second has a particular importance in real-time systems.

The most basic kind of behavior is called *simple*. The object performs services on request and keeps no memory of previous services. Each action is atomic and complete, at least from an external perspective. A simple object may maintain a collection of primitive data types and operations defined on them. A binary tree object, for instance, shows simple behavior. Another example is a $\cos(x)$ function. $\cos(\pi/2)$ always returns the same value, regardless of what value it was invoked with before. It retains no memory of previous invocations. This kind of object is also called *primitive*, because it adds no additional constraints on the use of its operations.

The second type of object behavior treats the object as a particular type of machine, which is called a finite state automaton or finite state machine (FSM). This kind of object possesses a bounded (*finite*) set of conditions of existence (*states*). It must be in one, and only one, state at a time. An automaton exhibits modal behavior—each mode constitutes a state. A state is defined as a mutually exclusive condition of existence defined by the set of events it processes and the actions it performs. Because objects with state machines react to events in well-defined ways, they are also called *reactive objects*.

Incoming events can induce transitions among object states in some predefined manner. A sample-and-hold A/D converter is such an object (see Figure 1-5). It shows the states of

- Enabled
- Sampling
- Holding
- Disabled

The third kind of object behavior is continuous. An object with continuous behavior is one with an infinite, or at least unbounded, set of

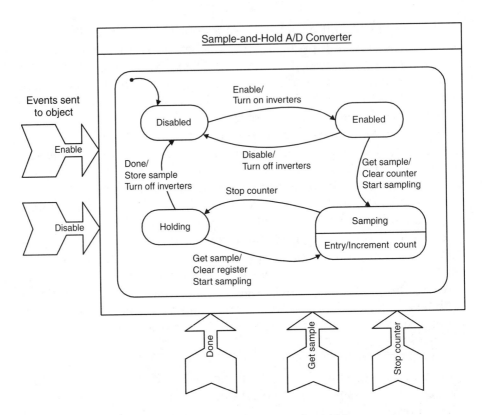

Figure 1-5: *State Machine for an Object*

existence conditions. One example is an *algorithmic object*. This is an object that executes some algorithm on a possibly infinite data stream. A moving-average algorithm performs a smoothing function over an incoming data stream. Objects with continuous behavior are objects whose current behavior is dependent on past behavior and inputs, but the dependency is of a continuous, rather than discrete, nature. Fuzzy systems, PID control loops, and digital filters are examples of continuous systems. Their current behavior depends on past history but in a quantitative, not qualitative, way.

The UML is a discrete modeling language and strongly emphasizes state behavior. To underscore their importance in the UML, state machines are the focus of the discussion in Chapter 4. See [5] for a more complete discussion of the integration of continuous models with the UML.

1.5.4 Messaging

The logical interface between objects is done with the passing of *messages*. A message is an abstraction of data and/or control information passed from one object to another. Different implementations are possible. For example:

- A function call
- Mail via a real-time operating system (RTOS)
- An event via an RTOS
- An interrupt
- A semaphore-protected shared resource
- An Ada rendezvous
- A remote procedure call (RPC) in a distributed system

Early analysis identifies the key messages. Later design elaborates an implementation strategy that defines the synchronization and timing requirements for each message. Internally, the object translates the messages into acceptor operations, state transitions, commands, or data to munch on, as appropriate. Messages occur only between object pairs that share an association (see Figure 1-6).

Use of message passing enforces loose coupling. In analysis, one does not specify interface details, such as synchronicity, function call format, rendezvous, time outs, and so forth. These are design and implementation details that can be decided later, once the overall problem is better understood.

An object's interface is the facade it presents to the world and is defined by the set of protocols within which the object participates. An interface protocol consists of three things:

1. Preconditions
2. Signature
3. Postconditions

The preconditions are the conditions guaranteed to be true before the message is sent or received. Preconditions are generally the responsibility of the object sending the message. Postconditions are the things guaranteed to be true by the time the message is processed and are the responsibility of the receiver of the message. The message signature is the exact mechanism used for message transfer. This can be a function

Figure 1-6: *Sending a Message to an Object*

call with the parameters and return type, RTOS message post/pend pair, or bus message protocol.

The interface should reflect the essential characteristics of the object that require visibility to other objects and should hide inessential details and enforce strong encapsulation. In C++, for example, common practice is to hide data members, but to publish the operations that manipulate the data.

1.5.5 Concurrency

Unlike subroutines in structure charts, objects are inherently concurrent (with respect to other objects) unless otherwise specified. It is theoretically possible for each object to run on its own processor. It is the physical structure of modern computers that drives sequential threads.

A thread is a set of actions executed in sequence. Concurrent threads can run on separate processors, meaning that the relative speeds with which they progress are uncoupled. On the same processor, we must rely on pseudo-concurrency provided by the underlying operating system or write our own executive. These concurrency mechanisms allow the threads to progress more or less independently.

In any system in which timeliness is a principal concern, the concurrency model is crucial. Through proper identification of the threads, mapping the identified objects to those threads, and selection of scheduling policies and properties, the timeliness constraints of the system are realized. As we will see later in Chapter 5, these are key architectural design decisions, but they are almost always done after the primary objects have been characterized in analysis.

1.5.6 Classes

In the object-oriented world, the term *class* is used in precisely the same way as in philosophy. A class is an abstraction of the common properties from a set containing many similar objects.

A class can be thought of as the type of an object.[12] The values 0, −3, and 7879 are all instances (objects) of the class integer. Further, all instances of a class have all the properties defined by the class. A mammal has fur, bears its young live, and is homeothermic. This is true of all members of the class mammals—cats, mice, bears, and even rock stars. This does not mean that instances of the class are all the same—cats are certainly different from rock stars—but they share at least some set of common properties.[13] The values of these properties may be different

---

[12] Strictly speaking, the type refers to the interface of the object—objects with the same interface are of the same type, regardless of their class. The class of an object defines its internal implementation. This is not usually a useful distinction, unless you are using languages that make the difference visible, such as Java.

[13] Most notably: fur, indifference to the needs of others, and a universal inability to sing.

among instances, but all properties must be present. For example, a bank checking account class may define a balance attribute—that is, all checking accounts have balances. Some checking accounts may have positive values while others hover around zero or even dip into negative numbers.

Object-oriented designers uncover classes much the same way as philosophers—by observing a number of objects and abstracting the common properties.[14] Some example classes are shown in Table 1-5.

In each of these cases, it is possible to imagine specific object instances of these classes. Just as a *struct* in C defines data structure, a class defines the type of objects created in its likeness (Figure 1-7).

Figure 1-7: *Classes and Objects*

---

[14] See Chapter 3 for a description of several object-discovery strategies.

Table 1-5: *Class Examples*

Class	Attributes	Behaviors	Example objects	Responsibilities
Bank account	Account type Account number Balance	Open Close Credit Debit	Sam's checking acct. Julie's savings acct.	Maintain updated balance to account for credits, debits, and interest. Also maintain an account history.
Elevator	Capacity Current floor Current direction	Go to floor Stop Open door Close door	Elevator 1, Blg 6 Elevator 3, Blg 1	Carry passengers to their desired floor
Marriage	Wedding date Number of children Children	Wed Divorce Create children	Cindy's first marriage	Maintain stable social group
Airline flight	Flight number Date Point of origin Destination Departure time	Take off Land Lose luggage	My flight to Jamaica	Carry passengers and luggage to destination safely
ECG Signal	Heart rate PVC count ST segment height Display rate scale factor	Get heart rate Set alarm limits. Display waveform	George's ECG signal	Monitor and report status of patient's cardiac function to the attending physician; alarm for possibly dangerous conditions

A class defines the attributes and behaviors of the objects it instantiates,[15] but not their responsibilities. All properties of objects of a class

---

[15] The term *instantiation* comes from the term *instance,* as in *making an instance* (that is, object) of a class.

are the same in *type,* but not in *value.* That is, if a class has an attribute, such as color or charm, then instances of the class have the characteristic, although their particular value of the attribute may differ. Responsibilities, however, are context-specific. They are determined by the use of the object within that context. A simple container object may hold checking accounts and be responsible for coordinating access to these accounts. A container object of the same class may hold inventory records and coordinate access for an inventory control system. The responsibilities are similar in type but differ in the specifics. An object's class defines the responsibilities of an object only when all such objects are used in the same context and in the same way.

UML classes are shown using rectangles with the name of the class inside the rectangle. A variation uses a three-segment box; the top segment has the name of the class, the middle segment contains a list of attributes, and the bottom segment contains a list of operations. Not all the attributes or operations need to be listed. Figure 1-8 shows a simple autopilot system consisting of an *autopilot* class and the various sensor and actuator classes it uses.

1.5.7 Relations Among Classes and Objects

As mentioned previously, objects collaborate and exchange messages to achieve system-level capabilities. For one object to send messages to another, they must relate with each other in some way. In UML, relationships exist among classes. Five elementary types of object relationships exist: *association, aggregation, composition, generalization,* and *dependency.*

Associations are relationships that typically manifest themselves at run-time to permit the exchange of messages among objects. Associations are shown using simple lines connecting two objects.[16] Unless otherwise specified, UML associations are bidirectional and support messaging in either direction. When it is clear that messages go only in one direction, an open arrowhead points to the receiving object.

Aggregation associations are shown with diamonds at the owner end of the relationship. Aggregation is used when one object logically or physically contains another. *Composition* is a strong form of aggregation in which the owner is explicitly responsible for the creation and destruction

---

[16] Almost all associations are binary—that is, between pairs of classes. However, tertiary and higher-order associations sometimes occur.

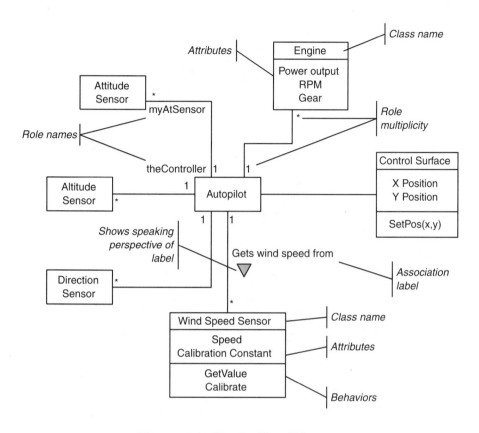

Figure 1-8: *Simple Class Diagram*

of the part objects. The directed lines with closed arrowheads indicate a *generalization* or *is-a-kind-of* relationship. Dependency is shown with an open arrowhead and a dashed line. Dependency relationships support generic or template elaborations of incomplete class specifications.

The numbers at each end of the relationship line denote the number of objects that participate in the relationship at each end. This is called the *multiplicity* of the role. We see in Figure 1-9 that one window object can have 0, 1, or 2 scroll bars. Because the window can have no scroll bars, this is an *optional* relationship. The scroll bar, for its side, works with only a single window, so the number at the window side of the relationship is 1. If multiple windows shared a scroll bar, then the cardinality would be "*" (an indicator for "unspecified but greater than or

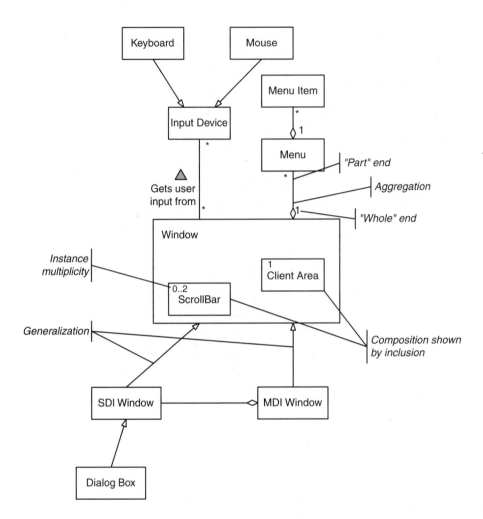

Figure 1-9: *Window Class Relationships*

equal to 0") or the fixed number, if known. Figure 1-10 shows a more real-time example, a sensor.

1.5.7.1 Association

When one object uses the services of another but does not own it, the objects have an association. *Associations* are appropriate when any of the following is true:

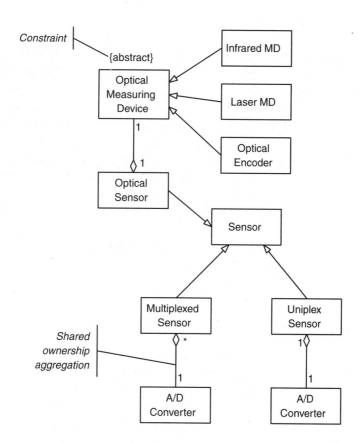

Figure 1-10: *Sensor Class Relationships*

- One object uses the services of another but is not an aggregate of it.
- The lifecycle of the used class is not the responsibility of the user class—that is, it is not responsible for the used object's creation or destruction.
- The association between objects is "looser" than one of aggregation.
- The association can be characterized as client-server.
- The used object is shared and used equally by many others.

The class diagrams show that a Window class *uses* (specifically, "gets user input from") various input devices. The two types shown are a mouse and a keyboard, but other devices are conceivable, including tablets, microphones, and even a modem for a remote session.

1.5.7.2 Aggregation

An aggregation relationship applies when one object physically or conceptually contains another. The larger class is referred to as the *owner*, or *whole*, and it contains the diamond end of the aggregation. The smaller class is the *owned*, *part*, or *component class*. The owner is typically responsible for the creation and destruction of the owned class. UML allows components of aggregates to be shared among owners. When an object has shared ownership, some application-specific rule must specify who has responsibility for its creation and destruction.

In Windows programming, a *window* is a kind of object that contains a *client area.* The client area cannot stand on its own, without being contained by a window. The client area comes into existence during the creation of the window and is destroyed when the window is destroyed. In the *Sensor* class shown, a *Pressure Sensor* class can optionally have an A/D converter.

1.5.7.3 Composition

Composition is a strong form of aggregation. Components are usually shown by actual inclusion of the component class within the composite. Alternatively, an aggregation association can be used, but with a filled diamond. Components of composites cannot be shared (that is, they can have only one owner) and the composite is required to create and destroy its components. A common use of composites is as active objects—that is, objects that are the roots of threads. These active objects create one or more threads in which they and their component parts execute. The composite receives messages and events from the RTOS and other threads and dispatches them to the appropriate components within its own thread(s).

1.5.7.4 Generalization

When one class is a specialization of another, the relationship is called *generalization.* It means that the child or descendant class is a specialized form of a more general class. This specialization may be done either by specializing behaviors—making them more semantically appropriate for the subclass—or by extension, which is the addition of new behaviors or attributes to the subclass. Fundamental to generalization is that it is an "is-a-kind-of" relationship between classes. A *mammal* is-a-kind-of *animal*, and an *infrared sensor* is-a-kind-of *sensor*.

In the *Window* class diagram in Figure 1-9, the *Window* parent class has two direct descendants, *SDI* (Single Document Interface) and *MDI* (Multiple Document Interface) classes. The *SDI* class is further subtyped into a *Dialog Box* class. A dialog box is an SDI window that does not have a menu[17] and has visual controls placed in its client area. Multiplicity makes no sense for inheritance relationships, and so is not depicted. Because the parent *Window* class *has* a client area, all its descendants do, as well.

Generalization is an extraordinarily powerful facility, despite its seeming simplicity. It allows objects to be *specified by difference* rather than from scratch each time. In standard structured methods, extending or specializing a function requires modification of the source code to produce a new routine that meets your needs. In object-oriented systems, you may subclass the parent to create a child class and merely add the additional attributes and behaviors needed. If a behavior needs to be implemented differently for a subclass, that's no problem either. You redefine the behavior in the subclass. The object-oriented paradigm ensures the correct version of the behavior will be called based on the object type you have.

In the UML, generalization implies two distinctly different, yet related, consequences. The first is called substitutability, also known as the Liskov Substitution Principle (LSP). LSP states that a subclass must be freely substitutable for its superclass. This means that a subclass must continue to act as though it also is an instance of its superclass. A dog may be a specialized, extended form of mammal, but an instance of dog is still a mammal and has all the properties of mammals. LSP requires that subclasses do not constrain superclass behavior, such as by "blocking" or "selectively inheriting" some properties.

The second consequence of generalization is called *inheritance*. Simply put, it means that whatever structural elements a class has, its subclasses will also have them. Thus, if a *Sensor* class has a *value* attribute and operations getValue() and enable(), then all classes using the *Sensor*

---

[17] Note that all subtypes of the class Windows can have a menu (the multiplicity of "0,1" makes it optional), but dialog boxes commonly do not.

as a parent will also have that attribute and those operations. It may specialize (redefine) the method that implements the operation if desired, but the parents' attributes and operations are passed on to their children subclasses. Attributes cannot be specialized and remain strongly typed in the same manner as they are in the parent class.

1.5.7.5 Dependency

Another important kind of relationship in the UML is *dependency*. In the UML, a dependency relationship means that some set of model elements requires the presence of another set of model elements for semantic completeness or correctness. The UML identifies various stereotypes[18] of dependency for different purposes and for different kinds of model elements.

The UML identifies a number of types of dependency.

- Relation between a type and a class that realizes it («realize»)
- Relation between an analysis class and a design class («trace»)
- Relation between two sets of model elements in which one can be computed from another («derive»)
- Relation between a high-level construct at a coarse granularity and a lower-level construct at a finer granularity («refine»)
- Relation in which one model element requires another for its proper functioning or implementation («use»)
- Relation in which a source class invokes an operation of a target class («call»)
- Relation in which a source class creates a target class instance («create»)
- Relation in which a source operation issues a target signal («send»)
- Granting of permission from elements of one package to access the public elements of another («access»)
- Granting of permission to add the elements of one package into another («import»)

---

[18] A *stereotype* is the class of an entity in the UML metamodel. Stereotypes are discussed in more detail in the next section.

- Granting of special access to otherwise inaccessible aspects of a model element («friend»)
- Relation between a parameterized model element with a formal parameter list and that model element bound to actual parameters («bind»)

One of the main uses of dependency is the taking of a generic, but incomplete, class specification and creating from it an instantiable class. A generic (*template,* in C++-speak) is an incomplete class specification with a formal parameter list. To create an instantiable class, a matching set of actual parameters must be supplied to filling in the missing details of the class description. The client in this case is called a *parameterized class.* You cannot construct an object from a parameterized class directly; a class must be instantiated first. This is called the «bind» dependency, because it binds the formal parameter list of a parameterized class to an actual parameter list.[19]

The «bind» dependency is similar to generalization in that it also creates more-specialized classes. At first glance, the distinction seems subtle indeed—in either case, you are specializing some entity to get a class. Inheritance is used when you want to specialize how some behavior is performed or how some class is constructed. Generic instantiation is used when you want the exact same behavior or structure but applied on a novel component type.

Collection or container classes are a common application of the «bind» dependency. A collection class is one that aggregates many component objects. These component objects are usually homogeneous (of the same class), or at least they are from a single inheritance hierarchy. Exactly the same behavior applies regardless of the class being collected. Things you want to be able to do with a collection of classes might be:

- Get the first object in the collection
- Get the next object in the collection
- Add an object to the collection
- Remove an object from the collection

---

[19] Note that other things than classes may be parameterized, such as free-standing operations. In C++, they are call function templates.

These behaviors are exactly the same regardless of whether you are dealing with a group of bank accounts, photodiode sensors, or waveform data. The behaviors of the objects themselves are vastly different, but the collection itself should behave in the same way, nevertheless.

This is difficult to implement using inheritance, but it is straightforward using parameterization. Figure 1-11 shows how parameterized classes are represented. The dependency relationship itself is a dashed line with an open arrowhead. The parameterized class is shown with a dashed box attached to an upper corner that contains the formal parameter list. The parameterization aspects can be shown in multiple ways, as shown in the figure.

- The actual parameters can be shown in a solid-line box attached to an upper corner of the instantiable class (most common).

- The actual parameters are shown on the association with a «bind» stereotype.

- More commonly, the actual parameters are shown in the class box between angled brackets (dependency is implied).

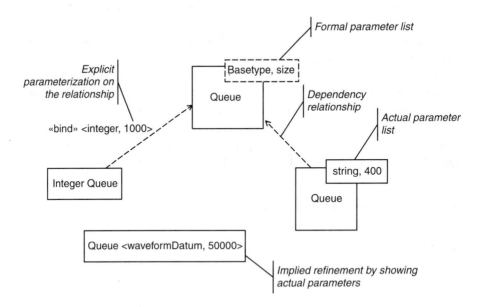

Figure 1-11: «bind» Dependency Relationship

The example in the figure declares a parameterized stack class with two parameters—the type of things to be put in the queue and the queue size—and then instantiates three different queue classes, one for integers, one for strings, and one for *waveformDatum* objects.

The use of parameterization is not limited to classes. Remember that collaborations realize use cases. Collaborations are depicted with ovals, like use cases, but with a dashed line style. *Design patterns* are parameterized collaborations; specific classes are substituted in the roles to instantiate the design pattern into a collaboration. Design patterns will be discussed in more detail in the chapters that deal with design, particularly Chapters 5 and 6.

There are many more things the UML can express than classes and their relationships, such as use cases, states, events, sequences of message flows, and so on. Yet, the most key aspects of object modeling in general, and the UML in particular, are expressed with classes and objects. We will defer the definition and use of these other elements to relevant chapters later in this book. Use cases, for example, are discussed in the next chapter in the context of requirements capture. States and statecharts are treated in detail under object behavioral modeling in Chapter 4. Armed with a basic understanding of objects and classes, we will explore the various aspects of the UML.

1.6 UML Diagrams and Notation

UML has a rich set of notations and semantics, which makes it applicable to a wide set of modeling applications and domains. In this chapter, we have only scratched the surface. In the coming chapters, new notations within UML will be presented as the context requires them. A concise overview of the notation is provided in Appendix A. Some notational elements we wish to present here include the text note, the constraint, and the stereotype, because they will be used in a variety of places throughout the book.

A text note is a diagrammatic element with no semantic impact. It is visually represented as a rectangle with the upper-right corner folded down. Text notes are used to provide textual annotations to diagrams in order to improve understanding.

A constraint is some additional restriction (above the usual UML "well-formedness" rules) applied against a modeling element. Timing constraints can be shown on sequence diagrams,[20] specifying the time between messages, for example. Constraints are always shown inside curly brackets, and they may appear inside text notes.

Figure 1-12 shows text notes and constraints used together. On the left, the class model for a doubly linked list is shown as a single class with constrained associations. On the right, the associations between classes *Worker* and *Team Member* are constrained in that the *Manager_of association* is a subset of the *Member_of association*.

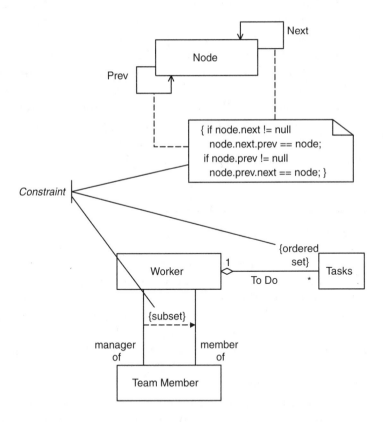

Figure 1-12: *Constraints in Action*

---

[20] Sequence diagrams are discussed in some detail in the next chapter.

A *stereotype* is the class of an entity in the UML metamodel.[21] Stereotypes provide an important extension mechanism to the UML, allowing users to extend the modeling language to better address their needs. Each modeling element in the UML is represented as a metaclass. A stereotyped metaclass is ultimately derived from an existing UML metaclass. For example, it is possible to create a new (meta)class of the UML class construct, which is just like the usual UML class but is extended, or specialized. An «active» class is just such a class.

The usual notation for stereotypes is to enclose the stereotype in guillemets[22] preceding the name of the entity, such as in "«active» ECG Waveform Acquisition," which is the name of a class that runs in its own independent thread of control. Special icons can be used instead of guillemets for common stereotypes. UML defines a number of common stereotype icons and you should feel free to add your own application-domain-specific icons.[23]

Figure 1-13 illustrates a few common UML stereotypes and icons. The "lollipop" is the icon for an *interface*. In earlier revisions of the UML, an interface was a stereotype of a class, but in UML 1.3 it is a first-order model element. An interface is a metasubclass of *Classifier*. Other kinds of *Classifiers* include *Class, Use Case, Actor, Data Type, Node,* and *Component*.[24] Even though an interface is not a class, when it is desirable to show the set of operations provided by the interface, it can be shown as a class with an «interface» stereotype.[25] The stick figure is the icon for an actor—an object outside the scope of the system that has significant interactions with the system. Similarly to an interface, an actor may be depicted with a class rectangle and an «actor» stereotype. The official

---

[21] The UML metamodel is the model of the UML itself, expressed in UML. It contains metaclasses, such as Classifier, Class, State, Operation, Signal, and so on. See [6] for a description of the UML metamodel.

[22] If guillemets are unavailable, then double angled brackets are an acceptable alternative. For example, <<interface>> may be substituted for «interface».

[23] At the risk of introducing some nonportability, of course.

[24] Each of these metaclasses (with the exception of Data Type) will be discussed at some point later in this book.

[25] Interfaces in the UML do not have attributes or methods. They have only operations. An operation is the specification of a method. An operation defined in an interface will be realized in an associated class by a corresponding method.

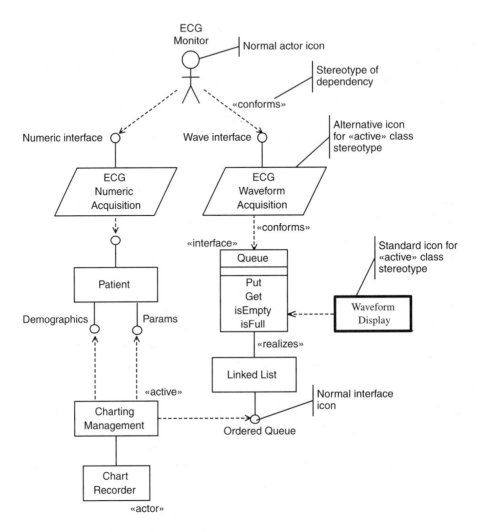

Figure 1-13: *UML Stereotypes and Icons*

icon for an «active» class is a class with a heavy border line. An alternative icon (nonstandard) is to use a parallelogram icon, which has the advantage of being more visually distinct. Usually, a single style is used—either the icon *or* the stereotype is shown, but not both. Both are shown in Figure 1-13 for illustrative purposes.

Notice in the figure, two actors are shown—*ECG Monitor* and *Chart Recorder.* These are independent devices to which our system must interface. Four active classes exist, two shown with the parallelogram icon, one with the standard UML heavy-bordered class icon, and one as a normal class with a stereotype. Also notice that the *Patient* class has three interfaces. It is not at all uncommon to present different interfaces to clients. And finally, notice that the *Queue* interface is shown using a stereotype class icon in order to show the operations visible to the client.

1.7 A Look Ahead

So far, we have touched on only the defining characteristics of real-time systems and the very basic aspects of the object-oriented perspective. In subsequent chapters, we'll apply these ideas to the process of creating real-time embedded applications. The process is broken into the overall process steps of analysis and design, as called out in Section 1.3. Analysis is subdivided into specification of external requirements and the identification of inherent classes and objects. Design is divided into three parts—architectural, mechanistic, and detailed levels of abstraction. Architectural design specifies the strategic decisions for the overall organization of the system, such as the design of the processor and concurrency models. Mechanistic design is concerned with the medium level of organization—the collaboration of objects to achieve common goals. Detailed design defines the internal algorithms and primitive data structures within classes. All the process steps are required to create efficient, correct designs that meet the system requirements. In the next chapter, we'll focus on capturing requirements using the UML via use cases.

1.8 References

[1] Leveson, Nancy G., *Safeware: System Safety and Computers.* Reading, MA: Addison Wesley Longman, 1995.
[2] Neumann, Peter G., *Computer-Related Risks.* Reading, MA: Addison Wesley Longman, 1995.
[3] Ellis, John R., *Objectifying Real-Time Systems.* New York: SIGS Books, 1994.

[4] Rumbaugh, James, Michael Blaha, William Premerlani, Frederick Eddy, and William Lorensen, *Object-Oriented Modeling and Design.* Englewood Cliffs, NJ: Prentice Hall, 1991.

[5] Douglass, Bruce Powel, *Doing Hard Time: Developing Real-Time Systems with UML, Objects, Frameworks, and Patterns.* Reading, MA: Addison Wesley Longman, 1999.

[6] Rumbaugh, James, Grady Booch, and Ivar Jacobson, *The UML Reference Guide.* Reading, MA: Addison Wesley Longman, 1999.

Chapter 2

Requirements Analysis of Real-Time Systems

Real-time systems interact with their external environment. The set of external objects of significance and their interactions with the system form the basis for the requirements analysis of the system. In the UML, this is captured by the use case model. A use case is a system capability that is detailed with accompanying text, examples (scenarios), or state models. The use case model decomposes the primary functionality of the system and the protocols necessary to meet these functional requirements.

Notations and Concepts Discussed

Actors   Use case diagram

Events   Sequence diagram

Scenarios   Statechart

State

49

2.1 Use Cases

A *use case* is a named capability of a structural entity in a model. Most often, use case analysis is applied only to the system as a whole, but use cases can be applied to any structural entity, including subsystems[1] or even classes. Use cases define a system-level capability, without revealing or implying any particular implementation of that capability. In fact, as we will see, use cases are implemented (*realized*, in UML-speak) by collaborations of classes.

Use cases exist within a structural context. In the case of the system, this context consists of the system and associated *actors*. An actor is an object outside the scope of the system under discussion, but that nevertheless interacts with it. In order to be a use case, it must return a result visible to one or more actors. If a capability of a system is invisible from the outside, then it is not a use case and should not be captured during requirements analysis (since it is an internal-only concern). Figure 2-1 shows a simple use case diagram.

Used primarily in early analysis, the *use case diagram* shows the black-box functional capabilities provided by the system. These capabilities manifest themselves as interactions among the system and the external objects.

One of the advantages of use case diagrams is their ability to capture a broad view of the primary functionality of the system in a manner easily grasped by nontechnical users. The use case diagrams can become a centralized roadmap of the system usage scenarios for people specifying the requirements of the system.

2.1.1 Actors

As mentioned earlier, an actor is an object outside the scope of the system under consideration but that has significant interactions with it. The icon for an actor, as shown in Figure 2-1, is a stick figure. Many people misconstrue this to mean that actors must therefore be human users of the system. An actor is *any* object that interacts directly with

---

[1] In the UML, a *subsystem* is a metasubclass (that is, a subclass of a metaclass defined in the UML metamodel) of both a package (since it contains many classes) and a class (since it binds together attributes and related behaviors).

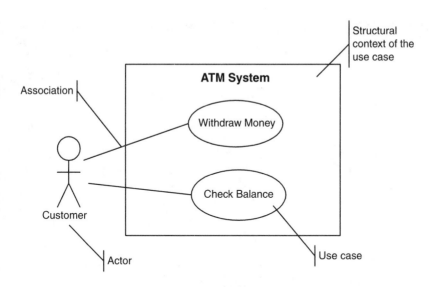

Figure 2-1: *Use Cases*

the system. Figure 2-2 shows some of the use cases for an air traffic control system. Note that of the several actors identified, only one of them (*Controller*) is a human user. All the rest are legacy systems or devices to which the system must integrate or interface.

Not all actors participate in all use cases. The two radar actors in Figure 2-2, for example, interact with *Locate Tracks,* but not with the other use cases. The use cases with which the actor interacts are indicated by the association drawn between the actor and the related use case. Of course, an actor can participate in more than a single use case, as well.

Associations are not drawn between actors (since they are outside the scope of the system), but sometimes they can be generalized. For example, a *user* in a library may participate in a *Check Out Book* use case, but only a certain type of *user,* called *Librarian,* may add new books to the library system or register a new *user.* Generalization is therefore sometimes shown among the actors.

At the system level, the actors for use cases are objects outside the entire system. However, if the use case is applied to an internal subsystem or class, then the actors will be truly external actors (as in the system case) plus the peer-level subsystems or classes with which the element under analysis associates.

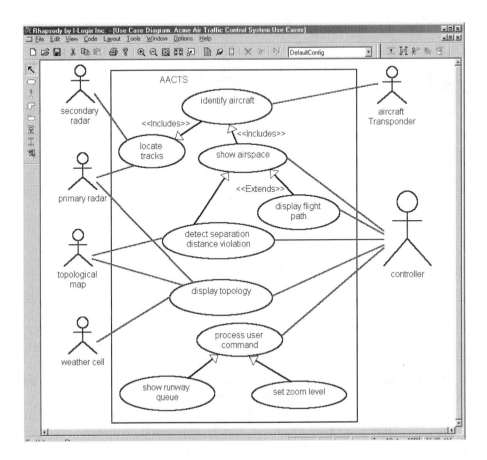

Figure 2-2: *Air Traffic Control Use Cases*

Consider the use cases in Figure 2-3. Here, the anesthesia system interfaces with an external ECG monitor and chart recorder. The other two actors are human users of the system—the physician and the patient.

Now let's consider a breakdown of the anesthesia machine into some large scale subsystems, as shown in the class diagram in Figure 2-4.[2] Use case analysis may be applied recursively to these subsystems.

_____

[2] The use of heavier lines for the association to external actors has no semantic meaning—they are just typical associations—but it does allow the interfaces that cross the system border to be easily identified.

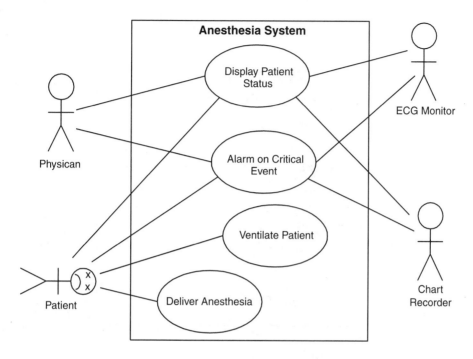

Figure 2-3: *Anesthesia Use Cases*

Figure 2-5 shows an example for one such subsystem, the user interface subsystem. Note that the external actors are shown by using the «actor» icon bitmap; the peer subsystems are drawn using a class icon but have the «actor» stereotype added to them. This is purely personal preference. I like to differentiate actors to a subsystem that are within the overall system (but, of course, outside the subsystem under consideration) from actors that are outside the entire system. Also note that actor generalization is shown in this example—actors of the *Monitor* superclass participate in the *Display Patient Status* use case, as well as independently participate in other use cases.

Use cases are interactions between the system and some set of associated actors. It is important, as well, to understand what use cases *are not,* as it is common to waste time during use case analysis either to capture design details or to functionally decompose the internals of a system. A use case is *not*

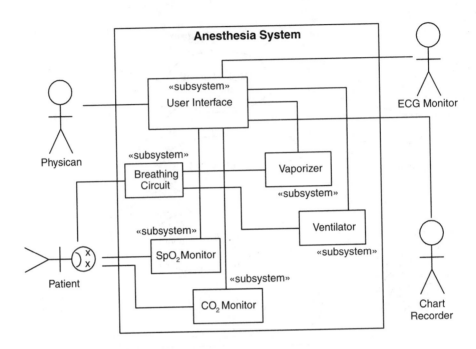

Figure 2-4: *Anesthesia Subsystems*

- A single message or event
  The details of a use case are represented with scenarios, consisting of potentially dozens of messages flowing back and forth between the system and the actors. If you identify a use case that consists of handling a single message or event, you have probably actually identified a (rather small) piece of another use case.

- A low-level interface
  Low-level interfaces are the means by which use cases are realized. For example, if a hard disk is an actor, the low-level commands passing between the system and the actor, such as *move head* and *spin up*, are not use cases. Remember that the use case is a reason *why* the actor communicates with the system, *not* how it actually does it.

- A functional decomposition of another use case
  Later, we will see relations among use cases, such as generalization and dependency. The point of these relations is *not* to decompose the system into a set of primitive functions that can be implemented

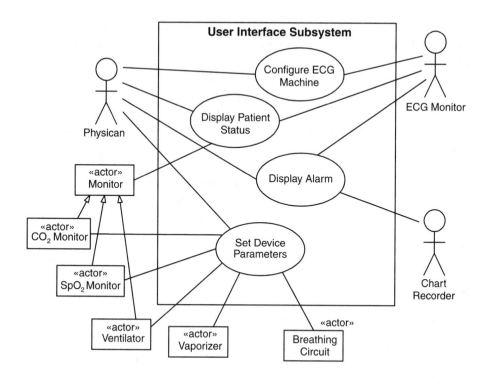

Figure 2-5: *User Interface Subsystem Use Cases*

in C! The purpose of use case relations is to allow a parsimonious description of the capabilities of the system.

Various authors will tell you different things about use cases, not all of them useful. Some will say that all use cases are initiated by actors. This precludes systems that have autonomous behavior—a property of many real-time and embedded systems. Other authors will say that all use cases have a single primary scenario. Again, this is often, but not always, the case. In fact, some use cases have a number of equally important scenario variations.

2.1.2 Requirements

Requirements captured by use cases and associated diagrams fall into two categories. *Functional requirements* are represented directly by the use cases themselves. In Figure 2-1, the use cases are *Withdraw Money* and *Check Balance.* Note that the use cases are primary capabilities of concern to the actor (in this case, *Customer*). The ATM system will also check user validity before allowing access, but that is a secondary behavior—no one uses an ATM machine to find out if he or she is a valid user. People use the ATM machine for the use cases. The less-significant behavior of validating a user may be modeled as an interaction within the scenarios of the primary use cases, or, as we shall see, as a secondary use case.

The other kind of requirement is called *quality of service* (QoS). QoS requirements capture *how well* the use case must be performed. Common QoS requirements for real-time systems include:

• Speed
• Timeliness
• Throughput
• Capacity
• Predictability
• Reliability
• Safety
• Security

QoS requirements are usually captured as *constraints* of some kind. A constraint is a rule applied to a set of model elements above and beyond the standard well-formedness rules defined by the UML itself. Constraints are usually textual, or formal, expressions contained within curly braces, such as:

{ The system shall return a balance check result within 30s. }

QoS requirements can be captured on use case diagrams, as shown in Figure 2-6. It is even more common to capture them in scenarios, but capturing them on use case diagrams is particularly appropriate when the QoS requirement applies to many or all scenarios. The QoS requirements in Figure 2-6 capture the requirements for setting the parameters, the reliability of the communications, and the accuracy of the performance of the pacing behavior.

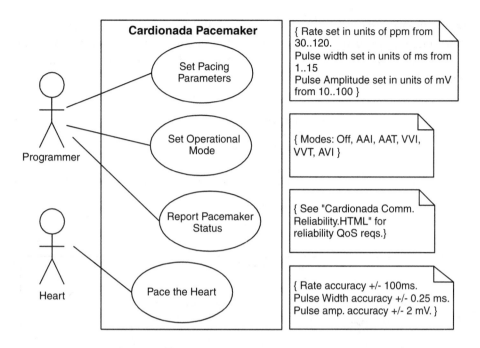

Figure 2-6: *Capturing QoS Requirements*

2.1.3 Use Case Relations

The UML version 1.3 defines three distinct relationships among use cases. *Generalization* means that one use case is a more specialized, or refined, version of another. For example, *Validate User* use case can be specialized into *Check Password, Check Fingerprint Scan,* and *Check Retinal Scan* use cases. Each of these sub-use cases is a specialized version of the base use case.

The other two kinds of use case relations are stereotypes of dependency. «includes» is used when the capability described in the client use case uses the capability described in another. «includes» should be used only when the behavior is shared among two or more use cases and is required for all client use case scenarios.

The third kind of relation is «extends», which is used when one use case provides an optional additional capability within a client use case. This optional capability is inserted at a named extension point. Figure 2-7 shows the syntax of the use case relations. Remember that the closed arrowhead indicates generalization with the arrow pointing toward the more general use case. Dependency is shown with an open arrowhead and a dashed line, with the arrow pointing toward the "smaller," or used, use case.

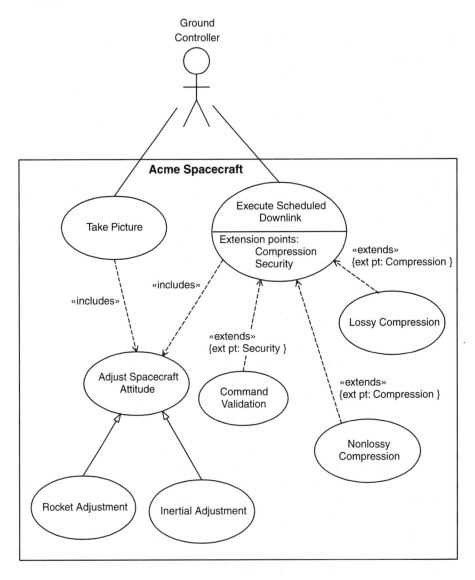

Figure 2-7: *Use Case Relations*

In the figure, the spacecraft turns in order to achieve two capabilities—to take a picture (under the premise that you must point at something to take its picture) and to execute a scheduled downlink of information. Because this common capability is required for both these use cases, it is extracted out and put into its own use case. The two means by which the spacecraft can be turned are specialized use cases of the *Adjust Attitude* base use case. In one case, rockets can be fired to turn the spacecraft, and in the other, reaction wheels are activated. Finally, the scheduled downlink can optionally compress images, either using lossy or nonlossy compression algorithms. Because this is an option, it is shown as an «extends» relation. Also, for risky command sequences, a high-level security clearance may be required. Note that the extension points are identified in the base use case and then referred to by the extending use cases.

A caution: Too often, beginners overuse the use case relations to capture the wrong things. Remember that you can model the requirements of systems without using generalization, «extends», or «includes». Their use can make a requirements model a little simpler, but not if they are misused.

2.1.4 Using Use Cases

Use cases can provide a unifying strategy for the entire project development. They are an embodiment of what the customer wants and expects to see when the dust settles[3] and the product ships. Use cases group together functionally related scenarios and provide valuable information on all phases, as shown in Table 2-1.

2.2 Filling Out the Details of the Use Cases

So far, we've identified what a use case is: a named system capability. We've also noted that use cases capture requirements, both functional and (with additional constraint annotation) quality of service requirements. However, a name alone isn't enough to understand what a use

---

[3] That is, the customer finally stops changing the requirements long enough for you to actually *build* the darn thing.

Table 2-1 Using Use Cases in Development

Phase	Application of Use Cases
Analysis	• Suggest large-scale partitioning of the domain • Provide structuring of analysis objects • Clarify system and object responsibilities • Capture and clarify new features as they are added during development • Validate analysis model
Design	• Validate the elaboration of analysis models in the presence of design objects
Coding	• Clarify purpose and role of classes for coders • Focus coding efforts
Testing	• Provide primary and secondary test scenarios for system validation
Deployment	• Suggest iterative prototypes for spiral development

case means. For example, consider the use case *Set Ventilator Tidal Volume:* The user turns a knob and sets the amount of mixed breathing gas pumped out per breath for the ventilator. That's not enough detail to understand how it actually works. For example:

• What happens if the knob is turned accidentally? Does tidal volume change directly or does it require confirmation?

• If there is a confirmation,

  ▼ How does the user cancel the operation?

  ▼ What happens if the user tries to set a different value, say *Respiration Rate,* before confirmation?

  ▼ How does the user know whether a value is currently being set (waiting for confirmation)?

• Does anything have to either precede or come after setting tidal volume?

In requirements capture, "the devil is in the details," and it is important to answer these questions. There are three main approaches to providing a greater level of detail. The first is to add textual annotation that describes the interaction. The second is to provide a set of interactions exemplifying the use case—that is, a set of scenarios. The third is to define all possible interactions in a single finite state machine.

Since the first of these is really outside the scope of UML per se, let's focus on the other two.

2.2.1 Scenarios

A *scenario* is a particular actor-system interaction corresponding to a use case—it is a specific example of a use case. Scenarios model order-dependent message sequences among objects collaborating to produce system behavior. Different scenarios within a use case show permutations of object interactions. Even early in analysis, the advantage of scenarios is that domain experts and users can usually easily walk the analyst through dozens of typical system usage scenarios. The domain expert can explain why each step is taken, who initiates it, what the appropriate responses are, and what kinds of things can go awry. In going through this process, the analyst uncovers many important facets of the system behavior not mentioned within the problem statement. Scenarios provide an invaluable tool for validating the problem statement against the user's expectations, as well as for uncovering the less obvious requirements. Late in analysis, they can be used to test the object structure by ensuring the appropriate participation by each object in each scenario.

Generally, a medium-size system will have a few to a few dozen use cases. Each use case will have anywhere from a few to a few dozen scenarios of interest. There are an infinite set of scenarios, but it is necessary to capture only the ones that are "interestingly different"—that is, the ones that capture all the different functional requirements. Quality of service requirements are added as constraints applied to the messages or groups of messages in the scenario.

Many (but certainly not all) use cases have a "sunny day," or *primary,* scenario. In this case, most or all the other scenarios for the use case are variants on the primary.

Every scenario has an underlying structural context. Early in analysis, the structural context is the use case diagram; the objects available for scenarios are the system and the actors identified on the use case diagram. Use cases are *realized* by collaborations of objects working together. Later analysis decomposes the system into objects, and the use case scenarios can be refined by adding additional levels of detail. It is important that you use objects in the scenario that appear only in the structural context. That means that if the use case diagram has two actors and the system, only three objects can appear in the scenario. If the system is "opened up" and internal objects are identified, these may then appear in the scenarios, as well. It is crucial to make sure you *always* know the structural context. Otherwise, you'll be making stuff up on the fly with only a vague notion about the underlying structural model. If you have a number of people doing this on different use cases, the chances the models will all play together later is vanishingly small. By drawing and agreeing upon the structural context, the scenarios from various use cases elaborated by different analysts will all play together when it comes time to decompose or implement the model.

It is important to stress that building and analyzing scenarios is a creative process of discovery. It is not simply a matter of starting with postulates and applying mathematical deduction to derive all possible behavior paths. Deep within the crevices of the domain experts' minds are hidden requirements that, if left to their own devices, will never be explicitly identified.[4] These cannot be deduced from the problem statement *per se.* The process of scenario modeling brings these hidden requirements to the surface, where they can be added to the system features.

Two primary scenario representations exist within the UML: sequence and collaboration diagrams. The first is the most commonly used and emphasizes messages and their sequence. The second is also popular and tends to stress the system object structure. Both diagrams show scenarios but differ in what they emphasize. Almost exclusively, in use case analysis, sequence diagrams are preferred over collaboration diagrams. Collaboration diagrams are not used until the object model of the system stabilizes (and even then, many people prefer sequence diagrams, anyway). Collaboration diagrams will be discussed later in the sections on object analysis.

2.2.2 Sequence Diagrams

Sequence diagrams show the sequence of messages between objects. The graphical syntax for sequence diagrams is shown in Figure 2-8. This

---

[4] At least not until the product is delivered!

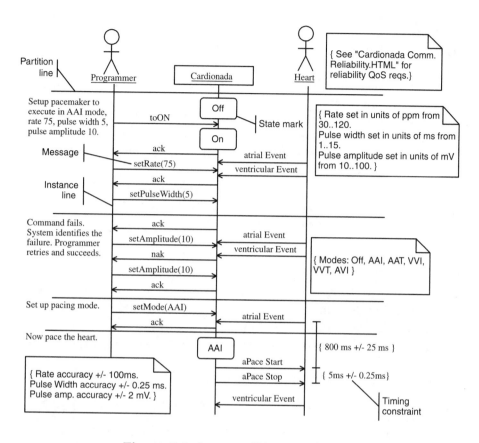

Figure 2-8: *Sequence Diagram Syntax*

figure shows all the elements used in most sequence diagrams. The vertical *instance lines* represent objects, with the name of the object written above or below the line. Some tools use a crosshatched line for actors. The horizontal arrows are messages. Each message line starts at the *originator object* and ends at the *target object* and has a message name on the line. This name might, in later phases, specify an operation with a parameter list and a return value. Time flows from the top of the page downward so that the *SetPulseWidth* is sent before the following *ack*, and so on. The time axis shows only sequence; the scale is not linear, nor is a scale provided.[5]

---

[5] The UML does allow a linear time ruler to be added, but no tool supports this at this time.

Note the textual annotation along the left side of the diagram. This descriptive text identifies initial conditions, actions, and activities not shown by the message sequence itself. QoS requirements are indicated by the constraints inside text notes and by the timing marks. States may be added to the diagram, as shown in the figure, as well. In use, the receipt of some message causes a change in state. At that point in the sequence, the new state is indicated by placing a state icon on the instance line. The object is assumed to be in that state until a subsequent state icon is indicated later on the instance line.

There are other things that can be shown on sequence diagrams, such as focus of control, but these are inapplicable to use case analysis. These forms are discussed later in the chapters on design.

2.2.3 Message Properties

Note: In this section, we'll get a little technical about the concepts of messages, signals, and events and how they're defined in the UML. For many people, it is sufficient to have a rather vague notion about these things. If you fall into that category, then this section may be skipped.

What Is the UML Metamodel?

The UML *metamodel* is a model of the UML itself. This metamodel is written in UML. The elements of the metamodel are called *metaclasses*. Examples include *Class, Classifier, Signal, Event, State, Message, Association*, and so on. These relate to each other using *metarelations*. The metamodel allows us to define, with at least some rigor, what we mean by terms like *Message, Signal, Operation*, and *Event* and the relations among them. Given that detailed understanding, we can then use these terms to reason about the applications we will model using them. When we talk about what a *Class* is, for example, we are delving into the arena of the metamodel. We will refer to the metamodel in various places in this book. In general, it is not usually necessary to understand the details of the metamodel unless a high precision is required in the discussion. For more details see [8] or visit the OMG Web site at *www.omg.org* or the I-Logix Web site at *www.ilogix.com*.

The UML defines a *Message* to be an abstraction of a unit of communication between two objects; one is the *source* or *originating object,* and the other is the *target* or *receiving object.* Most often, message passing will be realized with a simple direct call to a method in the target objects, but that is not the only realization. Other realizations include remote procedure calls, sending messages via an OS message queue, IPC, and sending messages across a bus or network.

The UML identifies two kinds of messages: the sending of a signal and the invocation of an operation. The primary difference between them is that signal sending is always asynchronous while the operation call may be either synchronous or asynchronous. Further, signal reception usually causes transitions to occur in state machines, but calls usually do not.[6] It is not quite that clear-cut, but this will suffice for our purposes. More details on messages, signals, and events are given in Chapter 4.

The essential properties of messages are:

- Sender
- List of target objects
- Action
- Parameter list and return value
- Arrival pattern
- Synchronization pattern

The sender and receiver(s) are the objects participating in the message transfer. Although in most cases, a single target object is identified, messages may be *multicast* to a list of objects. The UML has no intrinsic notion of broadcast, in which all objects receive a message without explicitly being part of a list.

The UML 1.3 specification defines several different kinds of actions, as shown in the segment of the UML metamodel depicted in Figure 2-9. In this figure, we can see that actions contain *Arguments* and may be contained in *ActionSequences.* Zero or more *Messages* associate to a given *Action.*

---

[6] The UML does permit the operation that is invoked with a call to trigger an event type called *CallEvent.* However, be very careful with synchronous calls triggering transitions on a state machine. It is very easy to construct state machines with race conditions and deadlock, particularly if you mix asynchronous and synchronous events in the same state machine.

There are many kinds of actions. Two are particularly relevant to our discussion: *SendAction* and *CallAction*. *SendActions* associate with a *Signal*—a specification of an asynchronous *Stimulus* sent from one object to a set of target objects. When a *Signal* is received by an object, it can asynchronously raise an event called a *SignalEvent*. This can cause a state machine to transition from one state to another. *CallActions* are another kind of action, which associate with operations. The receipt of a *CallAction* can raise a *CallEvent* on the receiving object, which is another kind of event. Figure 2-9 is only a portion of the metamodel,[7] but it shows a number of pieces coming together to provide the behavioral constructs as they commonly apply to objects.

The figure implies some relations that are of relevance to our discussion of messages on sequence diagrams. First of all, a message can associate with either a *CallAction* (synchronous or asynchronous) or a *SendAction* (asynchronous). Thus, a message can call an operation or send a signal. Either of these may trigger a transition on a state machine.

These metaclasses are relevant to the capture of requirements. In order to perform analysis of the timeliness and schedulability of a system, the arrival pattern, synchronization pattern, and execution timing of the operations must be captured. As mentioned in the previous chapter, messages may have different arrival patterns, such as periodic and aperiodic, and various properties of these arrival patterns, such as jitter and minimum interarrival time. These properties are often known from system analysis and must be captured in the use case model or on sequence diagrams to really understand the behavior of the system in its environment.

Similarly, synchronization patterns are often known early, particularly when interfacing with legacy systems with known rendezvous characteristics. One of the appropriate outcomes of use case analysis is to provide enough information for an early first-cut schedulability analysis to take place.

In UML terms, the arrival pattern is a property best associated with metaclass *Message*, while the synchronization pattern really applies to the metaclass *Action*.[8] Thus, a radar object may send a message with a periodic arrival pattern to the air traffic control system, resulting in the

---

[7] The author is, at the time of this writing, participating in the development of a modification to the action metamodel of the UML. For more details, see Appendix B.

[8] In UML 1.3, the *Action* metaclass has a metaattribute called *isAsynchronous*.

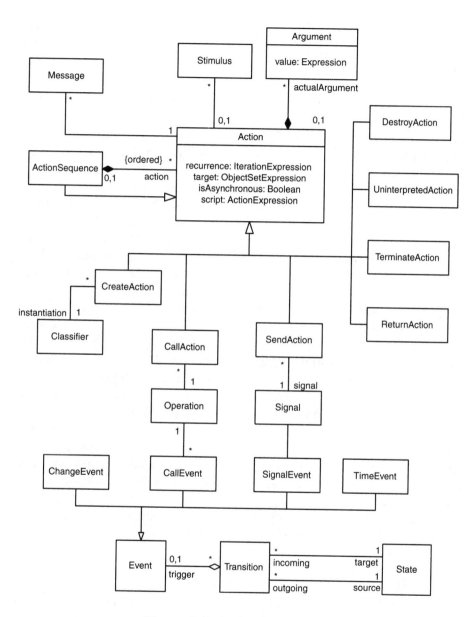

Figure 2-9: *Action Metamodel*

execution of an action with an asynchronous synchronization pattern. People often refer loosely to the arrival pattern of *Events* and *Message* synchronization patterns. This is fine, as long as the information is not lost and is treated consistently.

For detailed timing analysis, both the arrival patterns of the *Message* and the synchronization patterns of the *Action* must be specified. In addition, for early timing analysis, estimates must be made for the execution time for the *Action*, as well as its deadline (if RMA-style analysis is to be used).[9]

These values can be added to the diagrams and metaclasses of the use case and scenario models in a number of ways. The qualitatively different properties (such as whether a message is periodic or aperiodic) is best captured by creating stereotypes of the *Message* metaclass. Because we usually think about the *Message* as having both the arrival and synchronization patterns, we use stereotypes to indicate the instantiable message subclass, as in «periodic-asynchronous». If desired, iconic representations can be used instead of the stereotypes.

Figure 2-10 shows the iconic stereotypes I use for the arrival and synchronization patterns. These icons may be combined to form instantiable stereotypes, as shown in the figure. Both the standard guillemet notation and the iconic representation may be used. Naturally, if you are not concerned with the message arrival and synchronization types, the message stereotype may be omitted from the sequence diagram.

The quantitative values, such as the period and mean jitter, are best captured as *constraints*. A constraint, as mentioned in the previous chapter, is a user-defined rule applied to a metaclass. Constraints are usually represented as expressions between curly braces, although timing constraints are sometimes represented on sequence diagrams using alternative notations. Let us now turn our attention to the means by which we capture time-related requirements.

2.2.4 Capturing Time and Timeliness

The most differentiating characteristic of real-time systems is their concern and treatment of *time*, as discussed in the previous chapter. In the

---

[9] RMA stands for *rate monotonic analysis*. It is a set of mathematical techniques used to analyze schedulability of a set of tasks, given a set of assumptions and constraints. See [9] for more information.

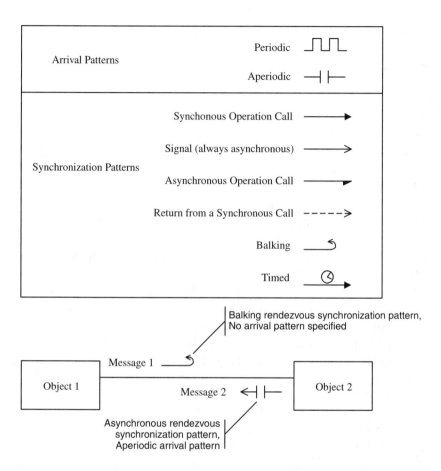

Figure 2-10: *Message Stereotypes*

realm of real-time systems, defining the external timeliness requirements is crucial to understanding the problem. However, most timing
requirements are derived, not primary, requirements. That is, a specific
timing constraint may arise from a need for accuracy or fault tolerance.
Because these requirements are derived, it is all too common for them
to be missed by systems designers, leading to unstable system performance. Thus, it is vital that these time constraints be captured as part of
the system model so that they can be treated appropriately.

A number of time values can be captured. Time values that are QoS
requirements can be captured as constraints applied against the actions or

messages. Time values that are estimates, used for the purpose of analysis, can be captured as tagged values (user-added properties of model elements). Tagged values are shown as *{property = value}* pairs in text notes.

A number of parameters are required to specify the timing requirements for real-time systems. Naturally, incoming messages must have their timing characterized. If they are periodic, then their periods and jitter must be identified. If they are aperiodic, then appropriate values, such as their minimum interarrival times and average rates, must be defined. The system response timing is commonly defined in terms of deadlines. If the response has a hard deadline, then missing the deadline constitutes a systems failure. In a soft deadline system, the average throughput must be specified. Soft systems are permitted to lag in their response but are expected to maintain an average throughput or system response. Firm deadlines have both a hard deadline and an average throughput requirement.

Response performance may be further specified into a worst-case hard deadline and an average response time, when appropriate. Some performance requirements must be met only in the long run, and occasionally missing a deadline creates no difficulties. These soft deadlines may be defined as average response time requirements or a bounded mean lateness. Firm deadlines have both a hard deadline and a shorter average response time.

More-complex timing behavior requires more-complex modeling. In some cases, scalars cannot adequately specify the timing of behavioral responses. Many actions require relatively long periods of time to perform, and intermediate responses may be important. For example, an emergency shutdown of a nuclear reactor is implemented by insertion of control rods into the core. This may be initiated by an event such as a coolant leak or an explosive temperature and pressure buildup. This takes some period of time. To avert an "incident," it is preferable to insert the rods 90% of the way as soon as possible, even if the remaining 10% takes much longer. Control loops are another example. Quick, if incomplete, responses stabilize PID control loops, even if the system response asymptotically converges much later.

These issues are domain- and system-specific. For many situations, the only concerns are service time and latency. Modeling 50% or 80% response times may be important in some special applications. In other applications, several points from a stimulus-response curve may be required to adequately characterize the performance requirements.

In most real-time systems, the time-response requirements are crucial because they define a performance budget for the system. As objects and classes are defined, this performance budget propagates through the analysis and design phases. Ultimately, they define a performance (sub)budget for each and every operation and function call in the thread of execution responding to the event. The sum of the (sub)budgets must meet the specified overall system performance requirement. For example, a message and the completion of its reaction may have a hard deadline at 500 ms. The overall response may be implemented via a chain of six operations. Each of these operations must be allocated some portion of the overall performance budget.

Figure 2-11 shows how timing and synchronization constraints may be captured on a sequence diagram using the stereotypes, tagged values, and constraints discussed above.

2.2.5 Statecharts and Use Cases

Although a full description of statecharts and state behavior won't be presented until Chapter 4, it is now useful to give a brief overview of statecharts and how they relate to use cases. A statechart is a diagram showing a state machine, as defined by David Harel [7] and refined in the definition of the UML. A statechart is a diagram consisting of rounded rectangles called *states*. A state is a *condition of existence of a Classifier that persists for a significant period of time and is distinguishable in some way from other such conditions of existence.* Distinguishability may be in terms of:

- Behavior of the object while entering, leaving, or existing in that state
- Events accepted while in that state
- Reachability graph of subsequent states

State machines are useful because they provide a means of decomposing a complex behavior into smaller pieces, each piece being only valid under a certain set of conditions. Statecharts are said to be *fully constructive*—that is, a single statechart depicts the total behavior of the *Classifier* that it represents.[10] A *Classifier* is a metaclass in the UML with common

---

[10] Realistically, not all *Classifiers* should have state machines; for example, it is difficult to image what the state machine of a *Signal* would specify.

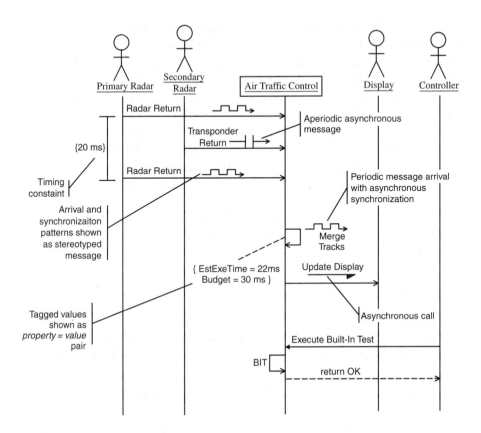

Figure 2-11: *Sequence Diagram Constraints*

properties, one of which is that they can have an associated state machine. Examples of the *Classifier* metaclass include *class* and *use case*.

A sample statechart is shown in Figure 2-12. It represents the state machine for the use case *Position Telescope* for a telescope controller system.

Statecharts are most appropriate for detailing use case behavior when the use case interaction must follow a fairly elaborate protocol to ensure correct behavior. Although statecharts are both powerful and expressive, they require some training to understand and so may not be helpful for communicating with nontechnical personnel.

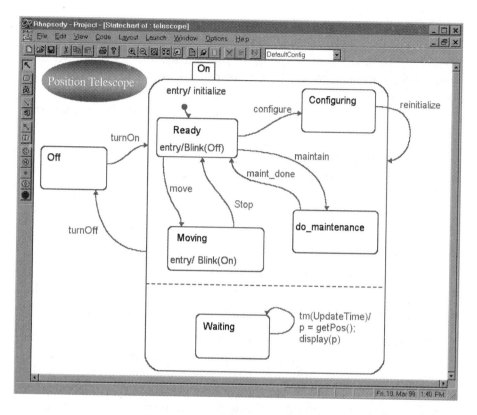

Figure 2-12: *Example Statechart*

2.3 Identifying Use Cases

There are three primary approaches to identifying use cases.

1. List the primary capabilities of the system, then identify the actors, and then identify the scenarios within each use case.

2. Identify the actors to the system, the messages they send or receive (the scenarios), and then group them into use cases.

3. Start with system scenarios, identify the actors that participate in them, and then lump them into use cases.

All of these approaches can work well.

How does the analyst extract the primary capabilities of the system? Although some domain experts may think in abstract terms, the vast majority will be more comfortable identifying specific scenarios rather than use cases. The analyst must identify the dozens (or hundreds) of scenarios that map the important system aspects and from these deduce the use cases. A number of approaches to identifying the scenarios are possible.

The analyst can sit with the customer and ask probing questions, such as:

- What are the primary functions of the system?
- What are the secondary functions of the system?
- Why is this system being built? What is it replacing and why?

The analyst must then identify for each use case:

- The role the actors and system play in each scenario
- The interactions (flows) necessary to complete the scenario
- The sequences of events and data necessary to realize the scenario
- The possible variations on the scenario (other related scenarios)

For example, the primary functions of an ECG monitor are to display waveforms for the physician, provide discrete patient numeric values (such as heart rate), and alarm when the patient is at risk. Secondary functions might be to provide a remote display for the surgeon, provide a reliable software upgrade facility, allow configuration, and even support a demonstration mode of operation for the sales reps. Why is the system being built? Perhaps it provides better arrhythmia detection, color displays for better differentiation of lead configurations, faster response times, or it interfaces to the hospital network and the operating room anesthesia machines. Figure 2-13 shows a reasonable use case model for an ECG monitor. Note that this use case diagram uses all three kinds of relations among use cases: includes, extends, and generalization.

Use cases are used primarily during requirements analysis, but Figure 2-14 shows that use cases have a role in other phases, as well. Once the system is broken down into its primary subsystems (in systems analysis phase), use cases may be applied to each of the subsystems in turn to define its requirements with respect to the other elements of the system. As the object model becomes fleshed out, the system and subsystem-context-level use cases may be refined in more detail, replacing the system with the objects collaborating within the system

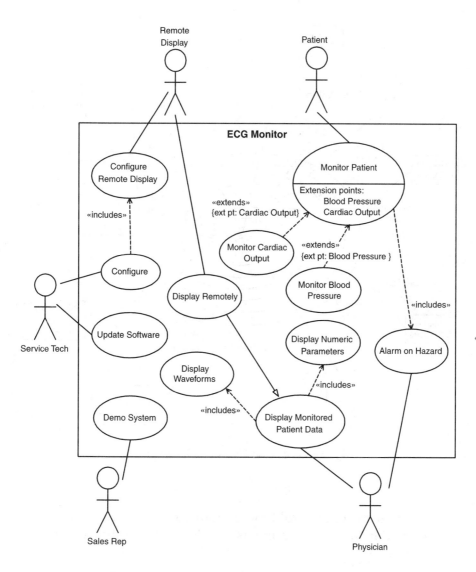

Figure 2-13: *ECG Monitor Use Case Diagram*

to realize the specific use case. Some additional use cases are typically uncovered during architectural design, as well, having to do with the concurrency and component models. Even in testing, the use cases and their associated scenarios form the key set of tests to be applied to the system.

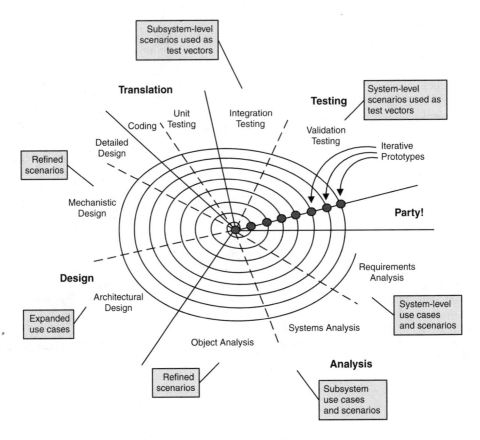

Figure 2-14: *Use Cases in Development*

Use cases are a powerful tool for both the capture of requirements and for binding those requirements into design and testing as development continues.

2.4 Looking Ahead

One of the first things done on any project is the determination of the detailed requirements of the system. These requirements may be either capabilities of the system or how well those capabilities are to be achieved. The UML provides use cases, scenarios, and statecharts to capture these requirements. Use cases identify the primary capabilities of a system. The details of how those capabilities are achieved—at least from an outside, black-box view—are captured in the scenarios or statecharts associated with the use cases. A use case is generally detailed by up to several dozen scenarios, shown on sequence diagrams. Alternatively, or collaboratively, a single statechart can provide the behavioral details of the entire system.

This is crucial in order to understand *what* system is to be built—that is, its capabilities and required characteristics. None of this, however, has anything to do with *how* it's built. Use cases are realized by collaborations of objects working together for a common purpose (to implement the use case). It is, at best, not obvious to go from a set of requirements, *regardless of how they are modeled,* to a set of objects. Many objects may work together to realize a use case, but the same object may participate in multiple use cases, as well.

The identification of objects and their classes is done in two phases. *Object analysis* identifies the essential set of objects necessary to realize the set of identified use cases. That is the subject of the next two chapters. Chapter 3 deals with how to "open the box" and identify the key concepts required to construct the essential logical object model of the system. Chapter 4 focuses on how to define the behavior of those logical elements and map them back to the use case behavioral details.

Chapters 5 through 7 go on to discuss *design.* Although object analysis identifies the set of objects required for *any* reasonable resolution of the requirements, design is all about *optimization.* Design selects one particular solution that optimizes total system quality with respect to all its quality criteria.

Armed with that understanding, let's go "open up the box" and peer inside.

2.5 References

[1] Laplante, Philip A., *Real-Time Systems Design and Analysis: An Engineer's Handbook.* New York: IEEE Computer Society Press, 1992.

[2] Gomaa, Hassan, *Software Design Methods for Concurrent and Real-Time Systems.* SEI Series in Software Engineering, ed. Nico Habermann. Reading, MA: Addison Wesley Longman, 1993.

[3] Ward, Paul, and Steve Mellor, *Structured Development for Real-Time Systems*. 4 vols. Englewood Cliffs, NJ: Prentice Hall, 1985.

[4] Ellis, John R., *Objectifying Real-Time Systems*. New York: SIGS Books, 1994.

[5] Booch, Grady, *Object-Oriented Analysis and Design with Applications*. 2nd ed. Redwood City, CA: Benjamin/Cummings, 1994.

[6] Booch, Grady, *Object Solutions: Managing the Object-Oriented Project*. Menlo Park, CA: Addison Wesley Longman, 1996.

[7] Harel, David "Statecharts: A Visual Formalism for Complex Systems," *Science of Computer Programming* 8 (1987): 231–274.

[8] *OMG Unified Modeling Language Specification (draft)*, Version 1.3 beta R1, Framingham, MA; 1999.

[9] Douglass, Bruce Powel. *Doing Hard Time: Developing Real-Time Systems with UML, Objects, Frameworks, and Patterns*. Reading, MA: Addison Wesley Longman, 1999.

Chapter 3

Analysis: Defining the Object Structure

Once the system's external environment is defined, the analyst must identify the key objects and classes and their relationships within the system itself. The chapter presents several strategies that have proven effective in real-time systems development for the identification of the key objects and classes. These strategies may be used alone or in combination. Relationships and associations among classes and objects enable their collaboration to produce higher-level behaviors. This chapter goes on to identify some rules of thumb for uncovering and testing these relationships.

Notation and Concepts Discussed

Object identification strategies

Object associations

Class relationships

Class diagrams

Sequence diagrams

3.1 The Object Discovery Process

In this chapter, we'll discuss object and class identification and how to infer relationships and associations among them. The next chapter will deal with the definition and elaboration of object behavior and state. The topics covered in this and the next chapter form the basis of all object-oriented analysis.

The use case and context diagrams constructed in the previous step provide a starting point for object-oriented analysis *per se*. The end result will be a structural model of the system, which includes the objects and classes identified within the system, their relationships, and generalization hierarchies. This structural model will be complemented by the behavioral model (see Chapter 4), and the entire analysis model will be elaborated in design.

The order in which the steps of object-oriented analysis are shown in Figure 3-1 is not particularly significant. Object-oriented analysis is a process of discovery that proceeds as much by free association as by sequential processes. Performing the steps in a different order may be better for some problems or some analysts. For example, it may some-

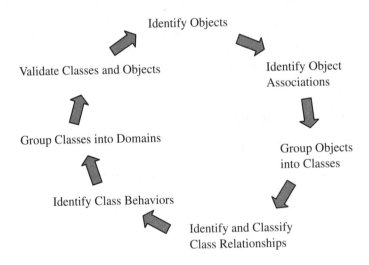

Figure 3-1: *Steps in Core Object-Oriented Analysis*

times be more profitable to first identify the object behaviors and then the class relationships rather than the other way around.

3.2 Connecting the Object Model with the Use Case Model

In the next section, we will present a number of strategies for identifying the objects and, subsequently, the classes inherent in a system. It is important to connect the object model with the preceding use case model for a couple of reasons.

First, the use case model *drives* the object model. Each use case will be realized by a set of objects working together. In the UML, this is called a *collaboration.* As a model element, it is represented as an oval, similar to a use case, but with a dashed line (see Figure 3-2). The collaboration represents a set of objects that assume specific roles in order to achieve the use case. By concentrating on one use case at a time, we can have help guiding our analytic efforts in fruitful directions.

Second, if we make sure to connect the identified objects to the use case model, we are more likely to build the best system that actually meets the requirements. Some developers ignore the requirements of a system, but they do so at their own peril. It is, unfortunately, too common to add features to a system so that it does more than is actually required. Although this may not sound like a problem, it makes testing more difficult, increases the cost of the product, and can lead to much higher maintenance costs. It is also all too common to omit features of a system because the requirements were not followed closely enough. Both of these problems can be avoided by allowing the use case model to drive the object analysis.

Once the object model has been created for the use case, the system-level use cases can be *refined* to take into account the identified objects and their relations. This allows checking that the object model actually does meet the requirements specified in the use cases, as well as illustrating *how* the objects work together to do it.

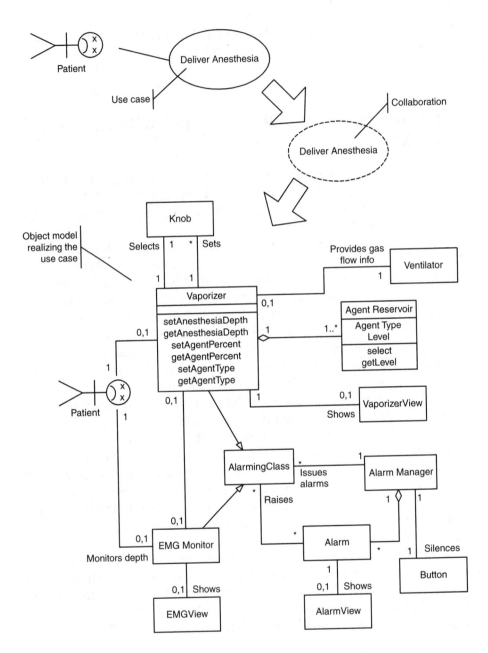

Figure 3-2: *Use Cases, Collaborations, and Objects*

3.3 Key Strategies for Object Identification

Over the years, I've consulted in an extremely varied set of problem domains, from medical systems to factory automation to avionics and fire control (weapons control systems). The *good* part about consulting in such a broad range of fields is that it is extraordinarily interesting and one gets to learn daily.[1] The *bad* part about that is that one is expected to sound intelligent about the problem almost immediately.[2] For any consultant to be successful in that kind of environment, he or she must have some effective strategies for working with engineers and managers who understand their problem domain very well but are often neophyte object wannabes. Table 3-1 outlines what I have found to be the most effective of these object-identification strategies.

This chapter will discuss all these strategies, but note that the analyst need not use them all on any project. These approaches are not orthogonal, and the objects they find will overlap to a significant degree. In fact, different subsets of the strategies will find exactly the same set of objects. Some methods fit some analysts' approaches better than others. It is common to select three or four strategies on a project and apply them. As with all modeling strategies, use those that work well for you and discard the ones that do not.

3.3.1 Underline the Noun Strategy

The first strategy works directly with the written problem or mission statement. Underline each noun or noun phrase in the statement and treat it as a potential object. Objects identified in this way can be put into four categories.

1. Objects of interest

2. Actors

3. Uninteresting objects

4. Attributes of objects

---

[1] Which has dropped me square in the middle of what I call the *knowledge paradox*: The more I *learn*, the less I *know*. I figure by the time I'm 60, I'll have learned so much that I will actually *know* nothing whatsoever!

[2] Good looks and charm get you only so far when they actually want to *fly* the thing!

Table 3-1: *Object Discovery Strategies*

Strategy	Description
Underline the noun	Used to gain a first-cut object list, the analyst underlines each noun or noun-phrase in the problem statement and evaluates it as a potential object.
Identify causal objects	Identify the sources of actions, events, and messages; includes the coordinators of actions.
Identify services (passive contributors)	Identify the targets of actions, events, and messages, as well as entities that passively provide services when requested.
Identify real-world items	Real-world items are entities that exist in the real world but are not necessarily electronic devices. Examples include objects such as respiratory gases, air pressures, forces, anatomical organs, chemicals, vats, and so forth.
Identify physical devices	Physical devices include the sensors and actuators provided by the system, as well as the electronic devices they monitor or control. In the internal architecture, they are processors or ancillary electronic "widgets."
Identify key concepts	Key concepts may be modeled as objects. Bank accounts exist only conceptually, but are important objects in a banking domain. Frequency bins for an online autocorrelator may also be objects.
Identify transactions	Transactions are finite instances of associations between objects that persist for some significant period of time. Examples include bus messages and queued data.
Identify persistent information	Information that must persist for significant periods of time may be objects or attributes. This persistence may extend beyond the power cycling of the device.
Identify visual elements	User interface elements that display data are objects within the user interface domain, such as windows, buttons, scroll bars, menus, histograms, waveforms, icons, bitmaps, and fonts.
Identify control elements	Control elements are objects that provide the interface for the user (or some external device) to control system behavior.
Apply scenarios	Walk through scenarios using the identified objects. Missing objects will become apparent when required actions cannot be achieved with existing objects.

The point of the exercise is to find objects within the first category—objects of interest. Actors have usually already been identified in the use case model, but occasionally some new ones are identified here. Uninteresting objects are objects that have no direct relevance to your system. Attributes also show up as nouns in the problem statement. Sometimes, an attribute is clearly just a property of an object. When in doubt, tentatively classify the noun as an object. If subsequent analysis shows the object is insufficiently interesting, it can be included as an attribute of some other object.

An elevator is a real-time system familiar to everyone. Below is a problem statement for an elevator system with the noun phrases in italics.

A software *system* must control a *set of eight Acme elevators* for a *building* with 20 *floors.* Each *elevator* contains a *set of buttons,* each corresponding to a desired *floor.* These are called *floor request buttons,* because they indicate a *request* to go to a specific *floor.* Each *elevator,* as well, has a *current floor indicator* above the *door.* Each *floor* has two *buttons* for requesting *elevators,* called *elevator request buttons,* because *they* request an *elevator.*

Each *floor* has a sliding *door* for each *shaft* arranged so that two *door halves* meet in the center when closed. When the *elevator* arrives at the *floor,* the *door* opens at the same time the *door* on the *elevator* opens. The *floor* does have both *pressure and optical sensors* to prevent closing when an *obstacle* is between the two *door halves.* If an *obstruction* is detected by either *sensor,* the *door* shall open. The *door* shall automatically close after a *timeout period* of five seconds after the *door* opens. The detection of an *obstruction* shall restart the *door closure time* after an *obstruction* is removed. There is a *speaker* on each *floor* that "pings" in response to the arrival of an *elevator.*

On each *floor (except the highest and lowest),* there are two *elevator request buttons, one for UP* and *one for DOWN.* On each *floor,* above each *elevator door,* there is an *indicator* that specifies the *floor* the *elevator* is currently at and another *indicator* for its current *direction.* The *system* shall respond to an *elevator request* by sending the nearest elevator that is either idle or already going in the requested *direction.* If no *elevators* are currently available, the *request* shall pend until an *elevator* meets the above *criterion.* Once pressed, the *request buttons* are backlit to indicate that a *request* is pending. Pressing an *elevator request button* when a *request* for that *direction* is already pending shall have no *effect.* When an *elevator* arrives to handle the *request,* the *backlight* shall be removed. If the *button* is pressed when an *elevator* is on the *floor* to handle the *request* (that is, *it* is slated to go in the selected *direction*), then the *door* shall stop closing and the *door closure timer* shall be reset.

To enhance safety, a *cable tension sensor* monitors the *tension* on the *cable* that controls the *elevator.* In the event of a *failure* in which the *measured tension* falls below a *critical value,* then four external *locking clamps* connected to running *tracks* in the *shaft* stop the *elevator* and hold *it* in place.

Many of these are clearly redundant references to the same object. Others are not of interest. The elevator *cable,* for example, is not nearly as interesting to the safety system as the *cable tension sensor.*[3] Likewise, the *passengers* (clearly actors) are not as interesting as the *buttons* they push and the *indicators* they read, which are likely to be inside the scope of the system under development. Other objects clearly need not be modeled at all.

A list can be constructed from the underlined noun phrases of the likely candidate objects. Table 3-2 shows object quantities, where specified, with parentheses and a few probable attributes of some of these objects, as shown in Table 3-3.

You can see that this strategy quickly identified many objects but also identified nouns that are clearly not interesting to the analyst.

3.3.2 Identify the Causal Objects

Once the potential objects are identified, look for the most behaviorally active ones. These are objects that:

- Produce or control actions
- Produce or analyze data
- Provide interfaces to people or devices

---

[3] That is, it need not be modeled within the system. The cable tension sensor, however, must be modeled.

Table 3-2: *Candidate Objects*

system (1)	elevator (8)	building (1)
floor (20)	request	button
floor request button (8*20)	elevator request button (20*2)	current floor indicator (8)
door (20*8 + 8)	optical sensor	obstruction
pressure sensor	speaker	UP button
door half	elevator door	indicator
DOWN button	floor door	secondary pressure sensor
internal door set	Open button	Close button
elevator control panel	alarm	central station
Emergency Call button	elevator request	door closure timer
electrical power	telephone	elevator occupants
Stop-Run switch	switch	message
emergency locks	alarm area	mechanical locking clamp
pressure sensor	tracks	electrical power source

Table 3-3: *Object Attributes*

Object	Attribute
Elevator	Direction
	Status
	Location
Button	Backlight
Alarm	Status
Cable tensor sensor	Cable tension
	Critical value

- Store information
- Provide services to people or devices
- Contain other types of fundamental objects
- Are transactions of device or person interaction

The first two categories are commonly lumped together as *causal objects*. A causal object is an object that autonomously performs actions, coordinates the activities of component objects, or generates events. Many causal objects will eventually become *active objects* and serve as the root composite object of a thread.[4] Their components execute within the context of the thread of the owner composite.

Clearly, the most behaviorally active objects are few in number.

Floor

Elevator

Door

Button

Request

Indicator

Cable tension sensor

Mechanical locking clamp

3.3.3 Identify Services (Passive Contributors)

Passive objects are less obvious than causal objects. They may provide passive control, data storage, or both. A simple switch is a passive control object. It provides a service to the causal objects (it turns the light on or off upon request), but it does not initiate actions by itself. Passive objects are also known as servers, because they provide services to client objects.

Simple sensors are passive data objects. An A/D converter might acquire data on command and return it to an actor, or as the result of an event initiated by an active object. Printers and chart recorders are common passive service providers as they print text and graphics on command. A hardware passive service provider might be a chip that performs a cyclic redundancy check computation over a block of data.

---

[4] Although the thread model for the system isn't determined until architectural design, as discussed in Chapter 5.

3.3.4 Identify Real-World Items

Object-oriented systems often need to model the information or behavior of real-world objects, even though they are not part of the system *per se*. A bank account system must model the relevant properties of customers, even though customers are clearly outside the accounting system. Typical customer objects will contain attributes such as:

- Name
- Social Security number
- Address
- Phone number
- Mother's maiden name

An ECG monitor might model a heart as containing:

- Heart rate
- Frequency of preventricular contractions
- Electrical axis

In anesthesia systems, modeling organs as "sinks" for anesthetic agent uptake can aid in closed-loop control of agent delivery, and prevent toxemia.

This strategy looks at things in the real world that interact in the system. Not all aspects of these real-world objects are modeled—only the ones relevant to the system. For example, the *color* of the heart or its neural control properties typically won't be modeled within an ECG system. Those aspects are irrelevant to the use cases realized by the ECG monitor. However, modeling its beat and PVC rate, as well as cardiac output, *is* appropriate and relevant. If the system manipulates information about its actors, then the system should model at least their relevant aspects as objects.

3.3.5 Identify Physical Devices

Real-time systems interact with their environment using sensors and actuators. These devices, in turn, must communicate through other devices called interfaces. The system controls and monitors physical devices inside and outside the system. Devices providing information used by the system are typically modeled as objects and must be configured, calibrated, enabled, and controlled so that they can provide services to the system. For example, deep within the inner workings of the system, processors typically perform initial Power-On Self Tests (POSTs) and periodic (or continuous) Built-In Tests (BITs). Devices frequently have nontrivial state machines and must provide status information on command. When device information and state must be maintained, the devices may be modeled as objects to hold the information about their operational status.

For example, a stepper motor is a physical device that can be modeled as an object with the attributes and behaviors, as shown in Table 3-4.

Generally, only the <u>interfaces to physical devices</u> are actually modeled within this kind of class, because the object presents an interface to client objects within the system. The object itself usually focuses on the communication with the device to achieve its client's purposes and *not* how the device actually works. The only exception to this rule is in constructing simulation systems, in which case modeling the internal behavior of the device is the *point* of the object.

3.3.6 Identify Key Concepts

Key concepts are important abstractions within the domain that have interesting attributes and behaviors. These abstractions often do not have physical realizations, but they must, nevertheless, be modeled by the system. Within the user interface (UI) domain, a *window* is a key concept. In the banking domain, an *account* is a key concept. In an autonomous manufacturing robot, a *task plan* is the set of steps required to implement the desired manufacturing process. In the design of a C compiler, *functions, data types,* and *pointers* are key concepts. These

Table 3-4: *Stepper Model Object*

Attributes	Position
Operations	Step(nSteps)
	GetPos
	Zero
Button	Backlight

objects have no physical manifestation. They exist only as abstractions modeled within the appropriate domains as objects.

3.3.7 Identify Transactions

Transactions are objects that must persist for a finite period of time and represent the interactions of other objects. Some example transaction objects are outlined in Table 3-5.

In the elevator case study, an elevator request is clearly a transaction. It has a relatively short life span, either:

- Beginning when the passenger pushes the elevator request button and ending when the elevator arrives and opens its doors, or

- Beginning when the passenger pushes the floor request button and ending when the elevator arrives at its destination and opens its doors

Other examples of transactions are alarms and (reliable) bus messages. Alarms must persist as long as the dangerous condition is true or until explicitly handled, depending on the system. Alarms will typically have attributes such as:

- Alarm condition
- Alarm priority
- Alarm severity[5]
- Time of occurrence
- Duration of condition

Reliable message transfer requires that a message persist at the site of the sender until an explicit acknowledgement is received. This allows the sender to retransmit if the original message is lost. Bus messages typically have attributes such as:

- Message type
- Priority

---

[5] Priority and severity are orthogonal concepts. *Priority* refers to how a scheduler resolves an execution order when multiple events are waiting to be handled (and is a combination of importance and urgency); the *severity* refers to how bad the outcome of the fault condition may be if unhandled. These concepts are discussed in more detail in [5].

Table 3-5: *Example Transaction Objects*

Object 1	Object 2	Association	Transaction Object
Woman	Man	Marriage	Marriage object: • Wedding date • Wedding location • Prenuptial agreement • Witnesses
			Divorce object: • Filing date • Decree date • Maintenance schedule • Amount paid to lawyers
Controller	Actuator	Controls	Control message over bus
Alarming class	Alarm manager	Issues alarms	Silence Activate
Customer	Store	Buys things at	Order Return
Display system	Sensor	Displays values for	Alarm Error
Elevator request button	Elevator	Issues request to	Request for elevator
Floor request button	Elevator	Issues request to	Request for floor
Task plan	Robot arm	Controls	Command

- Source address
- Target address
- Message data
- Cyclic redundancy check

3.3.8 Identify Persistent Information

Persistent information is typically held within passive objects, such as stacks, queues, trees, or databases. Either volatile memory (RAM or SRAM) or long-term storage (FLASH, EPROM, EEPROM, or disk) may store persistent data.

A robot must store and recall task plans. Subsequent analysis of the system may reveal other persistent data. For example, the information in Table 3-6 may be persistent.

Such data can be used for scheduling equipment maintenance and may appear in monthly or yearly reports.

3.3.9 Identify Visual Elements

Many real-time systems interact directly or indirectly with human users. Real-time system displays may be as simple as a single blinking

Table 3-6: *Possible Persistent Information Objects*

Information	Storage Period	Description
Task plans	Unlimited	"Programs" for the robotic system must be constructed, stored, recalled for editing, and recalled for execution.
Errors	Between service calls	Error log holding the error identifier, severity, location, and time/date of occurrence. This will facilitate maintenance of the system.
Alarms	Until next service call	Alarms indicate conditions that must be brought to the attention of the user, even though they may not be errors. Tracking them between service calls allows analysis of the reliability of the system.
Hours of operation	Between service calls	Hours of operation aid in tracking costs and scheduling service calls.
Security access	Unlimited	Stores valid users, their identifiers, and passwords to permit different levels of access.
Service information	Unlimited	Tracks service calls and updates performed: when, what, and by whom.

LED to indicate power status, or as elaborate as a full Windows-like GUI with buttons, windows, scroll bars, icons, and text.[6] Visual elements used to convey information to the user are objects within the user interface domain.

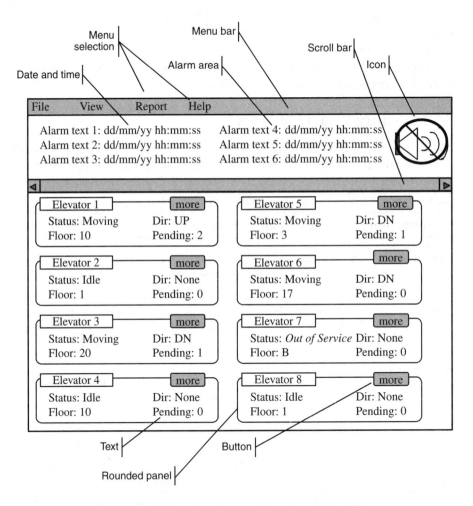

Figure 3-3: *Elevator Central Station: Main View*

---

[6] No doubt you've all heard this one: "How many Microsoft engineers does it take to change a light bulb? Ans: None. Bill Gates just declares 'Darkness at your Fingertips' to be the new standard graphical user interface."

In many environments, user interface (UI) designers specialize in the construction of visual interaction models or prototypes that developers implement.

For example, consider the sample screens for the elevator central control station shown in Figures 3-3 through 3-5.

We see a number of common visual elements:

- Window
- Rectangle
- Rounded panel
- Horizontal scroll bar

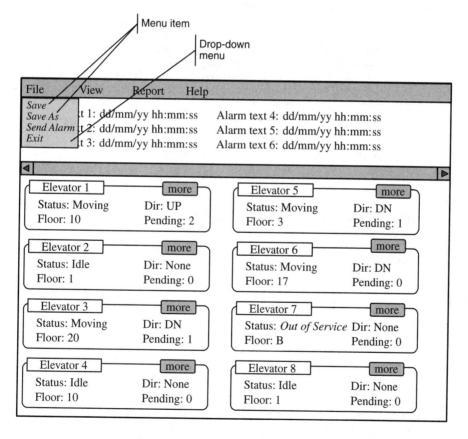

Figure 3-4: *Elevator Central Station: Menu View*

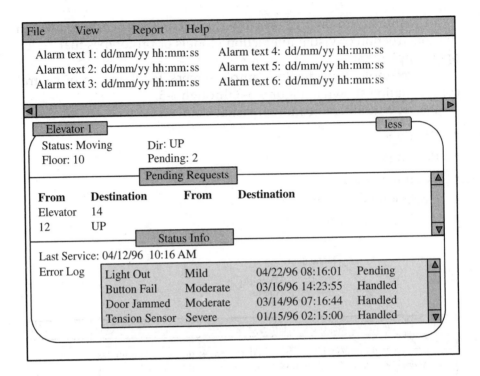

Figure 3-5: *Elevator Central Station: Zoom View*

- Scroll button (left, right, up, down)
- Button
- Menu bar
- Menu selection
- Drop-down menu
- Menu item
- List box
- Text
- Icon (for alarm silence)

Each of these is an object within the UI domain for the elevator central station. These UI objects are depicted in an object message diagram later in this chapter.

3.3.10 Identify Control Elements

Control elements are entities that control other objects and are specific types of causal objects. Some objects, called *composites,* often orchestrate the behaviors of their component objects. These may be simple objects or may be elaborate control systems, such as:

- PID control loops
- Fuzzy logic inference engines
- Expert system inference engines
- Neural network simulators

Some control elements are physical interface devices that allow users to enter commands. The elevator case study has only a few.

- Button (elevator and floor)
- Switch (elevator and floor)
- Keyboard (central station only)
- Mouse (central station only)

3.3.11 Apply Scenarios

The application of use case scenarios is another strategy to identify missing objects, as well as to test that an object collaboration adequately realizes a use case. Using only known objects, step through the messages to implement the scenario. When "you can't get there from here" occurs, it often identifies one or more missing objects.

Mechanistically, this is done by *refining* the use case scenario. Remember from Chapter 2 that the structural context for a use case scenario is the system and the actors participating in the scenario. This means that a use case scenario cannot show objects internal to the system—*because they are not yet known.* However, once we have identified and captured the set of objects in the collaboration, the single system object can be replaced by the set of objects in the collaboration. This provides a more detailed or refined view of the scenario and allows us to ensure that the collaboration does, in fact, realize the use case.

For example, consider the use case scenario in Figure 3-6. It shows the black-box behavior of the pacemaker with respect to the actors *Programmer* and *Heart.* Using the object identification strategies mentioned earlier, let's assume we construct the model in Figure 3-7. We can now

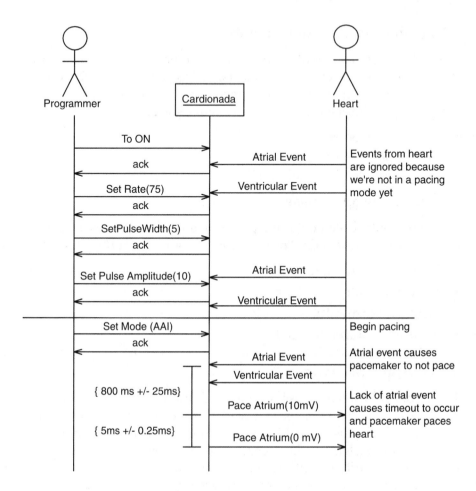

Figure 3-6: *Pace the Heart in AAI Mode (Use Case Level)*

refine the scenario by replacing the system object with the set of identified objects, as shown in Figure 3-8. This is now a white-box view that we can relate directly to our black-box use case view. This more refined view of the same scenario shown in Figure 3-6 shows how the objects in the collaboration work together. Note, for example, that when the *Programmer* instructs the pacemaker to go into AAI pacing mode, it tells the *Atrial Model* to go to *Inhibited* mode, and it tells the *Ventricular Model* to go to *Idle* mode. Figure 3-8 even shows the relationship between the scenario and the state models (not shown) of the *Atrial Model* and *Ventricular Model* objects.

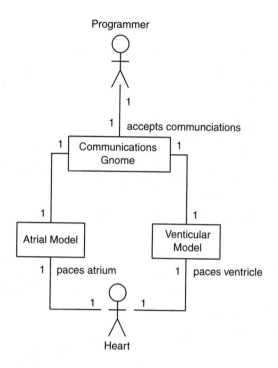

Figure 3-7: *Pacemaker Object Collaboration*

3.4 Identify Object Associations

Early in the analysis, some objects seem to relate to others, even though it is not always clear exactly how. The first step is to identify the existence of such associations. We will discuss the characterization of associations later in this chapter.

There are a few strategies for the identification of object relationships. Each relies on the fact that objects send messages to other objects and every message implies an association, as shown in Table 3-7.

In our elevator example, there are a number of associations, shown in Table 3-8.

Class and object diagrams capture these associations. A line drawn between two objects represents a link (instance of an association) between those objects that supports the transmission of a message from one to the other.

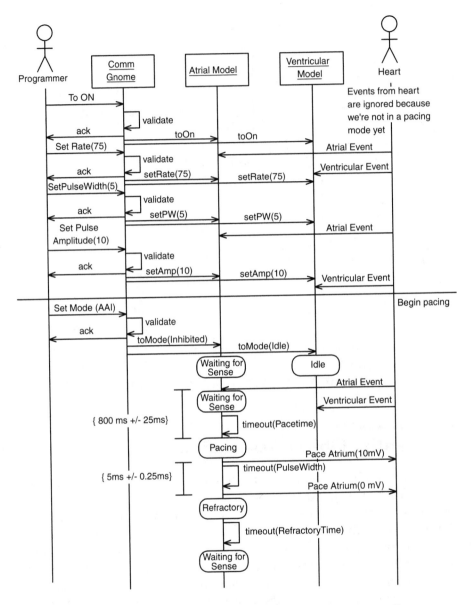

Figure 3-8: *Pace the Heart in AAI Mode (Object Level)*

Figure 3-9 is an object diagram showing the general structure of the identified objects and their neighbors. The system consists of 38 high-level objects: 8 shafts, 8 elevators, 20 floors, and one central station and

Table 3-7: *Object Association Strategies*

Strategy	Description
Identify messages	Each message implies an association between the participating objects.
Identify message sources	The sensors that detect information or events and the creators of information or events are all *message sources.* They pass information on to other objects for handling and storage.
Identify message storage depots	Message storage depots store information for archival purposes or provide a central repository of information for other objects. The depots have associations with the message sources, as well as with the users of that information.
Identify message handlers	Some objects centralize message dispatching and handling. They form connections to either or both message sources and message storage depots.
Identify whole/ part structures	Whole/part relations become aggregation relationships among objects. Wholes often send messages to their parts.
Identify more/ less abstract structures	Some objects are related to each other by differences in levels of abstraction. It is not uncommon for a single, higher-level abstraction to be implemented by a tightly knit set of objects at a more concrete level of abstraction. The larger object in this case becomes a composite object, and the smaller objects become its component parts. The relationship among them becomes a composition relation.
Apply scenarios	Walk through scenarios using the identified objects. The scenarios explicitly show how the messages are sent between objects.

one elevator gnome. The numbers at the upper-left corner of the object represents the instance count—that is, the number of instances of the object in the enclosing context. The shaft, elevator, and floor are all composites that strongly aggregate their components. The instance counts of their components are per instance of their context. That is, each *Elevator* has 20 instances of *Floor Request Button.*

Table 3-8: *Elevator Object Associations*

Message Source	Message Target	Message
Elevator request button	Elevator gnome	Request an elevator
Elevator gnome	Elevator	Request status
Elevator gnome	Elevator	Add destination for elevator
Elevator	Elevator gnome	Accept destination
Elevator	Floor speaker	Arrival event beep
Elevator floor sensor	Elevator	Location
Cable tension sensor	Locking clamps	Engage
Central station	Locking clamps	Release
Cable tension sensor	Central station	Alarm condition
Elevator	Central station	Status
Floor request button	Elevator	Add destination
Run-Stop switch	Elevator	Stop/Run
Run-Stop switch	Central station	Stop/Run
Alarm button	Central station	Alarm condition
Elevator	Door	Open/Close

3.5 Object Attributes

The UML defines an attribute to be "a named property of a type." In this sense, they are "smaller" than objects—they have only a primitive structure and, of themselves, no operations other than get_ and set_. Practically speaking, attributes are the data portion of an object. A sensor object might include attributes such as a calibration constant and a measured value. Attributes are almost always primitive and cannot productively be broken down into subproperties. If you find attributes to be structurally nonprimitive, then they should be modeled as objects owned by the main object rather than as attributes of that main object. For example, if a sensor has a simple scalar calibration constant, then it would be appropriate to model it as an attribute of the sensor object. If,

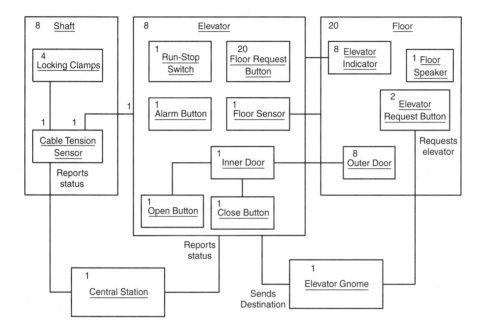

Figure 3-9: *First-Cut Elevator Object Diagram*

however, the sensor object has an entire set of calibration constants, each calibration constant should be modeled as an object aggregrated unidirectionally by the sensor object with a 1-* multiplicity. The set of constants would probably be managed by a container class (added in design), as shown in Figure 3-10. It is important to remember that modeling the table in this way *does not* necessarily entail additional overhead in terms of performance or memory usage, but it does provide superior encapsulation of concerns and easier maintenance.

Sometimes, the primary attributes of an object are obvious, but not always. Developers can ask themselves some key questions to identify the most important attributes of objects, such as:

- What information defines the object?
- Upon what information do the object's operations act?
- Take the object's viewpoint and ask yourself, "What do I know?"
- Are the identified attributes rich in either structure or behavior? If so, they are probably objects, not attributes.

Not this...

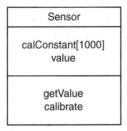

but this ...

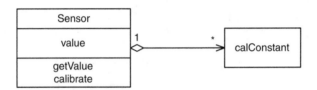

which will become (in mechanistic design) this...

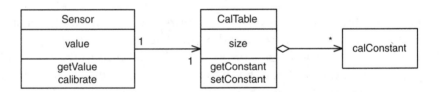

Figure 3-10: *Modeling Nonprimitive Attributes*

- What are the responsibilities of the object? What information is necessary to fulfill these responsibilities?

The *Elevator* class provides a good example of a real-time class with attributes. Let's ask these questions about this class.

- What information defines the object?
  The *Elevator* is a physical thing that must be controlled. To fulfill its function, it must know where it is, where it is going (destination list), and its current direction.

- Upon what information do the object's operations act?
  It has a goto() operation which must act on where it is, its current direction, and its state (moving, stopped, and so forth).

- Take the object's viewpoint and ask yourself, "What do I know?"
  I know where I am, where I am going, and what I am doing right now.

- Are the identified attributes rich in either structure or behavior? If so, they are probably objects, not attributes.
  The *Elevator* has a door that has state (open, closed, opening, closing), interlocks with the floor door, and operations. It is probably an object.

- What are the responsibilities of the object? What information is necessary to fulfill these responsibilities?
  The *Elevator's* primary responsibility is to transport passengers from one floor to another. It needs the attributes of where it is, which direction it is traveling, a list of current destinations, and its current state.

There are cases in which an object with no attributes is valid within the domain. A button is a reasonable class, but what attributes does it have? Probably none, in fact. Some composite objects are only aggregates of many objects, with no data specific in and of themselves. Other objects contain only functions and, therefore, are often called functoids or (in UML-speak) class utilities.

3.6 Discovering Candidate Classes

Of the many objects identified in the problem statement, many of them are structurally identical. In the elevator case study, for example, there are eight elevators, all the same. Similarly, there are scads[7] of buttons, but they all appear to be structurally identical. Each is activated by depression, acknowledges with a backlight, and so forth. Objects that are identical in structure are said to be of the same *class*. The next analysis activity is to propose candidate classes for the identified objects.

---

[7] Scad: a technical term meaning *a lot*. Antonym: *scootch.*

Classes are abstractions of objects. Objects that are identical in type (even if different in value) are abstracted into a class. In the elevator example, buttons differ in their purpose. Floor request buttons reside within the elevator and request a destination for that specific elevator. Elevator request buttons reside on the floor and request any elevator to come to the floor and take passengers in a specific direction. Each button is structurally identical and differs only in its context. It depresses when pushed and issues a message when released. When the message is accepted, the button is backlit. The *button* appears to be a good choice for a candidate class.

Similarly, other objects can be abstracted into candidate classes, such as:

- Elevator
- Door
- Floor
- Speaker
- Floor indicator
- Elevator indicator

and so on. From these classes, specific objects, such as "Elevator #2 Request Button for Floor #8," may be instantiated. Classes so identified can be put in a class diagram for a simpler structural view than the object diagram, especially since the object model of a system changes over time (as objects are created and destroyed).

3.7 Class Diagrams

Class diagrams are the most important diagrams in object-oriented analysis and design. They show the structure of the system in terms of classes and objects, including how the objects and classes relate to each other. Class diagrams are the primary road map of the system and its object-oriented decomposition. They are similar to object diagrams, except they show primarily classes rather than instances.

Figure 3-11 shows a class diagram for a banking application. The "0,1 - *" multiplicity between the *ATM Card* class and the *Checking Account* class shows that the *ATM Card* object is optional or a single

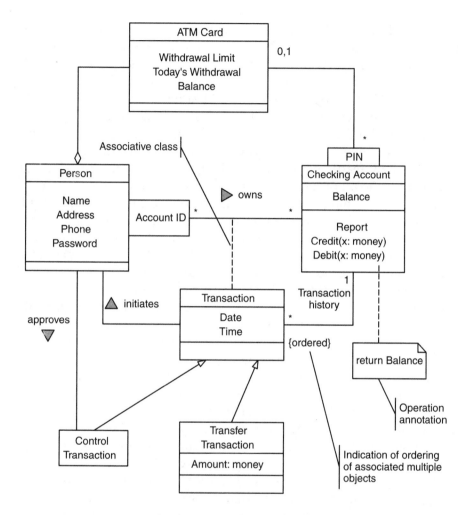

Figure 3-11: *Banking Class Diagram*

ATM Card object may participate. At the other role of the association, a single *ATM Card* object may reference multiple *Checking Account* objects. This can occur when a single bank customer has multiple checking accounts, all of which may be accessed via a single ATM Card and PIN.[8]

---

[8] PIN is a qualifier and will end up as an attribute within the ATM Card class.

Similarly, an "* - *" association exists between the *Person* class and the *Checking Account* class. This is because a person may have more than one checking account (hence the "*" at the checking account role end), and a checking account may be owned by more than one person (hence the "*" at the person role end). Although "* - *" associations are relatively rare, they do pop up from time to time. Note also that the association is bidirectional, so given a client you can get to his or her accounts, and given an account you can find its owner clients.

Three new features appear on this figure: an associative class, an annotation, and an ordering constraint. As noted in Chapter 1, associations themselves may have interesting attributes and behaviors. In this case, the *Transaction* class captures the interesting parts of the relationship between the *Person* and the *Checking Account* classes. Transactions may be things like transferring money (as in debits and credits) or may control checking account behavior (such as Open and Close).

Just to complicate things, these transactions persist in the form of a transaction history. The relationship between the *Checking Account* and *Transaction* classes is "1 - *." A single checking account object maintains a list (0 or more) of transactions. The checking account *report* operation prints a list of the transactions periodically. This "1-*" relationship is maintained as an ordered list, as indicated by the "{ordered}" constraint. This is usually a design detail, but it may be added whenever the requirement for the constraint becomes clear.

Annotations may be added for a variety of purposes. In this case, the annotation shows the return type of the checking account's debit operation. Other information of interest may be freely added.

Figure 3-12 shows some special types of associations. In Microsoft Windows, various controls, such as list boxes and buttons, are themselves windows. The owner window contains these controls and manipulates them via *handles*. This characteristic is an instance of a general method of accessing objects, called *access keys*. When appropriate, access keys may be indicated on the relationship to indicate how this relationship is managed. Relationships with access keys are called *qualified relationships*. Access keys, known as *qualifiers*, are special attributes of a class used to manage access.

This figure also shows two recursive relationships. The first, explained earlier, accounts for the fact that a window may contain controls and that controls are windows themselves. The second, from the multiple document interface (*MDI*) *Window* subclass, indicates links to

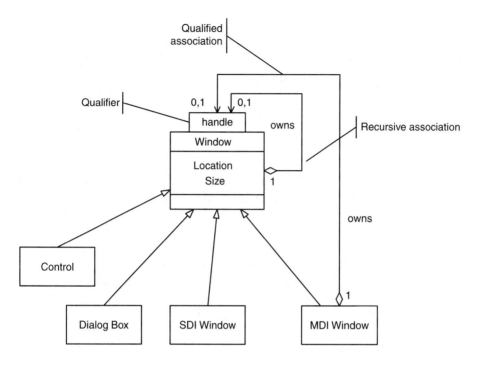

Figure 3-12: *Special Associations*

different objects, which happen also to be of class *Window*. This figure demonstrates that multiple relationships between a pair of classes can exist and do so for one of two reasons:

- Different associations with the same objects
- Associations with different objects

3.7.1 Elevator Class Diagram Example

Figure 3-13 shows the class diagram for an elevator system. It contains the fundamental classes, their (unrefined) associations, and the multiplicity of their associations. The multiplicity implies, but does not strictly define, the number of objects to be instantiated from a class. For example, the 1 to 1 association between the *Elevator* and its *Run-Stop Switch* component indicates that there is a single switch for each elevator. The 1-* relationship between the *Elevator* and the *Elevator Gnome* indicates that there are

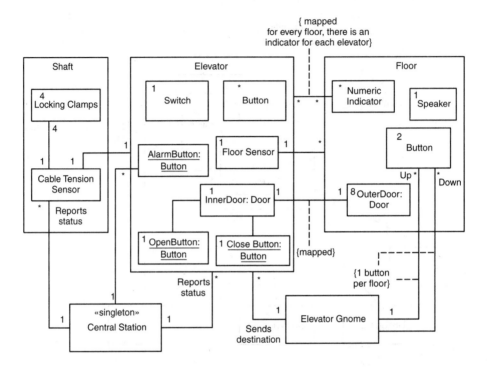

Figure 3-13: *Elevator Class Diagram*

many elevators for each gnome,[9] but it does not indicate the total number of gnomes. A large elevator system might have several banks of elevators, each with its own gnome controller. There is only a single instance of the *Central Station* class, so it includes the stereotype «singleton».

The *Elevator* has two associations to the class *Button*. The first is shown as the *Alarm Button: Button* object instance. The role name that would be used on the association line is used as the instance name. The second is the composition relation to the floor request buttons.[10] In addition *Open* and *Close* buttons define two more associations between the *Elevator* and *Button* classes.

---

[9] If desired, the explicit cardinality 8 can be used rather than *, but this limits the reuse of the model for other, similar systems that may have greater or fewer numbers of elevators.

[10] *Floor Request Button* is the name of the objects instantiated from the class *Button* within the class *Elevator,* which request the elevator go to a specific floor. Remember that all the buttons are structurally the same, so *Floor Request Button* is of the same class as *Elevator Request Button.*

The *-* association between the *Elevator* and the *Numeric Indicator* is due to the fact that each floor has an indicator dedicated to each elevator. Therefore, there are 20 indicators for each elevator, one for each floor, monitoring each elevator. From the perspective of the floor, each floor has one elevator indicator for each of the eight elevators. From the perspective of the elevator, there are 20 indicators, one per floor. The *{mapped}* constraint notes the fact that there must be a specific mathematical relation between these sets of objects.

3.8 Defining Class Relationships

The first part of this chapter presented strategies for identifying objects, grouping them into classes, as well as the initial identification of the associations among the objects and classes. This section will provide a taxonomy of object and class associations and strategies for their classification. This will aid in the identification of associations and how they can be effectively used to assist the required collaborations.

The UML provides several important types of relationships.

- Association
- Aggregation
- Composition
- Generalization
- Dependency

The existence of an association between objects means that one or both objects send messages to the other. Associations are *structural*, meaning that they must be part of the class from which the objects are instantiated. For that reason, analysis considers association as belonging to classes, rather than objects. Instances of associations, called *links*, occur between objects. Links may come and go during system execution as objects link and unlink to realize their roles in their collaborations. Aggregation and composition are specialized forms of association that imply increasing levels of ownership and responsibility.

Generalization is fundamentally a relationship between classes (rather than objects), because it defines a set of attributes, behaviors, and interfaces for the descendant classes. It is not implemented as messages sent to a parent class to invoke inherited behavior—subclasses already *have* these attributes and behaviors.

Dependency means that one model element depends upon another in some way. A common example is a compilation dependency among packages; another is the dependency between a parameterized class with a formal parameter list and an instantiable class bound with an actual parameter list. Because dependencies are not often identified during object analysis, their discussion will be deferred until the later chapters on design.

Figure 3-14 shows a class diagram with the primary classes of controller, sensor, and actuator. This figure has four types of relationships. It shows the structural arrangement of classes in terms of classes that send messages, have ownership relations, or are more general or specific versions of other classes.

3.8.1 Associations

Associations are logically bidirectional unless explicitly constrained. The association between a *dog owner* and his *dog* can be expressed in either direction, indicating this bidirectionality.

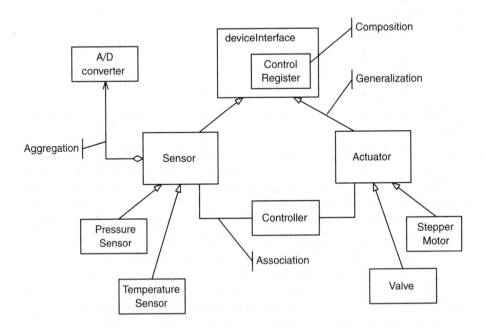

Figure 3-14: *Class Relationships*

He owns the dog.
The dog belongs to him.

or

The Floor Request Button sends requests to the Elevator.
The Elevator receives requests from the Floor Request Button.

It is rare that a relationship is actually implemented bidirectionally. In practice, such relationships are usually navigated only in a single direction. For example, the message would usually be sent as:

Dog.Send Tail->Wag

rather than

Tail.Send Dog->Wag

Associations are most often implemented as pointers or references to objects. Navigating in a single direction implies that one object may navigate to the other (via an operation in the latter), but not vice versa. For example,

```
class Dog {
    Tail* pT;
public:
    void BeHappy(void) { pT->Wag(20); );
    void BeSad(void) { pT->Wag(2); };
    void BeExcited(void) { pT->Wag(50); };
    void BeMelancholy(void) { pT->Wag(5); };
};
```

It may not be possible, given just a tail, to identify which dog is emoting. It is a question of navigability.

Associations navigable in a single direction are known as *client-server* associations. The client is the object with the reference, while the server is the object with the data or operation invoked by the client. Servers are mostly passive or reactive objects, responding to requests from their clients. Clients must know about the servers to be able to invoke their services. Servers should not know about their clients, because this introduces pathological coupling and makes the addition of new clients more difficult. In practical terms, it is necessary to use only a single role name for unidirectional association, typically at the server end.

An alternative to client-server association is *peer-to-peer* association. Although much less common than client-server, it does come up from time to time. A peer-to-peer association implies bidirectional message passing. Each object must know about the other. This is generally implemented as two independent client-server relationships, one in each direction. It is common to identify both role names on bidirectional associations.

3.8.2 Aggregation and Composition

An *aggregation* is a special type of association that implies logical or physical ownership. Some authors prefer the term *aggregation* for this type of relationship; others prefer the term *whole/part.*

Aggregation is further subtyped into *physical* and *catalog aggregation. Physical aggregation* is used when the multiplicity on the "part" end is 1. Note, however, that although the name suggests a physical relationship, the meaning is only that the "whole" directly accesses the "part."

When the multiplicity of the part is either optional or greater than one, then the relationship is *catalog aggregation.* The relationship must provide some means of navigating among the multiple parts.

Both physical and catalog aggregation support sharing of the same parts among different owners. This is shown adding the constraint of {shared} on an aggregate from a single class with the multiplicity of greater than one. If two different classes share a part, then the {shared} constraint must be applied to both aggregations. This syntax is shown in Figure 3-15.

Composition is a strong form of aggregation, similar to Booch's *aggregation by value* [2]. Composition means that part objects (called *components*) are solely the responsibility of the composite class. Composites must create and destroy their components. Components cannot be shared among composites. Composition is shown by graphical inclusions of the components within the composite or with a filled-in aggregation diamond. When inclusion is used, the multiplicity of the component is provided at its upper-left corner.

3.8.3 RTOS Example

Figure 3-16 shows a real-time example association and aggregation. This figure depicts the portion of a real-time operating system that

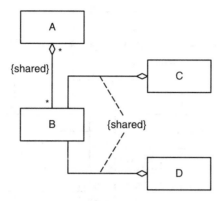

Figure 3-15: *Two Ways of Showing Shared Aggregations*

manages tasks. The RTOS Kernel contains a number of fixed-size heaps and tasks. In addition it provides services to post multiple events and messages to a task. RTOS kernels normally provide priority queues to the task for this purpose. However, the actual structure of these message depots is a job for design rather than analysis. Therefore, the relationship is shown as catalog aggregation. During design, classes to manage the events and messages must be added. For the purpose of analysis, however, it does not matter whether these components are arranged in a linear list, a binary tree, or some more-exotic organizational structure. It *is* important in the problem domain to order the components. In this case, the problem statement (supposedly) specifies a FIFO ordering, but ordering by task priority could have been specified, as well.

The *task* is clearly the central class in the figure. The RTOS must maintain a great deal of information about the tasks in order to properly schedule and manage their execution. From the RTOS perspective, tasks contain a number of critical components.

- Task stack
- Task context
- Executable code
- Static RAM blocks
- OS Event collection
- OS Message collection

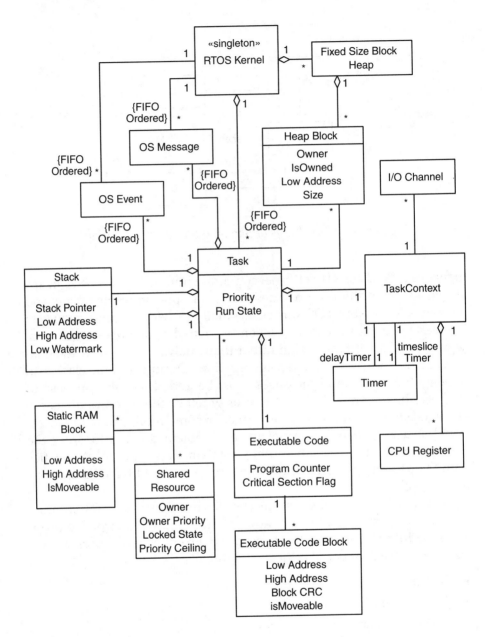

Figure 3-16: *RTOS Task Example*

A task also has important attributes.

- Priority
- Run state

When multiple tasks are ready to run, a priority-driven scheduler selects the task with the highest priority to run. In fact, it preempts currently executing tasks to run a ready higher-priority task.

The *task context* class contains information for internal use of the OS. It contains an image of CPU registers, so the RTOS can restore the task state exactly as it was prior to preemption.

The *executable code* class contains information about the task code. The program counter marks exactly where the program was preempted so that it can resume (note that this could be stored with the CPU registers, as well, but this model is somewhat more general). This particular RTOS does not constrain tasks to exist within contiguous memory. Tasks contain one or more *executable code blocks*, each of which has:

- Its memory block defined
- Define whether the block can be moved by the OS
- A CRC over the block

The CRC allows the OS to run a background watchdog task to check for executable code corruption. The allowance for multiple code blocks allows for some portions of executable memory to be in ROM, with other portions in RAM. Similarly, a task may contain multiple static RAM blocks for global memory, as well.

Each task has a separate stack. The stack pointer attribute could be stored with the CPU registers, but again this model is somewhat more general.[11] The low-water mark is an address an RTOS watchdog could check. Some RTOSs fill stack memory with a specific byte. The definition of a *low-water mark* allows for a watchdog task to check for a low stack condition.

The *isMoveable* attribute on static RAM and executable code blocks implies some design work is ahead. For RAM access, it indicates the need for multiple levels of indirection for static memory access. If the OS moves the location of the static RAM, then the task code must reference

---

[11] In particular, it allows for the simulation and execution of tasks at a level much higher than the underlying CPU hardware.

into an RTOS table that references the actual memory. When the memory is moved, the task references need not be modified. It is sufficient to change only the second reference within the RTOS itself. Executable code references must be indirect and the code position-independent.

Tasks have a couple of associations, as well. Notably, they use *heap blocks* from the heap and they share *shared resources.* The heap blocks allow the task to allocate memory dynamically. Fixed-size heap blocks mitigate the common memory fragmentation problem.[12]

Shared resources are a thorny issue for real-time systems. A task may require a resource in order to continue. Another client locking a resource required by a task blocks it from continuing. When this occurs, the RTOS sets the task's run state attribute to *blocked.* The RTOS kernel typically moves the task from the ready queue to the blocked queue until the OS posts an event indicating that the resource is available for the task. Resources can have a *priority ceiling*[13] attribute, as well. See Chapter 5 for more details on modeling shared resources.

3.8.4 Associative Classes

In distributed systems, the classic example of an associative class is a message class. In addition to the information being sent from one object to another, the message object may contain additional information specific to the relationship and even the link instance, for example:

- Message priority
- Message route
- Session identifiers
- Sequence numbers
- Flow control information
- Data format information

---

[12] Repeated allocation from the memory free store can result in memory being fragmented into small noncontiguous chunks. This can lead to memory allocation failure when no fragment is large enough to satisfy a request, even though the total available amount of memory is adequate.

[13] Priority ceiling is used in priority-ceiling scheduling algorithms. Such algorithms elevate task priorities dynamically when resources are locked to bound priority inversion. See [5] for a more detailed discussion.

- Data packaging information
- Time-to-live information for the message
- Protocol revision number
- Data integrity check information

In a transaction-oriented system, associative classes also contain information specific to the transaction.

An associative class is used when information does not seem to belong to either object in the association, or belongs to both equally. Marriage is an association between two people objects. Where do the following attributes belong?

- Date of marriage
- Location of marriage
- Prenuptial agreement

Clearly, these are attributes of the marriage and not of the participants.

Figure 3-17 shows a case of an associative class. In this distributed system model, one subsystem contains the sensor class and acts as a server for the data from the sensors. The client subsystem displays this data to the user. The association between the measurement server and measurement client is of interest here.

One way to implement the association is to have the client explicitly ask whenever it wants data to display. Another is to have the server provide the data whenever it becomes available. However, neither option may be the best use of a finite-bandwidth bus. In addition, what if another client wants to be added to the recipient list for the data? Some buses provide the ability to broadcast such data, but most target a specific recipient.

The associative class solution provided here uses a *session*. A session is a negotiated agreement between two communicating objects. Sessions save bandwidth because they negotiate some information up front so that it need not be passed within each message. Nonsessioned, or *connectionless*, communications are similar to postcards. Every time a postcard is mailed, it must contain the complete destination and source addresses. A session is more like a phone call. Once the destination is dialed and the connection established, communication of arbitrary length and complexity can be performed, without resending the phone number or reconnecting.

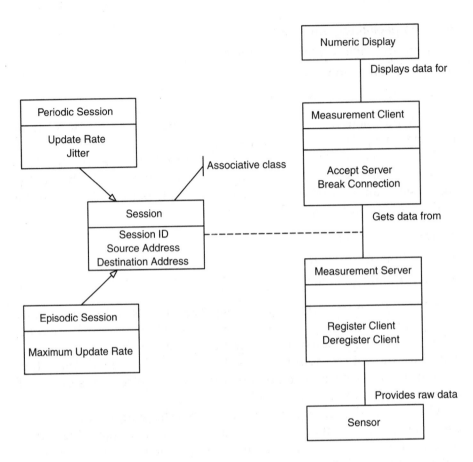

Figure 3-17: *Session Associative Class*

In this case, the session contains two important pieces of information: the source and target addresses. Two different session subtypes
are defined based on the update policy, which can be either *episodic* or
periodic. Episodic, in this context, means that the server sends data when
it changes—that is, when an episode occurs. Periodic means that the
server must send the data at a fixed interval. Episodic sessions, in this example, have a maximum update rate to make sure that a bursty system
does not overload the bus. Periodic sessions have a defined update rate.

The measurement server contains two operations to assist in session management. The first is *Register Client*. This operation accepts the
registration of a new client and participates in the negotiated construc-

tion of a session object. The *Deregister Client* operation removes a registered client.

The measurement client contains two operations to support its role in negotiating the session: *Accept Server* and *Break Connection.*

Who owns the session? Arguments can be made for both the server and the client. The server must track information about the session so that it knows when and how to issue updates. The client initiates the session and must also know about update policy and rates. The solution shown in the figure is that the session is an associative class and contains attributes about the relationship between the two primary classes. Because this is a distributed system, the implementation would involve creating two coordinating session objects (or a single *distributed object),* one on each processor node, providing session information to the local client or server.

3.8.5 Generalization Relationships

Generalization is a taxonomic relationship between classes. The class higher in the taxonomic hierarchy is sometimes called the *parent, generalized, base,* or *super class.* The class inheriting properties from the base class is called the *child, specialized, derived,* or *subclass.* Derived classes have all the properties of their parents, but may extend and specialize them.

Using Aristotelian logic and standard set theory, generalizing along a single characteristic guarantees that the classes are *disjoint.*[14] When the set of subclasses enumerates all possible subclasses along the characteristic, the subclassing is said to be *complete.*

The button subclasses in Figure 3-18 are specialized along the lines of behavior. Simple buttons issue an event message when pressed, but they have no state memory. Toggle buttons jump back and forth between two states on sequential depressions. Multistate buttons run through a (possibly elaborate) state machine upon each depression. Group buttons deselect all other buttons within the group when depressed.

In the UML, generalization implies two things: *inheritance* and *substitutability.* Inheritance means that (almost) everything that is true of a

---

[14] Disjoint means that the classes represent nonoverlapping or orthogonal alternatives. Male and female, for example, are disjoint sets. Fuzzy sets are inherently nondisjoint and allow partial membership. Object subclasses are assumed to be crisp sets (all-or-none membership) rather than fuzzy.

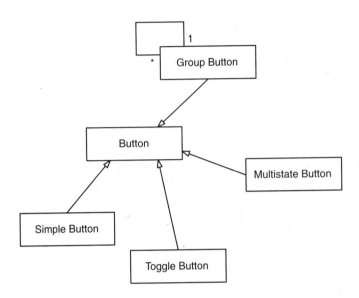

Figure 3-18: *Button Subclasses*

superclass is also true of all its subclasses. This means that a subclass has all its parent's attributes, operations, associations, and dependencies. If the superclass has a statechart to define its behavior, then the subclass will inherit that statechart. The subclass is free to both specialize and extend the inherited properties. Specialization means that the subclass may polymorphically redefine an operation (or statechart) to be more semantically appropriate for the subclass. Extension means that the subclass may add new attributes, operations, associations, and so forth.

Substitutability means that an instance of a subclass may always be substituted for an instance of its superclass, without breaking the semantics of the model. This is known as the *Liskov Substitution Principle* (LSP)[3]. It states that a subclass must obey polymorphic rules in exactly the same manner as its superclass. For example,

```
class Animal {
public:
    virtual void speak(void) = 0; // virtual base class
};

class dog: public Animal {
public:
```

```
        void speak(void) { cout << "Arf!" << endl; };
};

class fish: public Animal {
public:
        void speak(void) { cout << "Blub! " << endl; };
};

class cat: public Animal {
public:
        void speak(void) {
            cout << "<Aloof disdain>" << endl; };
};
void main(void) {
    Animal *A;
    dog d;
    fish f;
    cat c;
    A = &d;
    A->speak();
    A = &c;
    A->speak();
    A = &f;
    A->speak();
};
```

The base class (*Animal*) accesses the three subtypes through a pointer (A). Nonetheless, the access to the speak() method for each is identical, satisfying the LSP.

For the LSP to work, the relationship between the superclass and the subclass must be one of specialization or extension. Whatever is true of the superclass must also be true of the subclass, because the subclass *is a* type of its superclass. A dog *is* an Animal, so all the things true about *all* animals are also true about dogs. All the behaviors common to all animals can also be performed by dogs. If the abstraction *animal* had an attribute or behavior that was not true of dogs (such as being able to produce free oxygen via photosynthesis), a dog would not be "a type of" animal.

That being said, a subclass is free to specialize the behavior of a superclass. The speak() method defined within animal is an example. Each subclass does a different thing while still meeting the requirement of supporting the behavior speak(). Locomote() is another example. Dogs, cats, fish, and birds all locomote, but they implement it differently. This is what is meant by *specialization*.

Subclasses are also free to extend their inherited structure by adding new behaviors or attributes. We can add some new behaviors to the dog and cat classes that are not true of animals in general.

```
class dog: public Animal {
public:
   void speak(void) { cout << "Arf!" << endl; };
   void slobber(float slobberIndex);
   void AttackJogger(int fearLevel);
};

class cat: public Animal {
public:
   void speak(void) {
      cout << "<Aloof disdain>" << endl; };
   void ClawFurniture(long ClawLength);
   void SnubOwner(void);

};
```

Now dogs can slobber() and AttackJogger() while cats can Claw-Furniture() and SnubOwner(). Animals (and fish for that matter) can, in general, perform none of these charming behaviors.

Frequently, base classes cannot be instantiated without first being specialized. *Animal* might not do anything interesting, but dogs, cats, and fish do. When a class is not directly instantiated, it is called an *abstract class.* C++ classes are made abstract by the inclusion of a *pure virtual function.* A C++ virtual function is a class method that is denoted by the keyword *virtual.* It need be so indicated only in one class in the inheritance tree and it will be virtual for all derived classes. A virtual function is made *pure virtual* with the peculiar syntax of assigning to the function declaration the value zero. For example,

```
class widget {
public:
   virtual void doSomething() = 0;
};
```

Note that in C++, constructors and destructors cannot be made pure virtual. Furthermore, if a C++ class contains a virtual function, it is a logical error not to define the destructor as virtual.[15] C++ does not allow virtual constructors.

---

[15] Just one of many such opportunities provided by the C++ language.

3.8.5.1 Positioning Attributes in the Inheritance Tree

Generalization relationships form class hierarchies with the most-general classes at the top and the most-specialized classes at the bottom. Structuring these hierarchies is done by using the following three complementary approaches:

1. Derived classes that extend the capabilities of the parent (top-down)
2. Derived classes that specialize the capabilities of a parent (top-down)
3. Bubbling up attributes and behaviors that are common in peer children (bottom-up)[16]

The first strategy, extension, means that a subclass can add behaviors and attributes to those it inherits from its parents. This is an example of the Open-Closed Principle (OCP) [4]. The OCP states that for maximum reusability, a class should be open for extension but not for modification. The focus of the OCP is that changes in a well-designed class hierarchy should be made by subclassing rather than by modifying the hierarchy itself. Another term for this concept is *programming by difference*. The developer finds a class in the hierarchy that is close to what is needed, subclasses it, and extends the subclass to meet the particular needs. The OCP focuses on reuse, but it applies equally well to the construction of class hierarchies. Subclasses may extend the capabilities of their parents without modifying the parents.

Figure 3-19 shows a simple example of extending a subclass. The *Queue* superclass provides three methods: insert(), remove(), and clear(). It is subclassed by the *Cached Queue* class. This child class acts exactly like its parent for the defined methods—in fact, it does not redefine them but reuses them as-is from the parent. However, it adds two new methods: flush() and load(). The child class extends the functionality of the parent by providing only new behaviors.

Specializing a subclass redefines some of the class's (virtual) behaviors. The redefinition of the methods inherited from a parent specializes a subclass for an application. For example, Figure 3-20 shows a specialization of the class *Queue*.

---

[16] Note that restriction of the parent class is not included. All popular object-oriented languages allow the *augmentation* or *extension* of a class, but not *restriction* (removal of a behavior or attribute). To do so breaks the fundamental tenant of inheritance—that the child is a *type of* its parent—and therefore violates the LSP.

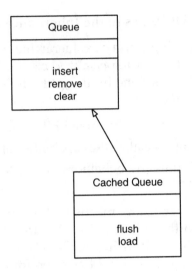

Figure 3-19: *Extending Parent Classes*

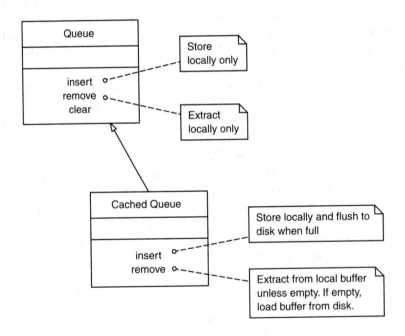

Figure 3-20: *Specializing Parent Classes*

The subclass *Cached Queue* implements the same methods as its parent, but specializes them. The parent class stores all its queue elements in normal memory. However, real-time systems often provide multiple read/write storage—dynamic RAM, static RAM, dual-ported RAM, FLASH memory, EEPROMs, disk storage, and so forth. The simple queue is limited to available memory for storing queue elements, but in some circumstances it may be necessary to queue more data than can be held in main memory.

The *Cached Queue* class provides one solution to this problem. It provides the same insert() and remove() operations as queue, but internally the methods work differently. A straightforward implementation for *Cached Queue* would maintain three areas: incoming, outgoing, and long-term blocks. The incoming and outgoing blocks in normal memory store the newest and oldest data, respectively. The long-term block in the slower memory stores the bulk of the queued data. Calls to insert() would put the inserted data into the incoming block. When this fills, insert() would flush the incoming block to the long-term storage. The overhead for slower memory is often the same whether the access is for a single byte or for a larger block. This makes caching the data more efficient than writing to the slower memory on each insert() call. Saving up data in higher-speed memory and writing to slower memory in blocks reduces the performance hit per insertion.

The remove() method works in reverse. If the outgoing block is not empty, remove() simply dequeues there. When a remove() call finds the outgoing block empty, it reads in the next block of values from the long-term storage area, and then dequeues the oldest item. If the long-term storage area is also empty, then it must move data from the incoming block directly into the outgoing block for maximum efficiency.

Clearly, this behavior is more elaborate than one would expect for a simple *Queue*. The cached queue must redefine the existing access methods to provide this more-complex implementation. Note, however, that LSP is still maintained. The client doesn't know whether it has a reference to a *Queue* or *Cached Queue*, because the effect is the same from its perspective.

The last strategy for constructing generalization hierarchies works from the leaves of the inheritance tree. After structuring the hierarchy, siblings subclassed from the same parent are examined for attributes and behaviors in common. If all siblings have the same property, the property belongs to the parent rather than being replicated in each

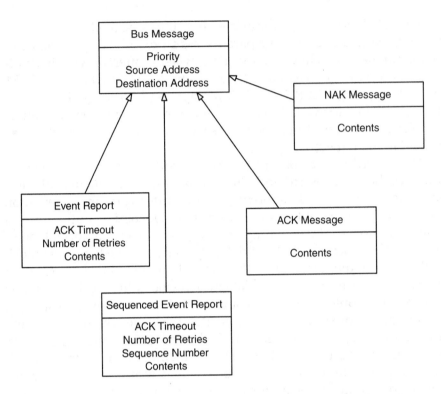

Figure 3-21: *Positioning Attributes in the Inheritance Hierarchy*

sibling. If the characteristic is common to some, but not all, of the siblings, then it may indicate a class is needed between the parent and the similar siblings.

Figure 3-21 shows an inheritance tree for bus messages. Each child class inherits the attributes *Priority, Source Address,* and *Destination Address.* We see, however, that each message has a *Contents* attribute. *Event Report* and *Sequenced Event Report* messages must identify the event in their *Contents* field. ACKs and NAKs must identify the message to which they are responding in their *Contents* field. Because all siblings have the contents attribute, it can be moved up into the parent class *Bus Message.*

Event Report and *Sequenced Event Report* messages share ACK *Timeout* and *Number of Retries* attributes. These do not appear in the ACK and NAK messages. Therefore, these may be abstracted into a class between *Event Report* and *Bus Message,* and *Sequenced Event Report* and *Bus Mes-*

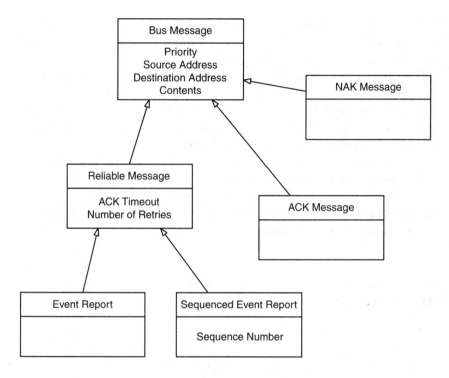

Figure 3-22: *Repositioned Attributes*

sage. This is called *Reliable Message,* because protocol mechanisms exist to support retransmission if no response to them is received. Figure 3-22 shows the resulting reorganization.

Of course, the astute analyst may mix all three strategies. It is possible to extend, specialize, and bubble up, all at the same time.

3.9 Looking Ahead

This chapter has discussed the first half of analysis—identification of objects, classes, and relationships. Many strategies can be used to identify objects and classes—underlining the nouns, identifying the physical devices, looking for persistent data, and so on. These objects have attributes and behaviors that allow them to fulfill their responsibilities. Classes are abstractions of objects so that all objects instantiated from a particular class are structurally identical.

To support collaboration of objects, classes have relationships to each other. These may be associations among class instances, such as association or aggregation, or they may be relationships between classes, such as generalization. Objects use these associations to communicate by sending messages to each other.

The other half of analysis is concerned with defining the behavior of the classes. As we shall see in the next chapter, class behaviors may be classified in three ways—simple, state, and continuous. The dynamic properties of these classes allows them to use their structure to meet the system responsibilities in real time.

3.10 References

[1] Cook, Rick, *The Wizardry Compiled*. Riverdale, NY: Baen Books, 1990.

[2] Booch, Grady, *Object-Oriented Analysis and Design with Applications*. 2nd ed. Redwood City, CA: Benjamin/Cummings, 1994.

[3] Liskov, Barbara, "Data Abstraction and Hierarchy," *SIGPLAN Notices 23*, no. 5 (May, 1988).

[4] Martin, Robert, "The Open-Closed Principle," *C++ Report 8*, no. 1 (1996).

[5] Douglass, Bruce Powel, *Doing Hard Time: Developing Real-Time Systems with UML, Objects, Frameworks, and Patterns*. Reading, MA: Addison Wesley Longman, 1999.

[6] Neumann, Peter G., *Computer Related Risks*. Reading, MA: Addison Wesley Longman, 1995.

Chapter 4

Analysis: Defining Object Behavior

The previous chapter showed how to define the system structure by identifying the fundamental objects and classes and their relationships. In this chapter, we define and refine operations and behaviors. There are a number of means for specifying overall object behavior; the most important of these is modeling the object as a finite state machine. Scenario modeling helps you test your behavioral models to ensure that the objects can collaborate to achieve the system responsibilities. The state and scenario models lead to the definitions of class operations required to process the incoming messages and events.

Notation and Concepts Discussed

Simple behavior	Or-state	Action
Continuous behavior	And-state	Pseudostate
State behavior	Event	Statechart
State	Transition	Operation

4.1 Object Behavior

Chapter 3 presented the analysis and decomposition of systems into their object structure and relationships. The other key pillar of object-oriented analysis is the specification of *dynamic behavior*. Behavior binds the structure of objects with their attributes and relationships so that objects can meet their responsibilities. Ultimately, an object's operations implement its behavior. There are means for constraining and controlling these primitive operations into permissible sequences, the most important of which is the finite state machine. This chapter will discuss these concepts in some detail.

4.1.1 Simple Behavior

We define three types of behavior: *simple*, *state*, and *continuous*. The object with simple behavior performs services on request and keeps no memory of previous services. A simple object always responds to a given input in exactly the same way regardless of its history. Some examples of simple behaviors are:

- Simple mathematical functions, such as cosine or square root
- A search operation of a static data structure that always starts from the same point, such as the search of a static binary tree
- Sort operations
- A knob that returns the number of clicks for a given user action

For example, $\cos \frac{\pi}{2} = 0$ regardless of what value the cos() function was called with previously. In other cases, the distinction is not as clear. Is the search of a binary tree simple or state-driven? If the behavior changes due to previous input, then it cannot by definition be simple. If the binary tree provides methods like next() and previous(), then it must maintain an internal state between calls.[1] If the tree provides only calls such as find(), then at least to its clients it exhibits stateless behavior.

---

[1] The caller can maintain this state, as well. This is the basis for the Container Pattern discussed in Chapter 6.

4.1.2 State Behavior

The second type of object behavior is called *state, state-driven,* or *reactive.* Our definition of a state is the following:

> A state is an ontological condition that persists for a significant period of time, is distinguishable from other such conditions, and is disjoint from them. A distinguishable state means that it differs from other states in the events it accepts, the transitions it takes as a result of accepting those events, or the actions it performs. A transition is a response to an event that causes a change in state.

Modeling an object as a *finite state machine* (FSM) attempts to reduce the behavioral complexity by making some simplifying assumption. Specifically, it assumes:

- The system being modeled can assume only a finite number of existence conditions, called *states*
- The system behavior within a given state is essentially identical and is defined by:
  - ▾ The messages and events accepted
  - ▾ The actions associated with entering or leaving the state
  - ▾ The activities performed while in the state
  - ▾ The reachability graph of subsequent states
  - ▾ The complete set of transition-target state pairs
- The system resides in states for significant periods of time
- The system may change these conditions only in a finite number of well-defined ways, called *transitions*
- Transitions run to completion, including the action execution, whether they are associated directly with the transition itself, or with entry with exit actions for the state entered or exited

The set of all possible behaviors of an object is bounded by the set of operations defined on the object. An FSM adds additional constraints on when and under what conditions those operations will execute.

4.1.3 Continuous Behavior

The third kind of object behavior is called *continuous*. Many objects show continuous behavior, including digital filters and PID[2] control loops. All that is required is that the current output depend on the previous history in a smooth way. An object with continuous behavior is one with an infinite, or at least unbounded, set of existence conditions. PID control systems, fuzzy sets, and neural networks all display continuous behavior.

The UML is expressly a discrete modeling language and provides no direct means for modeling continuous system behavior. However, one can define continuous behavior using a standard programming language, and the UML is really nothing more than a really high-level language. It is even sometimes appropriate to mix state and continuous behavior. For example, different sets of trajectory differential equations may be used, depending on whether the spacecraft is undergoing launch, achieving orbit, in orbit, or in cruise. The sets of equations used in this case depend on the state (in this case, phase of flight) of the trajectory object.

Because the UML relies so heavily on finite state machines to represent discrete behavior, let's now explore what that means in more detail.

4.2 Defining Object State Behavior

In state machines designed by traditional structured methods, the portion of the system that exhibits the state behavior is not clearly defined. Some set of functions and data collaborate in a way that lends itself to finite state modeling, but generally this set is only vaguely defined. In object-oriented methods, the programmatic unit exhibiting state behavior is clear—only *Classifiers*, such as classes and use cases, can define state models and only objects execute state machines.[3]

---

[2] Proportional integral-differential, a common type of control theoretic system using feedback, integration, and differentiation to smoothly control continuous systems.

[3] We use the term *state model* to mean the definition of a state machine, which, when used, must be defined within a class. The term *state machine* is an instance of a state model and therefore must belong to an object.

Consider a simple retriggerable one-shot timer. Such a timer is generally in one of two possible states: idle and counting down. When the timeout event occurs, it issues an event to a client object, (implicitly) resets the timer, and returns to the counting down state. This model is shown in Figure 4-1.

States are shown as rounded rectangles. Transitions are directed lines beginning at the starting state and finishing at the target state. Transitions usually have named event triggers optionally followed by actions (that is, executable statements or operations) which are executed when the transition is taken.

The example state machine shown in Figure 4-1 consists of two states and three transitions. In the *Idle* state, the timer isn't counting down; it sits patiently waiting for the *Start Cmd*. The *Start Cmd* event carries with it a single value, the length of time between timeouts. When the event occurs, the object transitions to the *Counting Down* state. As soon this state is entered, an implicit timer is started, because the state has an exiting timeout transition (shown using the common tm() event trigger). When the timeout occurs, the tm() transition is taken, and the actions in its action list are executed. Actions are shown in an action list, which is separated from the transition label with a

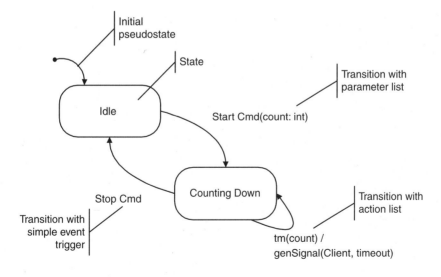

Figure 4-1: *Retriggerable One-Shot Timer*

slash ("/"). The action in the tm() transition's action list is to send a signal to a client object. The actions in the action list are typically short, but in any case they run to completion before the transition completes. The *Counting Down* state is then reentered. This again restarts the timer associated with the timeout transition.

In the *Counting Down* state, the object can respond to two transitions: a timeout and a *Stop Cmd.* In the latter case, the object enters the *Idle* state. The timer corresponding to the tm() transition is (implicitly) stopped as soon as its source state (*Counting Down*) is exited.

Another example of object state behavior is provided by a message transaction object within a reliable communication scheme. When one object (the sender) sends a bus message to a remote object (the receiver)

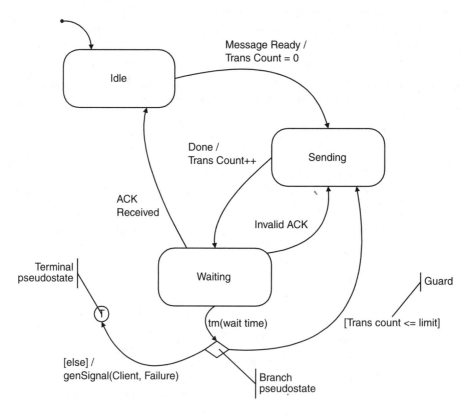

Figure 4-2: *Message Transaction Statechart*

using a reliable communication protocol, a transaction object is temporarily created until it can be verified that the receiver has received the message properly. If a timeout period elapses without the receipt of an explicit acknowledgment from the receiver, the message is retransmitted. Once an acknowledgment is received, the transaction object can be destroyed. In addition, the transaction object should be limited to a finite number of retries before giving up, informing the sender of the communications failure, and being destroyed. This behavior can be captured in a simple statechart.

The diamond represents a *branch pseudostate*[4] that allows one of a set of branching transitions to be selected based on some guarding condition. Guards are shown inside square brackets, such as "[Trans Count < = Limit]." If the event occurs and the guard evaluates to TRUE, then the transition branch is taken. If an event occurs that leads to a conditional connector and none of the exiting guard conditions evaluates to TRUE, then the event is discarded and the transition is not taken. The simple state diagram in Figure 4-2 represents the behavioral states of the message transaction object simply and clearly.

4.3 UML Statecharts

Harel statecharts [1] form the basis of UML statecharts. Statecharts overcome the limitations of traditional FSMs while retaining benefits of finite state modeling. Statecharts include the notions of both nested hierarchical states and concurrency while extending the notion of actions.

Statecharts consist of states, transitions, synch states, and a variety of different state-like things called pseudostates. As mentioned, a state is a condition of existence of an object that is distinguishable from other conditions of existence. A transition is the reification of a response of the object to an event when in a particular state. A synch state is a state vertex that helps model the synchronization of and-states. A pseudostate is a vertex in a state graph that is visited only transiently (unlike states that are visited for significant periods of time). A statechart is a directed graph consisting of *State Vertices* (such as states, synch states, and pseudostates)

---

[4] Pseudostates will be discussed shortly. ⓒ is also used as a notational alternative.

connected by transitions. The basics of each of these state modeling elements and how to link them together are the subjects of the next section.

4.3.1 Basic Statecharts

The essential syntax of statecharts is similar to traditional state diagrams in the simple case. In fact, Mealy-Moore state diagrams (M&Ms)[5] can be directly redrawn using statechart notation. The important basic features of statecharts are shown in Figure 4-3.

The most noticeable departure of statecharts from traditional state diagrams is the nesting of states within states. The outer enclosing state is called a *superstate*. The inner states are called *substates*. For example, state *State2* contains two substates, *State2::S1*[6] and *State2::S2*. While the system is in state *State2*, it must be in *exactly* one of its nested substates. The nested states may be shown physically within the superstate, or the superstate may be depicted on another statechart altogether (in which case, the elaboration of the state is called a *submachine*). This is an extremely powerful concept, as we will see later.

These states are called *or-states* because they are mutually exclusive. The object may be in one or-state or another, but it must be in *exactly one* or-state at a given level of decomposition. *S1* and *S2*, for example, are or-states. The object may be in either *S1* or *S2*, but not both. If *State2* is active, then either *S1* or *S2* must be active, but not both and not neither. *S1* and *S2* are or-states at the highest level of nesting.

When the object is created, or when a superstate is entered, an initial or default state must be identified. This is the job of the initial pseudostate (discussed in the next section). One can see in Figure 4-3 that the object enters *State1* when it is created. Similarly, when state *State3* is entered, its initial state is *S5*. Transitions may also be drawn to the specific substate, overriding the defined initial state. The figure shows an example of this with transition *T5*, which transitions from *State2* →

---

[5] Mealy FSMs allow actions only when a transition is taken, while Moore state models allow actions only upon state entry. In addition, M&Ms do not allow state nesting or orthogonal regions (and-states), topics discussed in more detail later in this chapter.

[6] Note that we use the scope resolution operator (':') to indicate the full state pathname when necessary. It can be used to indicate an arbitrary depth of nesting, as in A1::B7::C9::E2. The scope resolution operator is also used to indicate nesting of model elements within packages.

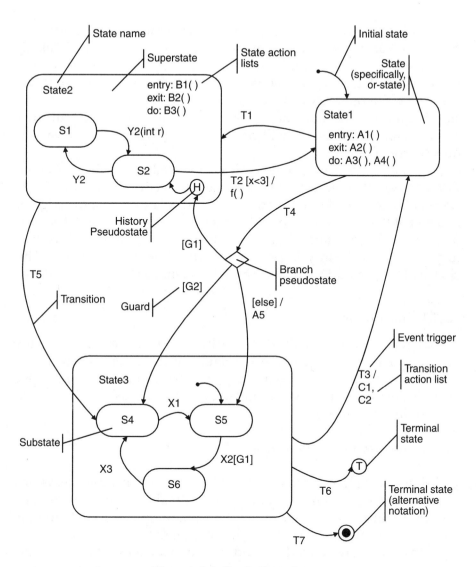

Figure 4-3: *Basic Statecharts*

State3::S4 (note that this transition applies to *either* substate of *State2*). If the transition is drawn to the enclosing superstate, then the defined initial state is used, as transition *T1*, which transitions from *State1* → *State2*.

In addition, a *history pseudostate* may be included, as in *State2*. The history pseudostate indicates that the initial or default state is that last active substate of the superstate. When present, the history pseudostate points with an arrow to a default state, just as does the normal default transition. This is the initial state in which the superstate has not yet been visited (that is, when there is no history). When the superstate has been active before (that is, when there is history), the last active substate becomes the next default. If the last substate was *S1* and transition *T5* was taken, the default will be substate *S1* when *State2* is subsequently reentered.

The UML identifies two kinds of history—shallow and deep. Shallow history means that the last active substate is the active default, but if that substate is further decomposed into sub-substates, no knowledge is retained of that nested history, only of the immediate substate. The normal default sub-substate within that substate will be entered. Deep history means that history is remembered to all levels of nesting. The circled H* indicates deep history; a circled H indicates shallow history.

4.3.1.1 Transitions

Navigation around a statechart is done by accepting events and executing transitions. Transitions are triggered by the receipt of an event while in a state that specifies an outgoing transition triggered by that event. Transitions may have parameters and guards, as well as actions. The syntax for transitions is:[7]

event-trigger (parameters) [guard] '/' action list

Table 4-1 explains fields of the transition. All of these fields are optional. Even the event-trigger may be omitted in the case of an null-triggered transition to be taken when a state completes its activities, if any, or immediately upon entering the state, if not.

Transitions may be made to and from either a superstate or a substate. When a transition is indicated to a superstate, then the default substate is entered. When a transition is indicated from a superstate, it means that the transition applies to *all contained substates*. This is a great help in simplifying diagrams, because a single transition from a super-

---

[7] Previous revisions of the UML used the '^' after the action list to denote events propagated to other state machines. This syntax was dropped after it was observed that sending events is a kind of action.

Table 4-1: *Transition Syntax*

Field	Description
Event-trigger	The name of the event triggering the transition. Together with the parameter list, this field forms the *event signature* of the transition.
Parameters	A comma-separated list containing the names of data parameters passed with the event signal.
Guard	A Boolean expression that must evaluate to TRUE for the transition to be taken. This is often used in conjunction with the conditional connector.
Action list	A comma-separated list of operations executed as a result of the transition being taken. These operations may be of this or another object.

state represents transitions from each of its contained substates. In Figure 4-3, transition *T3* can be taken from any substate of *State3*. In traditional M&M diagrams, a separate transition activated by the same event for each of the substates *S4, S5,* and *S6* would have to be drawn to represent the same behavior.

Transition *T2* contains a *guard expression,* or simply, a *guard.* The guard expression is a Boolean expression that must evaluate to either TRUE or FALSE and should not have any side effects (such as changing an attribute's value). If *State2::S2* is active and the object receives event *T2* and the expression "x<3" is TRUE, then the transition will be taken and the action f() will be executed. If the guard evaluates to FALSE, then the event *T2* is (quietly) discarded, the event is not taken, and the action f() will not be executed.

The branch pseudostate (branch pseudostates are a specialized form of junction pseudostates) is shown receiving the transition labeled *T4.* The branch pseudostate is the statechart equivalent of a switch-case statement. There are three transition segments exiting the branch, each of which is labeled with a *guard expression* enclosed in square brackets. In the same figure, if expression labeled *G1* evaluates to TRUE, then that branch is taken and *State2* becomes active. If *G2* evaluates to TRUE, then *State3::S4* becomes active. If neither evaluates to TRUE, the third branch is taken, because the *else* guard evaluates to TRUE if and only if all the other branches evaluate to FALSE. The [else] guard is optional; if it is missing and all guards on exiting transition segments evaluate to FALSE, then the event is discarded and the current state remains active.

Using guards with branch pseudostates can be tricky. The UML assumes that, at most, only a single guard exiting a branch pseudostate will evaluate to TRUE at any given time. If more than one branch evaluates to TRUE, then the model is said to be *ill-formed*. In that case, one branch will be taken, but you cannot predict which of the branches it will be (other than it will be one of the guards that evaluated to TRUE).

Events triggering transitions may have parameters. The parameters are accessible for use in the actions executed as a result of taking the transition. Figure 4-1 shows an example of a passed parameter, as does the transition between *Idle → Counting Down.*

Passing parameters with event signals allows information to be passed. The declaration of the parameters typically follows the

parameter name ':' parameter type

format, with multiple parameters separated from each other by commas. The declaration of the *formal parameters* is put on the transitions that *accept* the event; this formal declaration should include the data or object type of the parameter to be passed. The parameter can then be referred to by name in the transition action list. The *actual parameters* define the values passed when the signal event is created. The UML does not (yet) define a syntax for this. I recommend the following:

genSignal(signalName(parameter 1, parameter 2, ...), object Set)

Naturally, the parameters sent with the generated signal event must match (by type and number) the parameters expected in the formal parameter list, or it is an error. The objectSet is a list of target objects destined to receive the generated signal event. If this field is omitted, it is assumed that the target is the same object that generates the signal.

For example, an action that generates an event *T1* with two parameters, the first of which is an int and the second of which is a float, which is sent to objects *OB1* and *OB2*, might be generated like this:

genSignal(T1(17, 3.14159265), OB1, OB2)

The statecharts of objects *OB1* and *OB2* would define a transition (hopefully), that accepts this event and acts on it using the passed parameters in their action lists. Figure 4-4 shows this with a little-used notation that combines classes and their statecharts on a single diagram. In this case, note that both objects *OB1* and *OB2* accept the *T1* event and the formal parameter lists match the actual parameter list generated by object *ObjectSource*. If they did not match, as mentioned earlier, an error would result. Be aware that the object receiving the event is not required to have a transition with that event trigger; if it does not, the event is simply discarded.

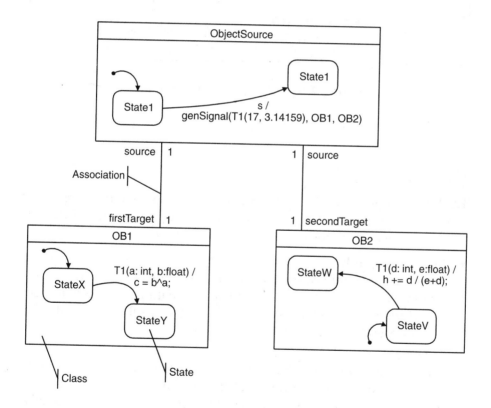

Figure 4-4: *Event Parameters*

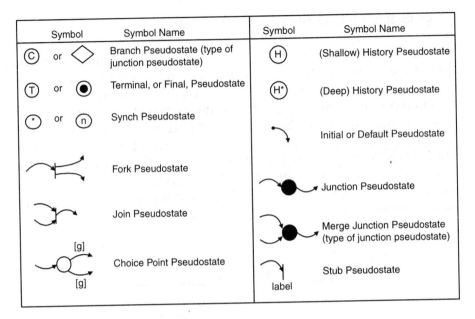

Figure 4-5: *UML Pseudostate Symbols*

4.3.1.2 Pseudostates

The UML defines a number of pseudostates, as shown in Figure 4-5. We saw some of these in Figure 4-3; others have not yet been introduced.

Briefly, these pseudostates are:

- Initial, or default
  Within a superstate context, the initial pseudostate indicates which substate is initially entered as a default. The initial substate may be overridden, either by transitioning directly to a substate or with the history pseudostate.

- Terminal, or final
  The final state indicates that the enclosing composite state is terminated. If the final state appears in the outermost level of nesting, it indicates that the object no longer accepts any event, usually because it is about to be destroyed.

- Branch, or conditional[8]
  The branch pseudostate indicates a set of possible target or-states; at most, one of which will be selected on the basis of a guarding condition. The branch pseudostate is nothing more than a junction with guards on exiting transition segments. However, it was called out in previous versions of the UML with a special icon (a © or a small diamond). It is still indicated using an independent icon by many modeling tools, so it is separately identified here.

- Shallow history
  This pseudostate indicates that the default state of a composite state is the last state visited of that composite state, *not* including nested substates.

- Deep history
  This pseudostate indicates that the default state of a composite is the last state visited of that composite state, including substates nested arbitrarily deeply.

- Junctions
  These are vertices used to join together multiple transitions or to divide a transition into a set of sequential transition segments. Regardless of the number of transition segments connected, they all execute in a single run-to-completion step.

- Merge junction[9]
  A merge junction is a junction in which multiple incoming transitions can be joined together to create a single transition entering an or-state. This is used as a shorthand, particularly when multiple transitions, triggered by different events, share a common action list and/or guard and a common target state.

- Choice point
  A choice point is a kind of junction that executes its action list before going on to the next transition segment. This allows actions bound

---

[8] This pseudostate was removed in the 1.3 revision of the UML, because it was noted to be just a kind of the junction pseudostate. However, since it is still widely used in tools, I include it here.

[9] The merge pseudostate is also just a kind of junction and was removed from the UML metamodel.

to the first transition segment to execute prior to the evaluation of subsequent guards.

- Join
  A join is a connector that joins together multiple incoming transitions from peer and-states into a single transition. This is not the same as a merge. (And-states are discussed in Section 4.3.2.)

- Fork
  A fork is a connector that branches into multiple transitions, each entering a different and-state, from a single input transition. This is not the same as a branch, because in a branch only a single transition activates; in a fork, all outgoing transition segments activate.

4.3.1.3 Branches and Junctions

We've already seen a number of pseudostates, including the branch, or conditional, pseudostate that break transitions into multiple segments. The UML allows the transitions to be broken up into any number of transition segments. Transitions may be joined at junctions, but they *do not* indicate a merging of control (unlike joins, as we will see later). Instead, they provide a shorthand for showing common transition elements in a single place. Figure 4-6 shows an example in which one transition segment adds a guard, while another adds an additional set of actions. The lower part of the figure shows an equivalent statechart, without the use of the junction pseudostate.

Because actions are executed only if a transition is taken, they are *not* executed when the guards are evaluated. This is because the guards must be evaluated *prior* to the execution of the actions. Sometimes, this is a convenient thing to do. In these cases, you should use choice points instead, as in Figure 4-7. A choice point is a specialized form of junction used when the result of an action executed during a transition is to be used in a guard. In this case, the actions on the initial segment of a compound transition are executed *before* checking the guard. It is important that exactly one of the guards evaluates to TRUE under all conditions. If no guard evaluates to TRUE, then the state machine is left in an undefined state. For this reason, an [else] guard is typically added to ensure a well-formed model.

Junctions and branches, together with the transition segments they connect, are different forms of *compound transitions*. Compound transitions are executed in a single run-to-completion step.

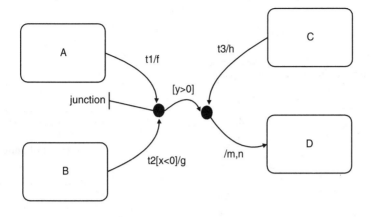

is equivalent to ...

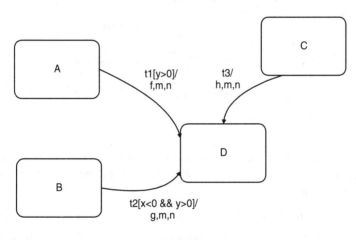

Figure 4-6: *Junctions*

4.3.1.4 Actions and Activities

Statechart behavior may be more elaborate than in traditional FSMs. Both states and transitions can have actions associated with them. States may have both *entry* and *exit actions,* as well as *activities.* Entry actions are performed when the state is entered, in the same run-to-completion step as the entering transition. Exit actions are performed when the state exits; they are executed in the same run-to-completion

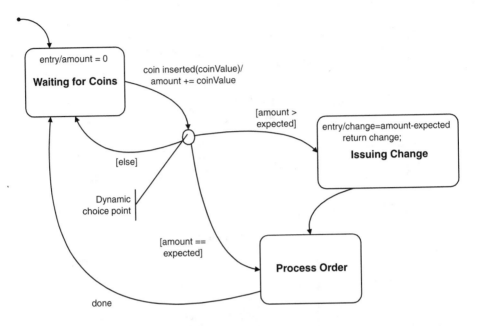

Figure 4-7: *Choice Points*

step as the transition causing the state to exit. All actions, in fact, run to completion and are not interruptible by new events sent to that object. Actions may be[10]:

- Calls to methods within the object owning the state machine
- Calls of methods defined in other objects (usually ones to which the current object has an association)
- Creation or destruction of other objects
- Assignments, such as "x += 6"
- Destruction of the object owning the statechart
- Creating and sending signals to other and-states or objects (called a *SendAction*) in the UML metamodel

---

[10] These are (almost) all the action metaclasses defined in UML 1.3 The Action Semantics Submissions Group, of which the author is an active participant, is looking into possibly adding more and refining their semantics. See Appendix B for more information.

Actions are distinct from *activities.* Activities may be performed as long as the state is active, and they may be interrupted and terminated by the receipt of an incoming event. Activities are indicated in the state activity list by the word "do/"

Actions are usually short, noninterruptible[11] behaviors, while activities are longer, interruptible behaviors. For example, an object might execute an activity to iteratively refine a trajectory solution as long as it is in the state of *Recalculating Trajectory.* It will stop as soon as an event, such as *tm(AdjustCourseTime)* occurs. When a state receives an event that triggers an exiting transition, any ongoing activities are terminated. If an activity terminates before an event is received, it results in the sending of a *completion event* to the object, activating any transitions specified without an event trigger (if any such NULL-triggered transitions exist).

Entry actions are executed in the same order as the nesting when entering a nested substate from outside its enclosing superstate. In Figure 4-8, when transition *T1* is taken, the sequence of actions is *f, g, w, x, y,* then finally *z.* When transition *T2* is taken, the reverse order applies (innermost -> out), so the sequence of exit actions is *p, n, m,* and *b.* When transitioning between states, as with transition *T3,* the exit actions of the source state are taken, followed by the transition actions, followed by the destination state's entry actions. In the case of transition *T3,* the sequence is *p, n, h,* then *s.* States may be nested arbitrarily deeply, and these rules apply recursively.

The UML defines several kinds of actions. A special kind of action, called *SendAction,* allows the issuance of events as a result of taking a transition. This allows one object to notify other objects of a change in state, a common synchronization mechanism. This is the *genSignal* action used in Figure 4-1 and other figures presented previously.

Actions are ultimately specified in terms of an *action language.* This action language consists of the semantics of the action language (the meaning of the syntactic elements) and the syntax itself. The UML 1.3 loosely specifies the former, but it does not specify the latter at all. This

---

[11] Noninterruptible in this sense means run-to-completion. That is, the object will complete its actions prior to accepting and acting on any incoming events. However, the object may be preempted in the middle of executing these actions by another, higher-priority thread. When the object regains the processor focus, the action execution will continue.

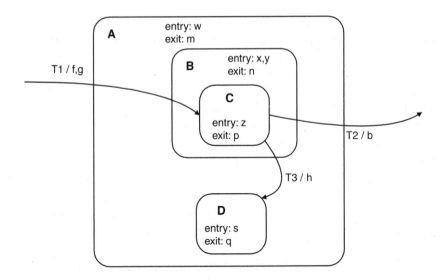

Figure 4-8: *Actions and Nested States*

is because of the diversity of the developer community. Some developers would like to have a complete, abstract action language that can be translated into a target programming language. This has a number of benefits, not the least of which is the portability of models that use such an action language.

Another camp of developers exists. They are typically experts in the target programming language and are unwilling to learn a second programming language in order to express action statements, especially when the statements they write in that language will ultimately be translated into a language they already know very well.

The UML allows the developer to use any reasonable language as an action language, provided that it supports the abstract semantics. In my own experience, C++ is an extremely viable action language, and is often used with good effect. This means that the statements in the action lists can be written as standard C++ statements—assignments, operation calls, and so forth.

4.3.2 And-States

Statecharts use *and-states* (also *orthogonal regions*) to represent independent states that may concurrently be active with other states. In Figure

4-9, the object has a color at the same time it has an operational mode. These are clearly not or-states (which would require that the object have either a color or an operation mode).[12]

Statecharts provide a very clear yet succinct representation of and-states, as shown in Figure 4-9. The dashed lines separate the peer and-states. And-states are always substates of a state. If they exist at the outermost level of the statechart, they are still drawn within a single encompassing state; this state is usually unnamed or given the class name.

Each of the orthogonal components is named and operates independently of the other components. An object with this state model

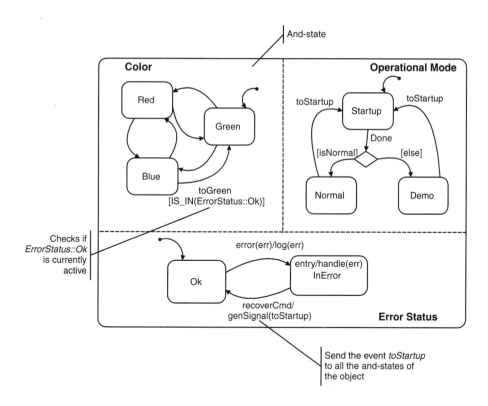

Figure 4-9: *Statechart of Object with And-States*

---

[12] And-states are commonly called *concurrent states*. While this is strictly true, the term *concurrent* implies to many people "thread" and that is only one possible implementation means.

must be in exactly one sub-state from *each of the and-states* as long as the enclosing superstate is active. An object of the class defining the state-chart in Figure 4-9 might be in state (*Red, Demo, and Ok*) or in state (*Blue, Normal, and InError*). The "complete" object state is the cross product of the substates within each active and-state.

When an object receives an event, it is received by all of its active and-states. That means that all those active and-states may act upon it.

The addition of and-states to your state-modeling paradigm is very powerful, but it also creates new questions. For example, how do I synchronize and communicate among peer and-states when necessary?

The UML provides a number of ways to synchronize and-states within a single object, or within states in different objects. These include:

- Join pseudostate
- Fork pseudostate
- Broadcast events
- Propagated events
- IS_IN( ) operator
- Synch pseudostate

When necessary or desirable, the branching or recombining of control can be explicitly shown, as in Figure 4-10. This is useful when the default substates of the orthogonal components are not entered. The fork is a true branch of control into different and-states that are active at the same time. There may be as many forking segments are there are peer and-states in the target superstate. The join pseudostate joins control from multiple source and-states. All predecessor segments leading to a join pseudostate must be triggered by the same event.

The next three means for synchronization are commonly used together. *Broadcast events* are simply events received by all peer and-states. Since all and-states on a statechart are in the same object, they all receive the same events. For synchronization of statecharts from two objects, the event must be multicast to the objects. In the UML, signals are sent to a set of objects, although most of the time, the set contains only a single object.

Propagated events are events that are sent as the result of a transition taken in one and-state or object. The UML defines a kind of action, called a *SendAction*, that can be put into an action list on a statechart. This action sends a signal (associated with an event) to a set of objects.

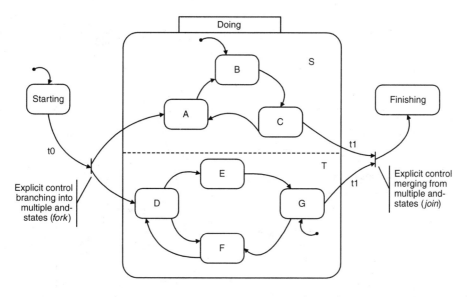

Figure 4-10: *Fork and Join*

This object set, if not otherwise defined, refers to the object owning the transition that executed the *SendAction*. It may also be a list of other objects.

Finally, statecharts provide a predefined operator, IS_IN( ),[13] which returns TRUE if another and-state is currently in the specified substate.

Figure 4-11 shows examples of both broadcast and propagated events among the three and-states, *State1*, *State2*, and *State3*, all and-substates of state *S*. Transition *T1* appears in both *State1* and *State2*, just as the transition *T3* appears in both *State2* and *State3*. If the object receives a *T1* event, it is logically sent to all currently active and-states. Of course, the event need not be acted on in all and-states. For example, if *State1* is in substate *A*, *State2* is in substate *E*, and *S3* is in substate *G* when the object receives the *T1* event, what happens? *State1* transitions to substate *B*; *State2* discards the event because *T1* can cause no transition while state *E* is active; *State3* simply discards it because it never acts on *T1*. If *State1* were in substate *A* and *State2* were in substate *D* when event *T1* occurs, then both and-states would perform substate transitions.

---

[13] IN( ) is another common form for this operator.

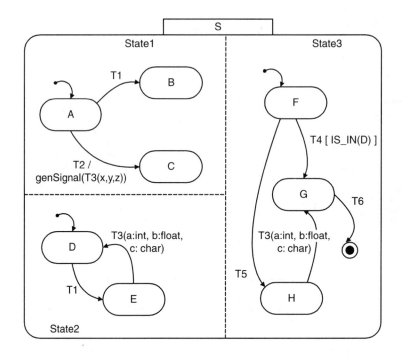

Figure 4-11: *Broadcast and Propagated Transitions*

There is no standard notation for the *SendAction.* For example, Rhapsody from I-Logix uses *GEN(signal).* We've used *genSignal(signal)* here for clarity. In *State1,* then, the transition labeled *T2* is taken; it sends the event *T3.* Since no object is specified, the event is sent to the same object represented by the statechart. The *T3* event is then sent to all currently active and-states of the object. In this case, it may cause transitions in and-states *State2* and *State3* (not in *State1,* because *T3* doesn't appear between any of *State1's* substates).

The IS_IN operator is used as a guard on transitions triggered by event *T4.* This allows the *State3* component to take transition *T4* only if state *State2::D* is currently active.

The last interesting thing about Figure 4-11 is the terminating connector, shown with a filled circle inside an unfilled one.[14] This has the

---

[14] An alternative syntax for this connector is to use a T circumscribed within a circle.

effect of ending and-state *State3* from accepting new transitions. Other and-states may continue to be active.

The IS_IN operator allows a transition to be guarded on whether or not a specific substate in another and-state is currently active. A more difficult problem arises when you want to guard a transition if a specific substate in another and-state has *ever* been visited. This more-complex synchronization requirement is one of the reasons for the final means for synchronizing and-states—the synch pseudostate.

A synch pseudostate can be thought of as a bin containing zero or more tokens. Synch states are used in conjunction with forks and joins that must cross and-state boundaries. A predecessor transition segment runs from a fork pseudostate to the synch state. When the fork's predecessor transition fires, it deposits a token into the synch state. A successor transition runs from the synch state to a join pseudostate. The other transition entering the join is allowed to fire only if the synch state has at least one token. If it does, a token is consumed (that is, removed from the synch pseudostate) and the join fires, transitioning to the subsequent state. If the joining transition fires and the synch state does *not* have a token, the event is discarded. Synch pseudostates act like guards, enabling a transition that it meets in a join to occur.

Synch pseudostates are essentially Petri net *places* and, as such, they have a *capacity*. The capacity of a synch pseudostate is the maximum number of tokens it can hold. This is indicated with a multiplicity symbol inside the synch pseudostate symbol. This capacity can be either a positive integer or '*', indicating an unbounded capacity. Synch pseudostates are particularly useful for modeling producer-consumer systems in which the producer and consumer rates are uncoupled.

Figure 4-12 shows the use of two synch states to coordinate three peer and-states. The first and-state is called *Data Processing*. This and-state waits for data and, when it gets it, goes on to process and then log the data before eventually ending up back, waiting for data. The *Alarm Processing* and-state waits until a specified duration has elapsed, and then *if there has been new data since the last time alarms were processed*, it applies the alarm filtering rules. This uses an unbounded capacity ('*') synch state so that if 10 data samples were processed since the last time the alarms were processed, the alarms processing will run 10 times, even if no new data were to occur during that time.

After the alarms are filtered, if there are no alarms, it transitions off to the *Waiting to Process Alarms* state. If there *are* alarms, then it displays

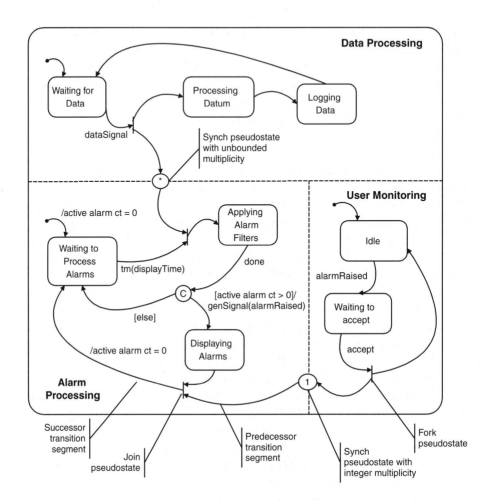

Figure 4-12: *Synch States*

those alarms and won't continue until the user explicitly acknowledges them. This explicit acknowledgment comes from the third and-state, *User Monitoring. User Monitoring* and-state starts in the *Idle* state. When an alarm is detected in the *Alarm Monitoring::Applying Alarm Filters* state, the transition propagates an event to *User Monitoring* and-state that causes it to get ready to receive a user acceptance of the displayed alarms. This prevents the user from "preaccepting" an alarm, because the user can accept it only after it is displayed. Once the user sends an *accept* event to the *User Monitoring* and-state, the *Alarm Processing* and-state is permitted to continue to the *Waiting to Process Alarms* substate once a subsequent *done* event occurs.

4.3.3 Submachines

Previously, we've seen that or-states and and-states can be nested within other states. In most cases, the entire state machine will be specified on a single statechart, using whatever level of nesting is called for. In large, complex statecharts, this can lead to diagrams that are difficult to decipher. For this reason, the internal state decomposition of a superstate can be defined on a separate statechart, called a *submachine*.

As long as transitions terminate on the border of the submachine state, they will transition to the specified initial state of the submachine. But how can transitions that terminate on a particular substate of the submachine be shown?

The answer is what is called a *stub pseudostate*. A stub pseudostate is a named connector that looks like a junction that appears on the containing statechart, as well as on the referenced submachine statechart. The stubs allows you to connect the containing and reference statecharts together. A special stub pseudostate is *subEnd*, which appears only in the submachine and only receives transitions from states inside the submachine. It is this stub to which the transitions emanating from the enclosing superstate on the containing statechart arise.

Figure 4-13 shows an example of the use of submachines. The top of the figure shows the containing statechart. It references two submachines—one for self-testing and one for operating. Note that the name of the submachine is shown in an "include /" clause in the state. Also note the small submachine icon in the corner of the two states elaborated by submachines. This indicator is optional, but it can be used to indicate states that are broken down into more detail in submachines, as well as for classes that have associated state machines.

Transitions that go to the enclosing superstate referencing the submachine are not explicitly depicted in the submachine. Instead, the active state will be the state identified as initial. Most of the remainder stubs appear in both the containing and the reference statecharts. For example, the *RAM Test* stub pseudostate appears in both. This test can be transitioned to directly from the *Normal* stub pseudostate in the

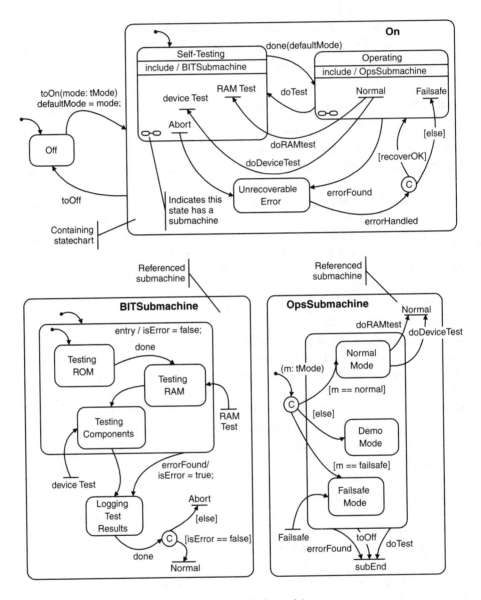

Figure 4-13: *Submachines*

Operating state, resulting in a transition to the *Testing RAM* substate of the submachine. From there, the submachine will progress, using its

standard state transitions. Assuming that all the tests pass, the submachine will wind up in its *Logging Test Results* state and then transition to
the *subEnd* stub. This causes an exit of the *Self-Testing* state in the containing statechart. Note that in this case, the containing statechart adds
a parameter to the *done* event and passes it on to the *Operating* state.

4.3.4 Inherited State Models

Two approaches are typically taken to support inheritance of class state
behavioral models. The simplest is to just ignore the parent class's state
model and reconstruct the child's state model from scratch. While this
has the advantage of flexibility, it hardly seems in the spirit of object-
orientation in general, and reuse in particular. The second approach is
to inherit the parent's state model but specialize and extend it where
necessary.

   In order to ensure compliance with the Liskov Substitution Principle (see Chapter 3), some rules must govern the modifications that can
be made to an inherited state model:

- New states and transitions may be freely added in the child class.
- States and transitions defined by the parent cannot be deleted (the
  subclass must accept all events and messages that can be accepted
  by the parent).
- Action and activity lists may be changed (actions and activities may
  be added or removed) for each transition and state.
- Actions and activities may be specialized in the subclass.
- Substates may not alter their enclosing superstate (including
  adding a new one).
- Transitions may be retargetted to different states.
- Orthogonal components may be added to inherited states.

   A simple example of inherited state models is provided in Figure
4-14. The class model is shown at the right of the figure. The class
Blower has a simple on-off state model. The *Switch On* transition has a
single action in its action list, the function f( ). The *Dual Speed Blower* class
extends the *Blower* class by adding *Low* and *High* speed substates to the
On state. Note that the action for the *Switch On* transition is now changed
to the execution of the function g( ) and that two actions are now added
to the *Switch Off* transition. The *Dual Speed Multiheat Blower* class

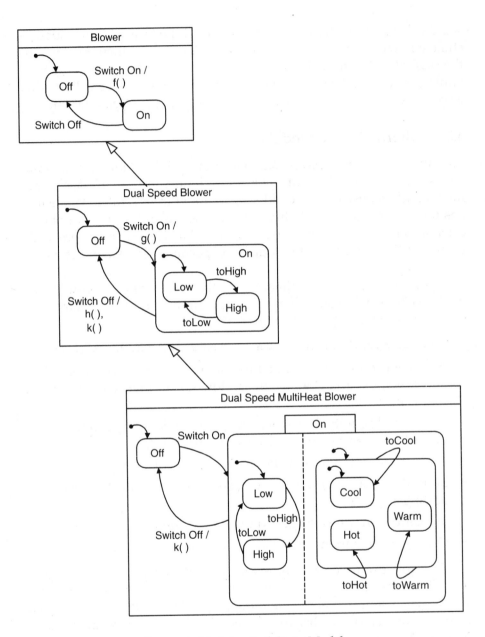

Figure 4-14: *Inherited State Models*

continues the specialization by adding three heat settings as an orthogonal component to the *Low* and *High* states added by the previous subclass. Also note that the g() action for the *Switch On* transition and the h() action for the *Switch Off* transitions have been removed.

4.3.5 Cardiac Pacemaker Example

A cardiac pacemaker is an excellent example of a system in which most objects use finite state machines. The problem statement below will be developed into a class model that will allow us to see how the various statechart features can be used in a real system.

Problem Statement: A Cardiac Pacemaker

A cardiac pacemaker is an implanted device that assists cardiac function when underlying pathologies make the intrinsic heart rate too low or absent. Pacemakers operate in different behavioral modes, indicated by a three-letter acronym. The first letter is either *A, V,* or *D* depending on whether the atrium, the ventricle, or both (dual), are being paced. The second letter is also *A, V,* or *D,* depending on which heart chamber is being monitored for intrinsic activity. The last letter is *I, T,* or *D,* indicating inhibited, triggered, or dual pacing modes. In an inhibited mode, a sensed heart event (that is, a detected cardiac contraction) will inhibit the delivery of a pace from the pacemaker. In triggered mode, a sensed heart event will immediately trigger a pace from the pacemaker. For example, VVI mode means that the ventricle is paced (the first *V*) if a ventricular sense (the second *V*) does not occur. If a ventricular sense does occur, then the pace is inhibited (the *I*). Dual modes are more complex and will not be discussed here.

   Most of the time, a pacing pacemaker waits for a sense event. When it decides to pace, the pacemaker conducts an electric current of a programmable voltage (called the *pulse amplitude*) for a programmable period of time (called the *pulse width*). Following a pace, the pacemaker is put into a refractory state for a set period of time, during which all cardiac activity is ignored. Following the refractory period, the pacemaker resumes monitoring for the next

continued

continued from previous page

cardiac event. The rate of pacing is determined by the programmable pacing rate. The period of time the pacemaker will wait in the waiting state is computed based on the pacing rate and the pulse width. The refractory period is fixed. This particular pacemaker operates in VVI, AAI, VVT, AAT, and AVI pacing modes, as programmed by the physician.

Pacemaker parameters are programmed via a telemetric interface to an external programmer. Telemetry is sent by pulsing an electromagnetic coil a certain number of times to indicate a "0" bit and a different number of times to indicate a "1" bit. To avoid inadvertent programming by electrical noise, a reed switch must be closed with a magnet before programming is enabled. The commands constructed from the bits must be checked prior to acting on them.

This short problem statement can be represented by a simple class model, as in Figure 4-15. The pacemaker itself is shown as a composite class containing the classes necessary for communicating with the external programmer and for pacing the heart. The *Reed Switch, Coil Driver,* and *Communications Gnome* and associated message queues form the *Communications* subsystem, while the *Chamber Model, Atrial Model,* and *Ventricular Model* form the *Pacing* subsystem. These two subsystems collaborate to achieve the overall system responsibilities of communications and cardiac pacing.

A statement about the generalization relationships in the pacing subsystem is in order. The *Chamber Model* class defines the basic behavioral model for pacing a cardiac chamber, so it seems as though the *Atrial Model* and *Ventricular Model* ought to be instances of the *Chamber Model* class rather than different subclasses. If, in fact, the behavior of the two chambers differed only in their context, then a single class, *Chamber Model,* would be appropriate. However, we are going to specialize the *Chamber Model* class in how the two cardiac chambers define their behavior in AVI mode. This will allow us to define the basic behavior in the superclass and specialize it for the two subclasses.

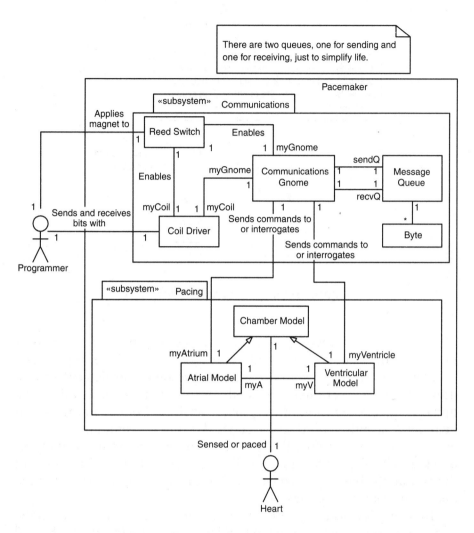

There are two queues, one for sending and one for receiving, just to simplify life.

Figure 4-15: *Pacemaker Class Diagram*

The *Reed Switch* has simple *On-Off* state behavior, as in Figure 4-16. It propagates events to other classes in the communication subsystem to enable and disable communications—specifically the *Coil Driver* and *Communications Gnome*.

The *Coil Driver* class has more-elaborate behavior (see Figure 4-17). The default initial state is *Disabled*. When the *Reed Switch* closes, it propagates an *Enable Comm* event to the *Coil Driver*, which then enters the

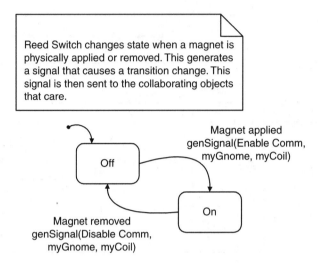

Figure 4-16: *Reed Switch State Model*

Idle substate. Once the *Coil Driver* is enabled, it can be idle, receiving incoming commands, or transmitting responses. The *Receiving Bit* state is entered when the *Coil Driver* is in its *Idle* state and detects a pulse transition in its electromagnetic coil. Once in that state, it waits for a timeout. If it receives another pulse transition before timing out, it increments a pulse count and restarts the timer. Eventually, when no more pulses arrive before the timeout, it transitions to the *Waiting for Bit* state. The actions for this transition are to decode the bit and shift the bit into the byte being constructed. If the byte is full, it is sent to the *Communications Gnome*[15] for processing.

Transmission is enabled by the receipt of a byte to transmit from the *Communications Gnome* while the *Coil Driver* is in the *Idle* state. The *Coil Driver* waits for a period of time (to separate transmitted bytes) and then begins transmitting the byte, one bit at a time. It pulses the electromagnetic coil for a specific period of time (depending on the value of the bit) and then transitions to the conditional connector if the guarding function *isDone()* evaluates to TRUE, the *Gnome* is signaled via a propagated *DoneTransByte* event, and the *Coil Driver* reenters its *Idle*

---

[15] This is a cousin of the *Elevator Gnome* we met earlier.

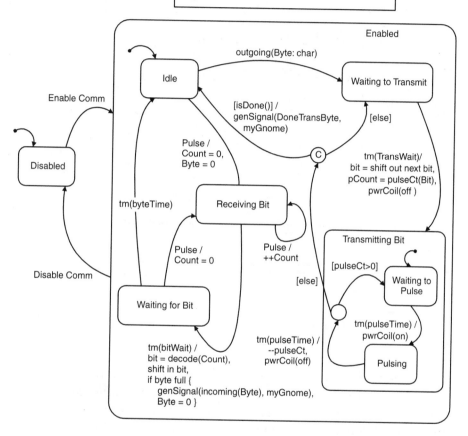

Coil Driver sends and receives a bit at a time by pulsing the coil a specific number of bits (to send) or counting the pulses (to receive). It communicates with the Communications Gnome a byte at a time.

Figure 4-17: *Coil Driver State Model*

state. Otherwise, it waits again to separate the bits in time and then sends out the next bit.

The *Communications Gnome* oversees the communication process for the pacemaker. It is enabled and disabled by the *Enable Comm* and *Disable Comm* events propagated from the *Reed Switch*. When enabled, but in the absence of incoming or outgoing messages, the *Communications Gnome* spends its time in its *Idle* state, as you can see in Figure 4-18.

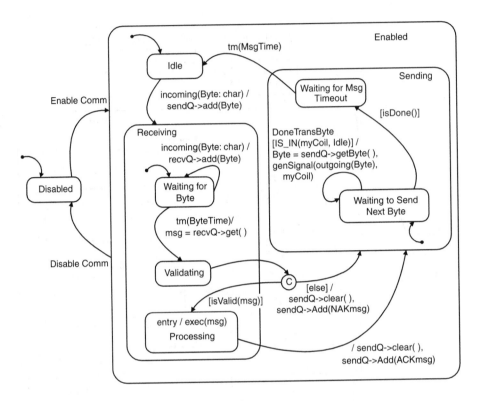

Figure 4-18: *Communication Gnome State Model*

The class diagram (Figure 4-15) names roles at both ends of the association between the *Coil Driver* and the *Communications Gnome*. These roles are used on the state machines to indicate the instance of the classes receiving the events. Specifically, the *Coil Driver* is sent the *outgoing(Byte)* event from the *Communications Gnome* by using this role name, as in *genSignal(outgoing(Byte), myCoil)*. Similarly, the *Coil Driver* sends the event *incoming(Byte)* using its role name for the *Communications Gnome: genSignal(incoming(Byte, myGnome)*. Note also the use of the IS_IN( ) operator to synchronize the two object's state machines.

The *Chamber Model* is where the pacing behavior occurs (see Figure 4-19). It changes mode only when commanded by the external programmer. When the *Communications Gnome* receives a command to set the pacing mode, it validates the command and, if valid, processes it. This processing is not quite as simple as just passing it along to the

Atrial Model or *Ventricular Model* objects, because the two objects must coordinate their actions. When the *Communications Gnome* receives a command to put the pacemaker in VVI mode, for example, it sends a *To Inhibited* event to the *Ventricular Model* object and a *To Idle* event to the *Atrial Model.* The large-scale coordination in this model is accomplished by this reasonably smart *Communications Gnome* controller.

Figure 4-19 shows a big empty state for the AVI mode. It is this state that will be specialized differently in the *Atrial Model* and *Ventricular*

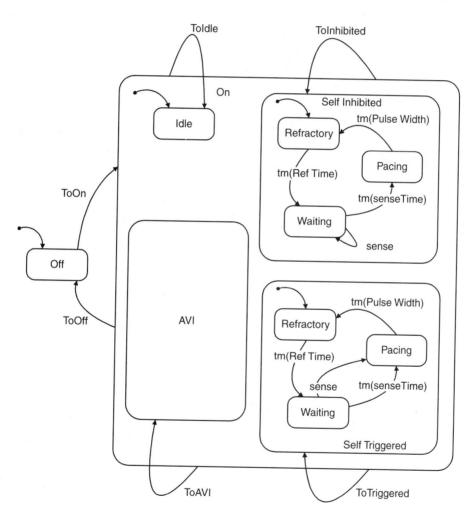

Figure 4-19: *Chamber Model State Model*

Model subclasses. The next two figures specialize the AVI state using the inherited state model rules given previously. By comparing the two specialized versions of the AVI state, you can see how the two objects communicate to coordinate their state machines.

The pacing is controlled by the *Atrial Model* (see Figure 4-20). When it gets a signal from the *Ventricular Model* in its *Waiting* state, the former propagates an *APace* event to the *Atrial Model*. Similarly, when the

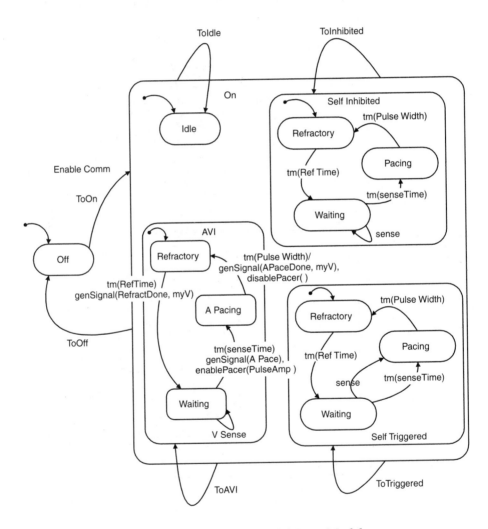

Figure 4-20: *Atrial Model State Model*

Atrial Model completes pacing, it sends an *APaceDone* event back to the *Ventricular Model*. The *Atrial Model* controls the refractory. When the *Atrial Model* is done with its *Refractory* state, it sends a *RefractDone* event to the *Ventricular Model* (see Figure 4-21). When the *Ventricular Model* sees a *Sense* event, it sends a *VSense* event to the *Atrial Model*. By sending events back and forth between the two collaborating objects, their state machines remain synchronized.

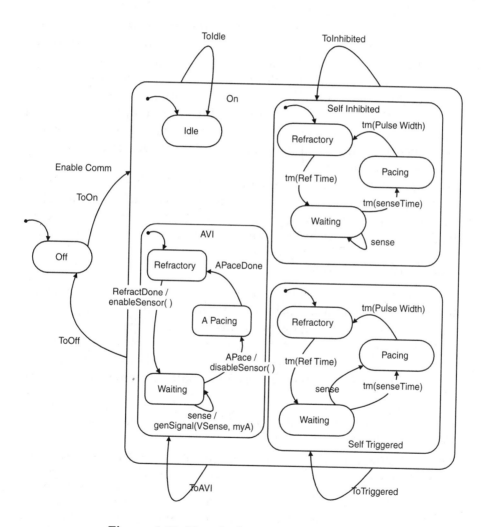

Figure 4-21: *Ventricular Model State Model*

4.4 The Role of Scenarios in the Definition of Behavior

A state diagram provides a static view of the entire state space of a system. Because the complete behavior of a state-driven object can be represented by a sufficiently detailed state model, state models are said to be *constructive*. This means that they can be used to fully generate executable code for the object.

What state diagrams do not show are typical paths through the state space as the system is used. These typical paths are called *scenarios*. Scenarios may not visit all states in the system nor activate all transitions, but they provide an order-dependent view of how the system is expected to behave when actually used. Because a scenario does not have enough information to fully define the complete behavioral model of an object, scenarios are said to be *semi-constructive*. They can add operations and event handling to a state model, but they do not fully define the model.

There are two methods for showing scenarios that are particularly useful in real-time systems. The first is the timing diagram, which is best used when strict timing must be shown. The other is the sequence diagram, which shows order but not strict timing.

4.4.1 Timing Diagrams[16]

Electrical engineers have used timing diagrams for a long time in the design of electronic state machines. A timing diagram is a simple representation with time along the horizontal axis and object state along the vertical axis. Of course, electrical engineers usually only concern themselves only with a small number of states for an individual circuit node, such as low, high, or high impedance.[17] Software engineers can use

---

[16] Timing diagrams are not explicitly supported by the UML at this time (although that may change—see Appendix B). If the reader wishes to stick to only explicitly defined UML features, this section may be omitted.

[17] In some cases, electrical engineers are concerned with a somewhat larger set of states, such as strongly but consistently driven (transistor driver) high and low, strongly and inconsistently driven (conflict), weakly driven (resistively driven) high and low, floating and undriven (high impedance, all outputs tri-stated) high, low and in the transition region, unknown transistor driven, unknown resistively driven, transitioning monotonically, transitioning with oscillation, and so on.

timing diagrams just as easily on more-elaborate state machines to show the changes of state objects over time.

State timing diagrams depict state as a horizontal band across the diagram. When the system is in that state, a line is drawn in that band for the duration of time the system is in the state. The time axis is linear, although special notations are sometimes used to indicate long uninteresting periods of time. The simple form of a state timing diagram is shown in Figure 4-22.

This timing diagram shows a particular path through the *Ventricular Model* state machine. It begins in the *Idle* state and remains there until it receives a command to begin pacing (*To Inhibited*). At this point, it jumps to the *Waiting* state. The vertical lines connecting states show that the time used for the transition is approximately zero, relative to the scale of the timing diagram. Later, a *Ventricular Sense* is detected (as shown by the transition annotation on the diagram) and the *Ventricular Model* returns to the *Waiting* state. Sometime later, the *Sense* timeout occurs and the *Ventricular Model* enters the *Pacing* state. In this state, the engine is actively putting an electrical charge through the heart muscle. When the pacing pulse width is complete, the object transitions to the *Refractory* state. Once this times out, the system reenters the *Waiting* state.

In this simple form, only a single object (or system) is represented. It is possible to show multiple objects on the same diagram. By separating these with dashed lines, the different (and possibly concurrent) objects

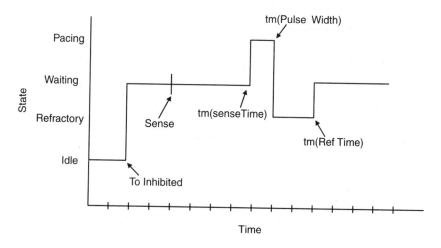

Figure 4-22: *Simple State Timing Diagram*

can be clearly delineated. Propagated transitions can be clearly marked with directed lines showing event dependency. Figure 4-23 shows just such a diagram depicting a scenario of collaboration between the *Atrial Model* and *Ventricular Model* while the pacemaker is in AVI mode.

Timing diagrams are very good at showing precise timing behavior and are often used to closely analyze the timing of periodic and aperiodic tasks. When used in this way, some common elements shown are:

Period   The time between initiations for the same state.

Deadline   The time by which the state must be exited and a new state entered.

Initiation   The time required to completely enter the state (that
time   is, execute state entry actions).

Execute   The time required to execute the entry and exit actions
time   and the required activities of the state.

Dwell time   The time the object remains in the state after the execute time before the state is exited. Includes time for exit actions.

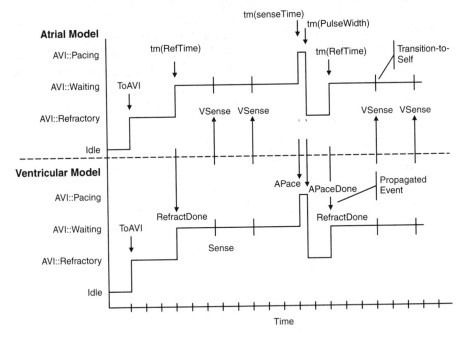

Figure 4-23: *Concurrent State Timing Diagram*

Slack time

The time between the end of actions and activities and the deadline.

Rise and fall time

The time required for the transition into the state to complete. This includes the time necessary to execute the transition actions.

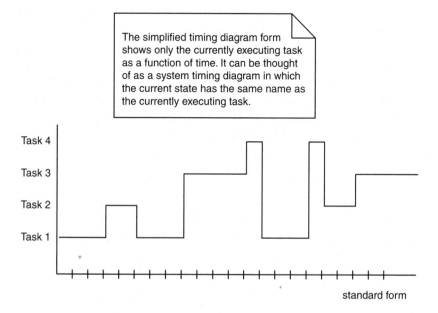

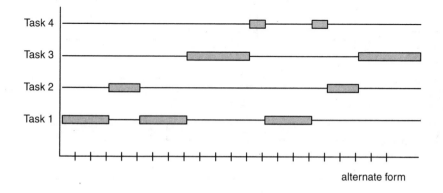

Figure 4-24: *Simple Task Timing Diagram*

Jitter   Variations in the start time for a periodic transition or event.

When there are many tasks to be shown on a single diagram, a common simplified form of the timing diagram shows only which task is executing at any point in time (see Figure 4-24). If desired, more details of the task state can be shown with pattern shading, as in Figure 4-25. Although timing diagrams show no information beyond that available in annotated sequence diagrams, the absolute timing of events and state changes and the relative timing among objects is much clearer and more obvious than on sequence diagrams even when explicit timing constraints are added. Furthermore, timing diagrams used in requirements elucidation can illustrate partial ordering (using the *Don't Care* state), whereas sequence diagrams show a choice among the possible partial orderings, which might unnecessarily restrict the design space.

4.4.2 Sequence Diagrams

Sequence diagrams are (by far) the more common way to show scenarios, as discussed earlier. Sequence diagrams use vertical lines to represent the objects participating in the scenario and horizontal directed lines to represent the messages sent from one object to another. Time

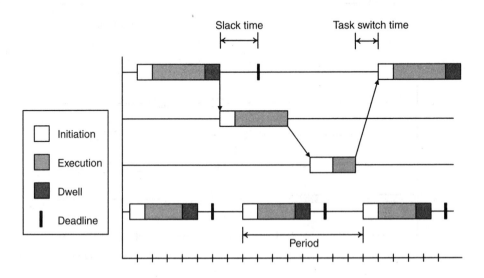

Figure 4-25: *Task Timing Diagram with Shading*

flows from top to bottom—that is, messages shown lower on the page take place later than ones above.

Sequence diagrams can be related more closely with associated state models when state marks are added to the instance lines, as shown in Figure 4-26.

Notice the timing marks shown in the figure. The notation is a standard way of expressing the time between two messages. In the UML 1.3, messages have added semantic elements that can be dereferenced for timing information. A message *msg* has the following operations defined in the metamodel:

- *msg.sendTime*

  This specifies the time at which the message is sent by the source object.

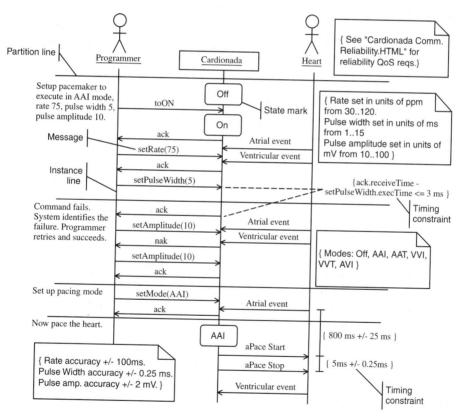

Figure 4-26: *Sequence Diagram Syntax*

- *msg.receiveTime*
  This specifies the time at which the message is received by the target object.

The modeler is free to add his or her own to meet the specific needs of the environment. Operations frequently useful in the development of real-time systems include:

- *msg.executionTime*
  This specifies the time required for the target object to perform the service executed in response to the message.

- *msg.arrivalPattern*
  This specifies whether the arrival pattern for the message is periodic or aperiodic.

- *msg.period*
  If the message arrival pattern is periodic, this operation returns its period. If the arrival pattern is aperiodic, the value returned may be interpreted as the average arrival time.

- *msg.jitter*
  If the message is periodic, this operation returns the jitter around the period. This is most commonly specified as a range, such as [–2..+4].

- *msg.minimumArrivalTime*
  If the message arrival pattern is aperiodic, this operation returns the minimum time between message arrivals, if it exists. If the arrival pattern is bursty, it may specify the minimum arrival time between bursts.

- *msg.maxBlockingTime*
  This operation returns the worst-case time the execution of the service provided by the message may be blocked due to the execution of a lower-priority thread that owns a resource required by that service.

- *msg.isBursty*
  If the message arrival pattern is aperiodic, this operation returns whether the messages tend to arrive in clumps.

- *msg.burstLength*
  For bursty message arrival patterns, this operation specifies the maximum number of messages between bursts.

- *msg.PDF*
  This operation returns the probability density function from which either the jitter or the minimum interarrival time is drawn.

- *msg.deadline*
  This operation specifies a well-formedness constraint on the message—namely, a point of time (the deadline) such that if the handling of the message completes after that time, the message is said to be *late.*

- *msg.utilityFunction*
  In some systems, the value of the completion of the operation corresponding to a message varies over time in a continuous way.[18] This operation returns a function that returns the value of the completion of the action as a function of time.

The addition of these operations to messages in your own metamodel can permit various types of schedulability analysis to be performed. These techniques provide the ability to make mathematical assertions about predictability of the system to meet deadlines and other measures of schedulability. These mathematical techniques are beyond the scope of this book; interested readers are referred to [3] and [4] for more information.

Sequence diagrams can be somewhat more elaborate than shown in Figure 4-26. In particular, focus of control, loops, and branching may be shown, as well. These act as annotation aids rather than add anything substantial to the diagram, and some developers may find them useful.

Focus of control is shown as a thick line (or a thin rectangle, if you like) on the sequence diagram. It means that the object instance has "focus" for the height of the rectangle. This is especially useful in synchronous message passing, because focus can be nested as one object blocks until an operation invoked on another message executes. Note on Figure 4-27 that operations can invoke operations on the same object. This is called *object recursion;* it differs from normal recursion in that the recursion may invoke different operations (but all in the same object).

Branching is shown using guards, and it provides a way of showing multiple scenarios on a single sequence diagram. Be careful as their

---

[18] Deadlines are just a special case of a utility function. The utility function for a message with a deadline returns 1 if the action completes prior to the deadline and zero thereafter.

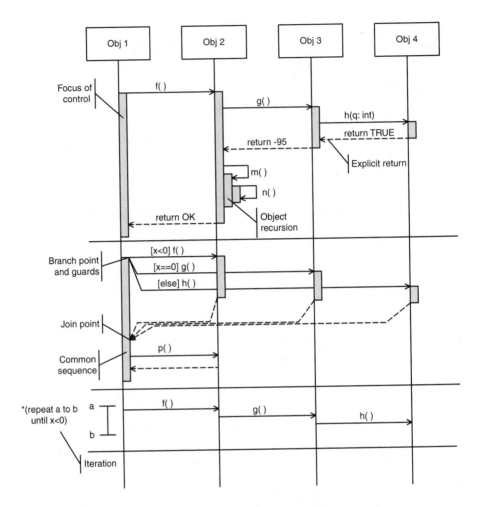

Figure 4-27: *Advanced Sequence Diagrams*

overuse can render the diagrams totally unreadable. Note that in the figure, the dashed arrows show explicit returns joining at the same spot on the object executing the branch.

Finally, the proper way to show a repetitive set of messages on a sequence diagram is to "unroll the loop" and show every message instance as it appears in sequence. This can lead to some very long sequences, so it is possible to show loops using an iteration expression. The UML does not require a particular iteration expression format, but common ones include:

```
*(for j=0 to n)
*(while x<10)
*(until Object1::IS_IN(OK_State))
```

These annotations are shown in Figure 4-27. The use of sequence diagrams as an aid in elaborating use cases is discussed in more detail in Chapter 2.

4.4.3 Event Hierarchies

Event instances are, themselves, objects. Because some events are specialized versions of others, it is possible to build event-class generalization hierarchies. Event hierarchies are useful because they allow polymorphic acceptance of events, which means that various objects can accept events at different levels in the hierarchy.

Figure 4-28 shows a simple hierarchy for user input events. A user input active object accepting *Input Event* objects would also accept any

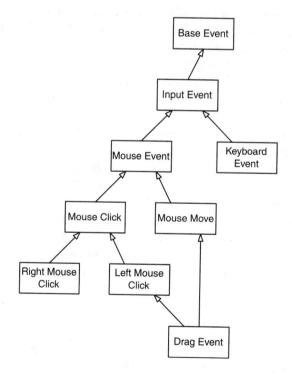

Figure 4-28: *Event Hierarchy*

subclass of *Input Event,* such as *Left Mouse Click* or *Keyboard Event.* The active object can then dispatch all mouse events to a mouse-handler class. This mouse-handler class would accept *Mouse Event* objects and any of its subclasses. The mouse handler can then delegate the handling of the different mouse event subclasses and act on them appropriately.

Exception event hierarchies are usually used in just this way. General handlers accept more-general exception instances and then dispatch them to more-specific handlers. Or specific exception handlers are tried first, and if they cannot accept the exception then the more-general handlers are executed. Either way, event hierarchies are an important structuring tool for the handling of events.

4.5 Defining Operations

All class operations either handle messages or assist in their handling. This means that once a class's state machine is defined and important scenarios elucidated, the messages and events shown on those diagrams become class operations.

In the UML, an *operation* is the specification of a behavior. This is distinct from a *method,* which is the realization of an operation. An operation is the fundamental quantum of object behavior. The overall behavior of the object is decomposed into a set of operations, some of which are within the interface of the class and some of which are internal and hidden. Naturally, all objects of the same class provide the same set of operations to their clients. An object's operations must directly support its behavior and, ultimately, its responsibilities. In the simplest case, a 1-1 mapping exists between a class's behaviors and its operations, but this is not true in general. Often, behaviors are decomposed into more-primitive operations to produce the overall class behavior. This is similar to the functional decomposition in structured system design.

Operations have a protocol for correct usage, which consists of the following:

- Preconditional invariants—that is, assumptions about the environment that must be satisfied before the operation is invoked

- A signature containing an ordered formal list of parameters and their types and the return type of the operation
- Postconditional invariants that are guaranteed to be satisfied when the operations complete
- Rules for thread-reliable interaction, including synchronization behavior

The responsibility for ensuring preconditional invariants are met falls primarily in the client's realm. That is, the user of the operation is required to guarantee that the preconditional invariants are satisfied. However, the server operation should check as many of these as possible. Interfaces are hotbeds for common errors, and the inclusion of preconditional invariant checking in acceptor operations makes objects much more robust and reliable.

In strongly typed languages, the compiler itself will check the number and types of parameters for synchronous operation calls. However, some language type checking is stronger than others. For example, enumerated values are freely and automatically converted to integer types in C++. A caller can pass an out-of-range integer value when an enumerated type is expected, and the compiler typing system will not detect it. Ada's stronger type checking[19] flags this as an error and will not allow it unless an explicit *unchecked_conversion* type cast is performed. Even in Ada, however, not all range violations can be caught at compile time. In such cases, the operation itself must check for violations of its preconditional invariants.

For example, consider an array class. Because C++ is backwardly compatible with C, array indices are not checked.[20] Thus, it is possible (even likely) that an array will be accessed with an out-of-range index, returning garbage or overwriting some unknown portion of memory. In C++, however, it is possible to construct a reliable array class:

```
#include <iostream.h>
template<class T, int size>
class ReliableArray {
T arr[size];
```

---

[19] It has been said "C treats you like a consenting adult. Pascal treats you like a naughty child. Ada treats you like a criminal."

[20] It is well documented that "the major problem with C++ is C."

```
public:
    ReliableArray(void) { };
    T &operator[](int j) {
        if (j<0 || j >=size)
            throw "Index range Error";
            return arr[j];
    };
    const T *operator&() { return arr; };
    T operator*() { return arr[0]; };
};

int main(void) {
    ReliableArray<int, 10> iArray;
    iArray[1] = 16;
    cout << iArray[1] << endl;
    iArray[19] = 0; // INDEX OUT OF RANGE!
    return 0;
};
```

Classes instantiated from the *ReliableArray* template overload the bracket operator ("[]") and prevent inappropriate access to the array. This kind of assertion of the preconditional invariant ("Don't access beyond the array boundaries,") should be checked by the client,[21] but it is guaranteed by the server (array class), nevertheless.

4.5.1 Types of Operations

Operations are the manifestations of behavior. This behavior is typically specified on state diagrams (for state-driven classes) and/or scenario diagrams. These operations may be divided into several types. Booch [2] identifies five types of operations:

1. Constructor
2. Destructor
3. Modifier
4. Selector
5. Iterator

---

[21] If known—clearly a negative index into an array is probably nonsensical, but the client may not know the upper bounds of the array. If you always put range checking in the server array class, you can be assured that even if the client forgets, the array integrity will be maintained.

Constructors and *destructors* create and destroy objects of a class, respectively. Well-written constructors ensure the consistent creation of valid objects. This usually means that an object begins in the correct initial state; its variables are initialized to known, reasonable values; and required links to other objects are properly initialized. Object creation involves the allocation of memory, both implicitly on the stack, as well as possibly dynamically on the heap. The constructor must allocate memory for any internal objects or attributes that use heap storage. The constructor must guarantee its postconditional invariants; specifically, a client using the object once it is created must be assured that the object is properly created and in a valid state.

Sometimes, the construction of an object is done in a two-step process. The constructor does the initial job of building the object infrastructure, while a subsequent call to an initialization operation completes the process. This is done when concerns for creation and initialization of the object are clearly distinct and not all information is known at creation time to fully initialize the object.

Destructors reverse the construction process. They must deallocate memory when appropriate and perform other cleanup activities. In real-time systems, this often means commanding hardware components to known, reasonable states. Valves may be closed, hard disks parked, lasers deenergized, and so forth.

Modifiers change values within the object, while *selectors* read values or request services from an object without modifying them. *Iterators* provide orderly access to the components of an object. They are most common with objects that maintain collections of other objects, called *collections* or *containers*. It is important that these three types of operations hide the internal object structure and reveal instead the externally visible semantics. Consider a simple collection class:

```
class Bunch_O_Objects {
    node* p;
    node* current_node;
public:
    void insert(node n);
    node* go_left(void);
    node* go_right(void);
};
```

The interface forces clients of this class to be aware of its internal structure (a binary tree). The current position in the tree is maintained by the current_node pointer. The implementation structure is made visible by the iterator methods go_left() and go_right(). What if the design changes to an n-way tree? A linked list? A hash table? The externally visible interface ensures that any such internal change to the class will force a change to the interface and therefore changes to all the clients of the class. Clearly, a better approach would be to provide the fundamental semantics (the concept of a next and a previous node), as in:

```
class Bunch_O_Objects {
    node* p;
    node* current_node;
public:
    void insert(node n);
    node* next(void);
    node* previous(void);
};
```

However, even this approach has problems. This interface works fine provided that marching through the objects in the collection will always be in a sequential manner and only a single reader is active.

The first problem can be resolved by adding some additional operations to meet the needs of the clients. Perhaps, some clients are able to restart the search or easily retrieve the last object. Perhaps, having the ability to quickly locate a specific object in the list is important. Considering the client needs produces a more elaborate interface:

```
class Bunch_O_Objects {
    node* p;
    node* current_node;
public:
    void insert(node n);
    node* next(void);
    node* previous(void);
    node* first(void);
    node* last(void);
    node* find(node &n);
};
```

This interface isn't primitive or orthogonal, but it does provide common-usage access methods to the clients.

Providing support for multiple readers is slightly more problematic. If two readers march through the list using next() at the same time, neither will get the entire list; some items will go to the first reader; others will go to the second. The most common solution is to create

separate iterator objects, one for each of the various readers. Each iterator maintains its own current_node pointer to track its position within
the collection:

```
class Bunch_O_Objects {
    node* p;
public:
    void insert(node n);
    node *next(node *p);
    node *previous(node *p);
    friend class BOO_Iterator;
};

class BOO_Iterator {
    node* current_node;
    Bunch_O_Objects& BOO;
public:
    BOO_Iterator(Bunch_O_Objects& B) : BOO(B) {
        current_node = BOO.p; };
    node* next(void);
    node* previous(void);
    node* first(void);
    node* last(void);
    node* find(node &n);
};
```

This strategy is reified into the Container Pattern identified in
Chapter 6.

4.5.2 Strategies for Defining Operations

Defining a good set of operations for a class interface can be difficult.
There are a number of heuristics that can help decide on the operations:

- Provide a set of orthogonal primitive interface operations.
- Hide the internal class structure with interface operations that show
  only essential class semantics.
- Provide a set of nonprimitive operations to enforce protocol rules
  and capture frequently used combinations of operations.
- Operations within a class and class hierarchy should use a consistent set of parameter types where possible.
- A common parent class should provide operations shared by sibling classes.

- Each responsibility to be met by a class or object must be represented by some combination of the operations, attributes, and associations.
- All messages directed toward an object must be accepted and result in a defined action.
  - ▼ Events handled by an class's state model must have corresponding acceptor operations.
  - ▼ Messages shown in scenarios must have corresponding acceptor operations.
  - ▼ Get and set operations provide access to object attributes when appropriate.
- Actions and activities identified on statecharts must result in operations defined on the classes providing those actions.
- Operations should check their preconditional invariants.

Just as with strategies for identifying objects, classes, and relationships, these strategies may be mixed freely to meet the specific requirements of a system.

By providing the complete elemental operations on the class, clients can combine these to provide all nonprimitive complex behaviors of which the class is capable. Consider a *Set* class, which provides set operations. The class below maintains a set of integers. In actual implementation, a template would most likely be used, but the use of the template syntax obscures the purpose of the class, so it won't be used here.

```
class Set {
    int size;
    SetElement *bag;

    class SetElement {
    public:
        int Element;
        SetElement *NextPtr;
        SetElement(): NextPtr(NULL); {};
        SetElement(int initial): Element(initial),
NextPtr(NULL) { };
    };
public:
    Set(): size(0), bag(NULL) { };
    Set union(set a);
    Set intersection(set a);
```

```
        void clear(void);
        void operator +(int x); // insert into set
        void operator -(int x); // remove from set
        int numElements(void);
        bool operator ==(set a);
        bool operator !=(set a);
        bool inSet(int x); // test for membership
        bool inSet(Set a); // test for subsethood
};
```

This simple class provides a set type and all the common set operations. Elements can be inserted or removed. Sets can be compared for equality, inequality, and whether they are subsets of other sets. Set unions and intersections can be computed.

Often, a series of operations must be performed in a specific order to get the correct result. Such a required sequence is part of the protocol for the correct use of that object. Whenever possible, the operations should be structured to reduce the amount of information the clients of an object must have in order to use the object properly. These protocol-enforcing operations are clearly not primitive, but they help ensure the correct use of an object.

A sensor that must first be zeroed before being used is a simple example. The sensor class can simply provide the primitive operations doZero() and get(), or it can provide an acquire() operation that combines them:

```
class sensor {
    void doZero();
    int get();
public:
    int acquire(void) {
        doZero();
        return get();
    };
};
```

The acquire() operation enforces the protocol of zeroing the sensor before reading the value. Not only does this enforce the preconditions of the get() operation, it also simplifies the use of the class. Since the doZero() and get() operations are always invoked in succession, combining them into an operation provides a common-use nonprimitive.

Polymorphic operations are operations of the same name that perform different actions. Depending on the implementation language, polymorphism may be static, dynamic, or either. Static polymorphism is resolved at compile time and requires that the compiler have enough context to unambiguously determine which operation is intended. Dynamic polymorphism occurs when the binding of the executable code to the operator invocation is done as the program executes. Both static and dynamic polymorphism are resolved on the basis of the type and number of parameters passed to the operation.[22] Ada 83 operator overloading is purely static. C++ polymorphism may be either static or dynamic. Smalltalk polymorphism is always dynamic.

4.6 Looking Ahead

We have now seen both parts of analysis. The previous chapter covered means to identify the object structure of a system, find the classes of those objects, and link them together with relationships and associations. This chapter covered the dynamic aspects of objects—the definition of behavior, with special attention to state-driven objects, and the operations necessary to implement those behaviors.

The task of analysis is to find the object structure required of all acceptable solutions to the problem. Put another way, analysis finds the essential objects, classes, and relationships inherent in the system under study. Analysis defines the "what" of the system. The next process step, design, will add the "how." We have deferred many questions about implementation strategies and structures, such as the number of tasks running, how messages will be implemented, and the internal design of the objects themselves. Let's continue with the large-scale architectural design in the next chapter.

4.7 References

[1] Harel, David, "Statecharts: a Visual Formalism for Complex Systems," *Science of Computer Programming* 8 (1987): 231–274.

---

[22] C++ class operations have an invisible *this* pointer in their parameter lists. Thus, even an operation with an otherwise identical parameter list can be polymorphic if a subclass redefines the operation, since the *this* pointer is a pointer to a different type.

[2] Booch, Grady, *Object-Oriented Analysis and Design with Applications.* 2nd ed. Redwood City, CA: Benjamin/Cummings, 1994.

[3] Douglass, Bruce Powel, *Doing Hard Time: Developing Real-Time Systems with UML, Objects, Frameworks, and Patterns.* Reading, MA: Addison-Wesley, 1999.

[4] Klein, Mark, Thomas Ralya, Bill Pollak, Ray Obenza, and Michael Gonzalez Harbour, *A Practitioner's Handbook for Real-Time Analysis: Guide to Rate Monotonic Analysis for Real-Time Systems.* Boston: Kluwer Academic Publishers, 1993.

Chapter 5

Architectural Design

The last three chapters have dealt with analysis of the system. Chapter 2 looked at ways of capturing requirements using use cases, scenarios, and statecharts. Chapters 3 and 4 presented approaches for identifying and characterizing classes and objects inherent in the problem. Analysis looks at key concepts and structures in the system that are independent of how the solution is implemented.

Now we're ready for design. Design specifies a particular solution that is based on the analysis model. Design can be broken into three parts according to the scope of decisions made: architectural, mechanistic, and detailed. This chapter discusses the first: architectural design.

Architectural design identifies the key strategies for the large-scale organization of the system under development. These strategies include the mapping of software packages to processors, bus and protocol selection, and the concurrency model and task threads. The UML provides notation and semantics for the specification of large-scale architecture. This chapter presents the features available in the UML for architectural design and shows how they can be applied to real-time systems.

Large-scale design strategies can be based on architectural patterns that may be found useful in a variety of similar systems. A few patterns are presented in this chapter that exemplify how pattern-based architectures can simplify architectural design.

Notation and Concepts Discussed

Design phases	Node	Communication
Architectural design	Component	Deployment diagram
Active object	Multiprocessor systems	Component diagram
Architectural patterns		Task diagram

5.1 Overview of Design

If you've been following this book, you should have a good grasp by now of the process and products of analysis. Analysis identifies the criteria of acceptance of any solution. The first part of analysis studies system-environment interaction and explores and captures this interaction with context and use case diagrams. The second part of analysis "drills down" inside the system to identify the fundamental concepts within the system that must be represented in terms of both structure and dynamics. These concepts are captured as classes and objects.

Design is the process of specifying a solution that is consistent with the analysis model. The ROPES process divides design into three primary categories based on the scope and breadth of decisions within that category: architectural, mechanistic, and detailed design (see Figure 5-1 and Table 5-1). Architectural design details the largest-scale software structures, such as subsystems, packages, and tasks. The middle layer of design is called mechanistic design; it includes the design of mechanisms composed of classes working together to achieve common goals. Detailed design specifies the internal primitive data structures and algorithms within individual classes.

For simple systems, most of the design effort may be spent in the mechanistic and detailed levels. For larger systems, including avionics and other distributed real-time systems, the architectural level is crucial to project success. This chapter will focus on the process of architectural design.

The design process can be either translative or elaborative. Translative design takes the analysis model and, using a translator, produces an executable system more or less autonomously. Great care must be

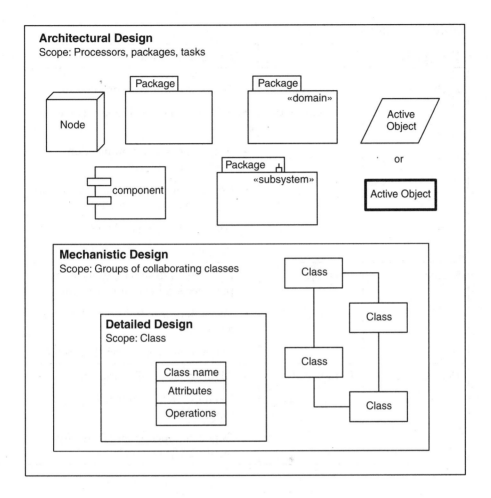

Figure 5-1: *Three Levels of Design*

put into the design of the translator, and this is often highly customized for a particular problem domain and business environment. The other approach elaborates the analysis model by adding increasing amounts of design detail until the system is fully specified. The UML is process-independent and applies equally to both design approaches. Since the elaborative approach is more common and generally applicable, we will continue in an elaborative spirit in this book.

Table 5-1: *Phases of Design*

Design Phase	Scope	What Is Specified
Architectural	System-wide Processor-wide	• Number and type of processors • Packages of objects running on each processor • Interprocessor communication media and protocols • Concurrency model and inter-thread communication strategies • Software layering and vertical slices • Global error-handling policies
Mechanistic	Interobject	• Instances of design patterns of multiple objects collaborating together • Containers and design-level classes and objects • Medium-level error-handling policies
Detailed	Intraobject	• Algorithmic detail within an object • Details of data members (types, ranges) • Details of function members (arguments, internal structure)

5.2 What Is Architectural Design?

The analysis model identifies objects, classes, and relationships, but it does not specify how they are organized into large-scale structures. As shown in Table 5-1, architectural design is concerned with large-scale design decisions that involve collaborations of packages, tasks, or processors.

System architectural design is broader in scope than simply software and involves the physical architecture, as well, including electronic and mechanical design. Naturally, physical architecture has a great impact on the software architecture. Together, physical and software architectures combine to form the *system architecture.* In most embedded systems, the system architecture is by necessity a collaborative effort that includes engineers from a wide variety of disciplines, such as software, electronics, mechanics, safety, and reliability. The system design must ensure that all the pieces will ultimate fit together and achieve the system objectives in terms of functionality, performance, safety, reliability, and cost.

The software must ultimately map to the physical structure. This mapping occurs primarily at the architectural and detailed levels of design. The detailed design level deals with the physical characteristics of the individual hardware components and ensures that low-level interface protocols are followed. The architectural level maps the large-scale software components, such as subsystems, packages, and tasks, onto the various processors and devices. Mechanistic design is insulated away from most aspects of physical architecture.

5.2.1 Physical Architecture Issues

The electronic design decisions that are particularly relevant to the software architecture are the number and type of devices in the system (particularly the processors) and the physical communications media linking them together.

It is crucial to the success of the system that the electrical and software engineers collaborate on these decisions. If the electrical engineers don't understand the software needs, they are less able to adequately accommodate them. Similarly, if the software engineers don't have a sufficient understanding of the electronic design, their architectural decisions will be at best sub-optimal, and at worst unworkable. For this reason, both disciplines must be involved in device selection, particularly processors, memory maps, and communication buses. It is an unfortunate truth that many systems do not meet their functional or performance requirements when this collaboration is missing in the development process.

The software concerns for each processor are:

- Envisioned purpose and scope of the software executing on the processor
- Computational horsepower of the processor

- Availability of development tools, such as compilers for the selected language, debuggers, in-circuit emulators
- Availability of third-party components, including operating systems, container libraries, communication protocols, and user interfaces
- Previous experience and internal knowledge with the processor

How the processors are linked together is another far-reaching set of electronic design decisions. Should the communication media be arranged in a bus or star topology? Should it be bus-mastered or master-slave? Should it arbitrate on the basis of priority or fairness? Point-to-point or multidrop? How fast must the transmission rate be? These are the requirements of just the physical communications media. The software must layer appropriate communications protocols on top of that to ensure timely and reliable message exchange.

Naturally, these electronic design decisions can have a tremendous impact on the software architecture. Smaller processors can be used if there are more of them and they are linked together appropriately, or a smaller number of larger processors can do the same work. If the bus-mastering is not arbitrated in hardware, it becomes more difficult to implement a peer-to-peer communications protocol required for distributed processing. Only by working together can the electronic and software engineers find an optimal solution, given the system constraints. The optimal solution itself is specific to both the application domain and the business goals and approaches.

5.2.2 Software Architecture Issues

Within the confines of the physical architecture, the software itself has large-scale structures. The UML defines a subsystem as a subordinate system within a larger system [1]. In the embedded world, it is useful to further constrain our use of the term to mean *an integrated set of software components residing on a single physical processor.* These components are typically packages that, in turn, contain other packages, tasks, objects, and classes. Software architecture then becomes the process of designing subsystems, packages, tasks, and their interconnections.

The building blocks of subsystems are packages and tasks. Packages may contain subpackages, but their primary components are objects and classes. Packages can be used to model a single area of concern, or *domain.*[1] Specifically, they contain objects and classes that represent important concepts within a given domain. Class generalization hierarchies are always within a single domain package. Another common use for packages is to represent *subsystems.* A subsystem is a type of package that organizes run-time elements (objects and components) using common behavior as the organizing principle. The icons used to represent these features, shown in Figure 5-1, are elaborated in this chapter.

Subsystems are often organized as a set of layered packages. Many complex systems have several layers ordered hierarchically, from the most abstract (closest to the system problem domain) down to the most concrete (closest to the underlying hardware). For example,

- Application
- User interface
- Communication
- OS
- Hardware abstraction

Layering packages and subsystems in this way is an example of the Microkernel Architecture Pattern discussed in Section 5.4.

Just because the subsystems and packages are logically layered in terms of abstraction does not imply that system should be implemented in a layered fashion. In fact, the opposite is true. It is most efficacious to design a layered architecture and actually implement the system as a series of vertical slices of functionality that cut through all layers.

The OSI's seven-layer reference model is a common layered architecture for communications protocols, as shown in Figure 5-2.[2] The lollipop at the left of each package represents its *interface,* a set of classes and objects that may be externally accessed.[3] The dashed arrow is the dependency relationship and indicates that each package depends on the packages below it. This is an example of the Microkernel Architecture Pattern, described in Section 5.4.2.

---

[1] We use the term *domain* to refer to an independent subject matter that has its own set of concepts that can be modeled as classes and objects. Domain is a useful stereotype of package, although it is not defined within the UML specification.

[2] The physical layer is not shown in the figures because it does not usually involve software.

[3] These are service access points (SAPs), in OSI's nomenclature.

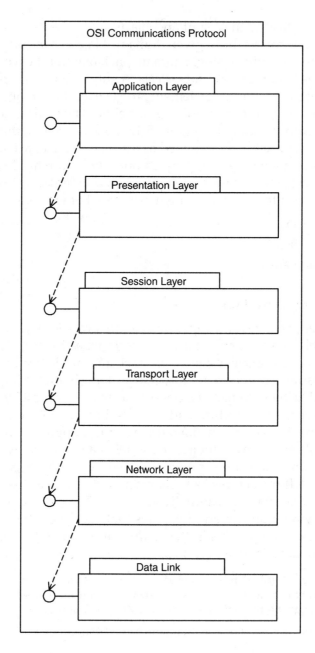

Figure 5-2: *OSI Model's Layered Architecture*

The Microkernel Architecture Pattern is fundamentally a set of client-server relationships among the layers. The more abstract layers are the clients that invoke the services of the more concrete layers. This one-way dependency makes it possible to use the same lower-level server layers in different contexts, because they know nothing of their clients. Similarly, because the lower layers offer a well-defined set of interfaces, they can be replaced with different lower layers, making the entire subsystem easily portable to other physical environments.

A layered implementation strategy would build each layer independently and link them together as they are completed. However, this approach has been proven to be risky and expensive in practice because fundamental flaws that affect the overall subsystem functionality are not caught until integration. A better implementation strategy is to implement vertical slices, as shown in Figure 5-3.

Each vertical slice implements only the portion of each layer relevant to the purpose of the slice. This approach to implementation is called *iterative prototyping,* and each slice is called a *prototype.* The prototypes are implemented so that each prototype builds upon the features implemented in its predecessors. The sequence of prototypes is decided based on which features logically come first, as well as on which represent the highest risk. By doing "risk-based development," higher-risk items are explored and resolved as early as possible. This typically results in less rework and a more integrated, reliable system.

The figure shows a set of *components* (more on components later) with a *refinement* relation between successive versions. The refinement relation is a stereotyped dependency in which one model element represents a more refined version of another. Also note that two tagged values indicate the version and date using the normal { tag = value } syntax.

A typical set of prototypes for Figure 5-3 is shown in Table 5-2.

Note how the later prototypes build upon the services implemented in their predecessors. This is the essence of the iterative prototyping development philosophy—gradually add capability until the entire system is complete. Naturally, iterative prototyping applies to more than just communications protocol design. Any sufficiently complex piece of software can be broken down into a set of hierarchical layers in a client-server topology.[4]

---

[4] The formal inductive proof of this statement is left as an exercise to the reader.

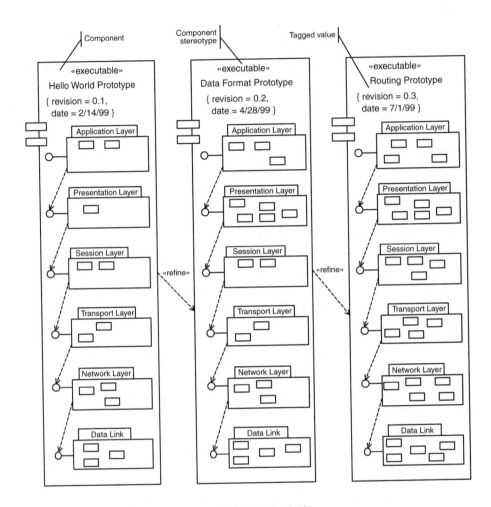

Figure 5-3: *Vertical Slices*

It is common for these components to contain one or more threads. The concurrency model is another piece of architectural design that can greatly effect system performance. In a soft real-time environment, average throughput must be ensured, but individual deadlines are not crucial to system correctness. In hard real-time environments, however, each deadline must be met and the concurrency model must ensure the ability of the system to meet all deadlines. For most multitasking systems, this is a nontrival problem, because the exact arrival patterns are

Table 5-2: *Typical Protocol Implementation Strategy*

#	Prototype Name	Description
1	Hello World	Implement enough of each layer (and stub the remainder) to send a message from one node to another.
2	Data Format	Mostly presentation layer—implement data encode, decode, and network data format conversions. Also include timed ACK/NAK transport layer protocol.
3	Routing	Mostly network and data link layers to control routing of messages.
4	Flow Control	Data-link Xon/Xoff flow control, and message CRCs to implement data integrity checks with automatic retry on message failure.
5	Connections	Connections and sessions (transport, data-link, session layers).
6	Performance	Performance tuning of all layers to optimize throughput.

not periodic and synchronous. Commonly, the system must respond to periodic events with vastly different periods, as well as to aperiodic events, which may be bursty.[5] Concurrency design is the subject of the latter half of this chapter.

The last primary architectural goal is to design the global error-handling policies to ensure correct system performance in the presence of faults.[6] Many strategies are possible, ranging from each object assuming full responsibility for all errors to a single global error handler that decides the correct action to take in all error conditions. Most systems are a hybrid of approaches. One popular strategy is to have

---

[5] A bursty event arrival pattern is one in which the events often arrive in great numbers that are separated by relatively long "quiet" intervals. To make a system deterministic, this bursty behavior must be bounded in both the maximum number of events and the minimum arrival time between events within a burst.

[6] Note that a requirement for fault tolerance almost always translates to a hard deadline for fault detection and handling, even in otherwise soft real-time systems.

multiple levels of error handling with the general rule that each error will be handled at the point at which enough context is available to make the correct decision. An object with enough redundancy of its data members (such as triple storage for important data) might process an invalid data value by reconstructing the appropriate data value or assigning a default value in the event of an error. A subsystem might reboot itself and let the remainder of the system function when it discovers a particular error. Some errors may require a global handler to intervene and coordinate a correct system shutdown, such as in the event of a failure in a nuclear power plant.

Error-handling policies are usually at least as complex as the primary software functionality and may result in systems three times as large and an order of magnitude more complex. Complicating error handling is the fact that it is highly system-dependent, yet only through clear error-handling policies can safety-critical systems be deployed safely.[7] This is an important aspect of the software architecture.

5.3 Representing Physical Architecture in UML

The UML represents physical architectures with deployment diagrams. The are several important diagrammatic elements, as shown in Figure 5-4. The icon of primary importance on deployment diagrams is the *node*. Nodes represent processors, sensors, actuators, routers, displays, input devices, memory, custom PLAs, or any physical object of importance to the software. Typically, nodes are stereotyped to indicate the type of node. Interconnects represent physical interconnections among nodes. They are most commonly electronic, but they can as easily be optical or telemetric.

Classes and objects are part of the *logical* architecture of the system. That is, they represent the logical concepts of the system and how they are inherently linked together. *Components* are part of the *physical* architecture. A component is an artifact of development that exists at runtime. Typical components are executables, libraries, files, configuration tables, and so on.

---

[7] Something for you to think about the next time you fly off to visit Grandma.

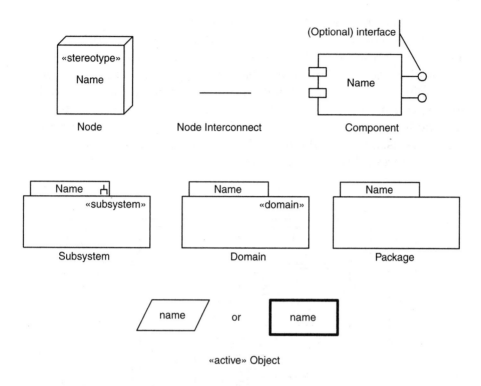

Figure 5-4: *Deployment Diagram Notation*

There are always many ways that a logical architecture can be mapped to a physical architecture. In fact, the same logical architectural elements may end up instantiated in multiple components. For example, many components may have to communicate with each other across a bus. They may all contain classes to assist the marshalling and unmarshalling of resources for bus transfer.

Processor nodes are occasionally shown containing classes or objects, but usually processor nodes contain components that may be broken down into subcomponents and tasks (represented as «active» objects). To show tasks, include the «active» objects in the component on the diagram. Of course, these components are the realization of objects and classes, but classes and objects usually appear only on class and object, not deployment, diagrams.

Another element commonly shown in deployment diagrams are *subsystems*. In the UML, a subsystem is a metasubclass of *both* a *Classifier* and a *Package*. It is usually shown as a package with a fork symbol in the package icon, or as a package with a «subsystem» stereotype. While a domain represents a set of classes organized around a common subject matter and vocabulary for the logical model, a subsystem organizes model elements together on the basis of behavior for the physical model. When both domains and subsystems are used in the same system model, the logical elements (for instance, classes) should reside in the domains, and only the instances (for instance, objects and component instances) should reside in the subsystems. This means that the

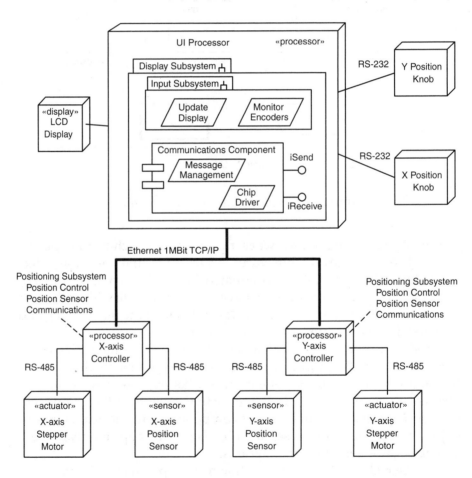

Figure 5-5: *Telescope Position Controller Deployment Diagram*

classes are used *by reference* in the subsystems because they are defined in the domains.

Subsystems may be divided into two compartments, one for behavioral specification and one for realization.

Figure 5-5 shows a simple example of a telescope position control system. The user interface consists of an LCD display and two rotary encoder knobs, which are tied to the same processor. The positioning subsystem consists of two independent subsystems, each containing a stepper motors and an independent sensor. The processors are linked together across an Ethernet network, and both use Ethernet controller boards to access the network.

This figure shows two methods for specifying the software running on the processors. The first is shown in the *UI Processor* node, which contains subsystems, components, and «active» objects. The software components are shown as nested packages. The other notation is to list the packages in a textual annotation, as is the case for the position controllers.

The description for the user interface processor in the figure shows that it contains two primary threads—one for monitoring the encoders and one for updating the display. The positioning subsystem also has two threads—one for controlling the stepper motor and one for monitoring the position of the telescope. Both processors have additional task threads for communicating across the network. Because this is a large-scale view, it does not typically include individual classes and objects.

5.4 Architectural Patterns

So far, we've discussed some issues that must be addressed by a system architecture and we've even given a simple example of one. Rather than give dozens of concrete examples of architectures in real-time systems, let's present some abstractions of architectures and weigh their pros and cons.

Architectural design may be approached in many ways. Each approach to solving a problem can be generalized into a pattern of organizing and marshalling these large-scale structures to achieve system goals. The UML defines a *pattern* as a parameterized collaboration in which the formal parameter list is the set of object roles defined. An instantiable collaboration can be created by supplying the specific classes that will play the roles in the collaboration. In use, a pattern is the formalization of a generalized approach to a common problem within a context [4].

Many useful software patterns have been identified in the literature, and the next chapter will present several patterns that appear at the mechanistic level of design. In following sections, we'll present some architectural patterns that have been particularly useful in the design of real-time systems.

The UML notation for a design pattern is an oval with a dashed border.[8] It connects to a participating entity with a dashed line. The label on the association is the role of the entity within the pattern. Patterns can be applied to nodes and packages, as well as to objects, and that will be how they are used in this chapter. We will show both the structure and a scenario illustrating the use of each pattern.

The patterns presented in this section are shown in Table 5-3.

The interested reader can find a larger selection of patterns for real-time systems in [7]; a number of patterns can be found in other references, such as [3], [4], and [5], but they are not focused on real-time systems.

Table 5-3: *Architectural Patterns*

Pattern Name	Purpose
Master-Slave	Coordinates the activities of several processors
Microkernel	Decomposescomplex components into sets of hierarchical abstraction layers to facilitate portability and reuse
Proxy	Handles the distribution of data from a central server to multiple remote clients
Broker	Handles the distribution of data from a central server to multiple remote clients when the location of the servers and clients is not known at compile time

---

[8] This is also the notation for a *collaboration* (the realization of a use case). Even though a pattern is really a parameterized collaboration, the formal parameter list is usually not shown, because the class roles in the pattern constitute this parameter list. If desired, however, the formal parameter list can be shown by attaching a dashed rectangle in the upper corner of the oval with the parameter list. This graphical syntax is similar to that used for parameterized classes.

5.4.1 Master-Slave Pattern

The master-slave pattern is a control pattern in which an intelligent controller issues commands and receives inputs from slave devices. The slaves typically don't initiate communication but must be actively polled by the master (see Figure 5-6).

This pattern applies to both symmetric and asymmetric multiprocessing. In *symmetric multiprocessing,* the slave nodes are more-or-less identical and the master distributes tasks to the slaves dynamically.

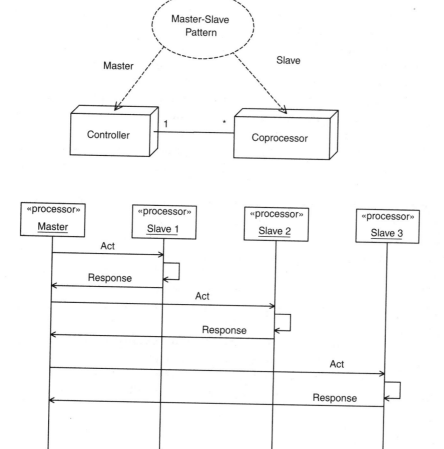

Figure 5-6: *Master-Slave Pattern*

This is particularly useful when the master must dynamically balance the processing load among a set of processors. An advantage of symmetric processing is that the addition of processors to an existing system can result in improved performance with no modifications to the software, because the symmetric RTOS dynamically loads tasks to lightly loaded processors.

Asymmetric multiprocessing means the processors are dedicated at compile-time to specific tasks. This approach makes smaller demands on the RTOS scheduling software and is more efficient for a specific configuration, but it is less flexible. Most real-time systems are asymmetric, because each processor has different interfaces to particular hardware devices.

A third approach that I've found useful for larger, hard, real-time systems is what I call *semi-symmetric multiprocessing (SSM)*. In this compromise approach, the allocation of tasks is not determined at compile-time but, rather, during system boot. A task broker queries the set of available processors and allocates tasks that are not tightly coupled to the hardware to the processors. The advantage of SSM is that it remains highly flexible and has minimal software run-time impact.

The advantages of the master-slave pattern lie in its simplicity. It can be used to implement distributed concurrent processing algorithms or simplify arbitration of shared resources. Master-slave control is usually performed as a cycling executive in which the master cycles through actions that invoke services of the slaves in a predefined sequence. When the action sequence is known at design time, the master-slave pattern is an obvious choice. The cyclic scheduling of actions makes the system extremely deterministic. It is possible to stop the CPU clock at any known point in time and tell from the design which CPU instruction it is executing. Aperiodic events are handled with polling, but because the scheduling is so deterministic, it is a simple matter to compute the worst-case latency for event handling.[9]

The simplicity of the master-slave pattern is also its primary disadvantage. Many systems must respond to episodic events that are impossible to predict. Depending on the complexity of the control

---

[9] Many modern CPUs are significantly less deterministic due to instruction caching and reordering. This is a case of better average performance coming at a cost of lessened predictability.

algorithms and the computational horsepower available on the master, it may be difficult to meet all deadlines in a master-slave arrangement. Cyclic schedulers are simple, but they tend to be inefficient in their use of CPU resources. It is possible to meet all deadlines using a preemptive scheduling policy and be unable to do so with a cyclic scheduler.[10]

5.4.2 Microkernel Pattern

This pattern is also known as the Layered Pattern. The basic concept of this pattern is to layer the structure of the subsystem into distinct sets of classes that can be arranged in a set of hierarchical client-server associations (see Figure 5-7). Commonly, the lowest level in the hierarchy directly interfaces with the underlying hardware or operating system, while the highest layer contains high-level application domain objects.

The layer interfaces are transparent from above, but opaque from below. The classes defined in the package interface are visible only to classes in packages at or above the package in the hierarchy. A *closed-layered architecture* is one in which each layer knows only about the layer immediately below it in the hierarchy. In an *open-layered architecture*, a layer can request services of any layer lower in the hierarchy. Closed-layered architectures tend to sacrifice some performance for increased encapsulation and reusability.

There is much to recommend layered designs as they provide good portability at both the top and bottom layers. The bottom layers can be reused with different upper layers, because the former are more concrete and more primitive. For example, a device I/O layer can be used in a wide set of applications on the same hardware platform. The upper layers can be reused on different hardware platforms by replacing only the device-specific lower layers. This is a great aid in porting a system to new physical architectures.

The primary disadvantage of the Microkernel Architecture is a loss in performance. A layered strategy often means that an execution path must pass through several layers in order to invoke the required service, when it would be more efficient to call the service directly. Also,

---

[10] Although most current avionics flight-control systems for both planes and spacecraft, such as the Galileo Jupiter probe, use cyclic schedulers, the Mars Pathfinder mission used priority-based scheduling with great success.

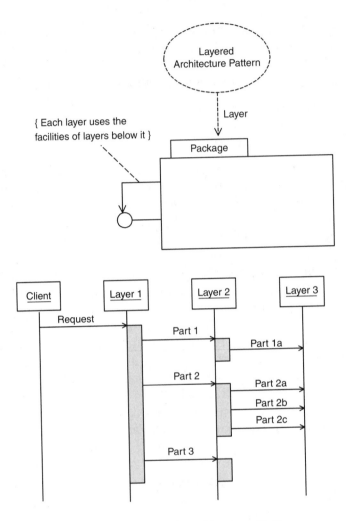

Figure 5-7: *Layered Architecture Pattern*

because the lower layers know nothing of the higher layers, they must, of necessity, be general and not apply any optimization that would require knowledge of their clients. This inefficiency can be mitigated by identifying the high bandwidth among the objects and optimizing the propagation of the data along those paths.

5.4.3 Proxy Pattern

The Proxy Pattern is only marginally an architectural pattern, but it is included here because it serves as the basis for the Broker Pattern, which is clearly architectural. The Proxy Pattern is applicable when a normal reference or pointer to an object is inappropriate or impossible, such as when the object resides in another thread or processor. This pattern de-couples clients from their servers by creating a local proxy, or stand-in, for the less-accessible server. When the client needs to request a service from the server, such as retrieving a value, it asks its local proxy. The proxy can then marshal a request to the original server or it can use an asynchronous policy that periodically or episodically receives updated values from the server.

The decoupling of client and server means that the server can reside in a different address space than the client, and it is useful in distrib-uted systems for this reason. Diverse proxy objects can provide differ-ent access rights to data, such as when your system must interface to third-party systems over which you have little or no control. Finally, the Proxy Pattern can provide reference counting for load-on-demand objects and assist in the creation and destruction of servers when mem-ory is extremely tight.

Figure 5-8 shows the Proxy Pattern and an example. In this sce-nario, the server contains the heart rate as measured from its ECG leads. The client resides on a separate display processor and displays the current heart rate. Because the objects reside on different proces-sors, the display processor uses a proxy object to hold a local copy of the heart rate. This proxy can have many clients, such as an alarm manager (to check for arrhythmia), a trending client, and several dis-play clients. The proxy maintains its own link over the communica-tions bus to the heart rate server. The proxy subscribes to the server (which might have several proxy clients distributed throughout the system), and every so often the server sends an update to its prox-ies. The proxy insulates the clients from knowing anything about the location of the server and how to marshal bus messages to get the data. Further, the proxy is more efficient when multiple clients reside on the same processor because bus bandwidth is usually at a premium, and this way only the proxy must communicate with the server directly.

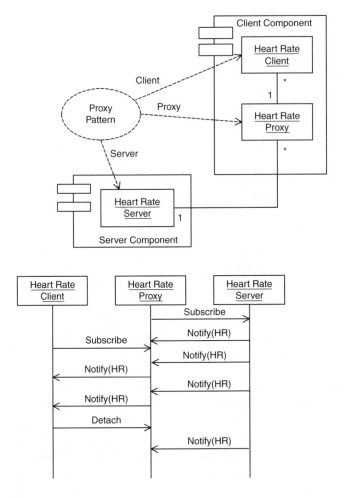

Figure 5-8: *Proxy Pattern*

The primary disadvantage of the Proxy Pattern is again a possible loss of performance when only a single client resides on the processor. Another weakness of it is the coupling between the proxy objects and the server. The proxy must know how to find the server, so it must know not only the operational syntax for requesting the data, it must also know the location of the server and how to marshal requests using the communication protocol. The Proxy Pattern can be elaborated to decouple the proxy from the server using the Broker Pattern, described below.

5.4.4 Broker Pattern

The Broker Pattern is an elaborated Proxy Pattern and goes another step toward decoupling the clients from the servers. An object broker is an object that knows the location of other objects. The broker can have the knowledge *a priori* (at compile-time) or can gather the information dynamically as objects register themselves, or a combination of both. The primary advantage of the Broker Pattern is that it is possible to construct a Proxy Pattern when the location of the server isn't known as the system is compiled. This makes it particularly useful for systems using symmetric or semi-symmetric multiprocessing.

The architectural components of the Broker Pattern are the *Object Broker, Client,* and *Server* components. It is rare to have a broker with an isolated client and server, and when it is used, the Broker Pattern is typically a key strategic design decision. Although many real-time systems may be able to use commercial object brokers, it is not uncommon to implement a custom broker to optimize system resource usage.

In fault-tolerant and safety-critical systems, the object broker may play a key role in the maintenance of system integrity. For example, the broker can contain a watchdog that maintains connections with all safety-relevant subsystems.[11] When a subsystem becomes unstable or shuts down, the object broker can initiate safety actions, such as de-energizing lasers, inserting control rods into the nuclear reactor core, and so on. The broker can also be involved in startup and shutdown sequences for distributed real-time systems.

The scenario in Figure 5-9 shows how the participant objects collaborate with two levels of indirection. The first level is provided by the proxies, insulating the clients and servers from each other. The second level is provided by the object broker, which insulates the proxies from the servers. Note that the server object first registers with the broker so that it can handle incoming requests for the server. When the client subscribes to its local proxy, the proxy in turn subscribes to the server proxy. The object broker handles this request because only it knows the location of the server.

---

[11] This connection is often implemented with special *life tick* (also known as *heartbeat*) messages that indicate that the client subsystem is alive and well.

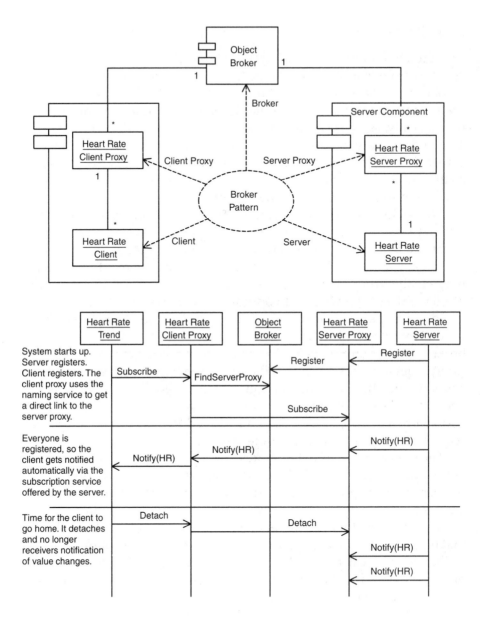

Figure 5-9: *Broker Pattern*

5.5 Concurrency Design

Real-time systems typically have multiple threads of control executing simultaneously. A *thread* can be defined as a set of executable *actions* that execute sequentially. Actions are statements that execute at the same priority in a particular sequence or that perform some cohesive function. These statements can belong to different objects. The entirety of a thread is also known as a *task.* Multiple objects typically participate within a single task. In some systems, a distinction is made between *heavyweight* and *lightweight* threads. Heavyweight threads use different data address spaces and must resort to expensive messaging to communicate data among themselves. Such threads have relatively strong encapsulation and protection from other threads. Lightweight threads coexist within an enclosing data address space. Lightweight threads provide faster inter-task communication via this shared "global" space, but they offer weaker encapsulation. Some authors use the terms *thread* or *task* to refer to lightweight threads and *process* to refer to heavyweight threads. We shall use the three terms synonymously in this book.

5.6 Representing Threads

The UML can show concurrency models in a couple of ways. Class and object diagrams can show the threads (represented as active objects) directly and, less frequently, state diagrams can show the orthogonal components participating in multiple threads. Collaboration and sequence diagrams show specific scenarios of these active objects and their components with other threads.

Class and object diagrams can use the stereotype «active» or the active object stereotype icon to represent threads. By showing only classes and objects with this stereotype, the task structure can be clearly shown. A task diagram is nothing more than a class diagram showing only active objects and their associations.[12]

---

[12] The system specification must be kept distinct from the diagrams. The specification resides in the repository, while diagrams provide a view into that repository. Many different and redundant views are possible, so it is perfectly all right to create new diagrams that contain only partial information, such as the system task diagram.

State diagrams show the state space for classes and objects. Because active objects are just a special kind of object, their behavior can be captured on state diagrams, as well. Using the complex transition notation (for example, join and fork), it is possible to show multiple threads rooted within a single active object. Multicast and propagated events show the event communication between active objects. These concepts were dealt with in some detail in the previous chapter.

Scenarios can be single or multithreaded. In multithreaded scenarios, threads are included in the message label by preceding the sequence number with the thread name.

5.6.1 System Task Diagram

Class and object models are fundamentally concurrent. Objects are themselves inherently concurrent, and it is conceivable that each object could execute in its own thread.[13] During the course of architectural design, the objects must be aligned into a smaller set of concurrent threads solely for efficiency reasons. Because of this, the partitioning of a system into threads is always a design decision.

In the UML, threads are rooted in a single active object. The active object is a composite that aggregates the objects participating within the thread. It has the general responsibility to coordinate internal execution by dispatching messages to its constituent parts and providing information to the underlying operating system so that the latter can schedule the thread. By showing only the classes with the «active» stereotype on a single diagram, you can create a system task diagram.

Packaging objects appropriately into nodes and threads is vital for system performance. The relationships among the threads are fundamental architectural decisions that have great impact on the performance and hardware requirements of the system. In addition to identifying the threads and their relationships to other threads, the characteristics of the messages must themselves be defined. These characteristics include:

- Message arrival patterns and frequencies
- Event response deadlines

---

[13] This is, after all, how biological neural systems work (see [6]).

- Synchronization protocols for inter-task communication
- "Hardness" of deadlines

Answering these questions is at the very heart of multithreaded systems design.

The greatest advantage of a task diagram is that the entire set of threads for the system can be shown on a single diagram, albeit at a high conceptual level. It is easy to trace back from the diagram into the requirements specification and vice versa. By elaborating each thread symbol on the task diagram into either a lightweight task diagram or an object diagram, the threads can be efficiently decomposed and related to the class, object, and behavioral models.

The elevator class diagram in Figure 3-13 identified the primary classes from the original problem statement, along with their relationships and multiplicity. Figure 5-10 shows the task diagram for the same set of classes, subsumed within the shown «active» objects. The diagram shows a number of useful things. First, notice that the processors have been identified. The *Elevator Gnome* is a singleton processor because it acts as a controller/event dispatcher. The *Central Station* is likewise a singleton. The *Elevator* and *Floor processors* are not—there is an instance of the elevator processor for every elevator, and an instance of a floor processor in every floor. Note the instance multiplicity defined in the upper-left corner of each processor icon.

Within each processor, objects are busy collaborating to achieve the goals of that processor. However, on the system task diagram, only the threads are shown. Remember that each thread is rooted in a single «active» composite object that receives the events for that thread and dispatches them to the appropriate object within the thread.

The associations among the threads are shown using conventional association notation. These associations indicate that the threads must communicate in some fashion to pass messages.

Compare Figure 5-10 with Figure 3-13. Can you identify in which threads the various objects and classes in the latter diagram reside?

5.6.2 Concurrent State Diagrams

Rumbaugh [2] has suggested a means by which concurrent threads can be diagrammed using the statecharts. He notes that concurrency with

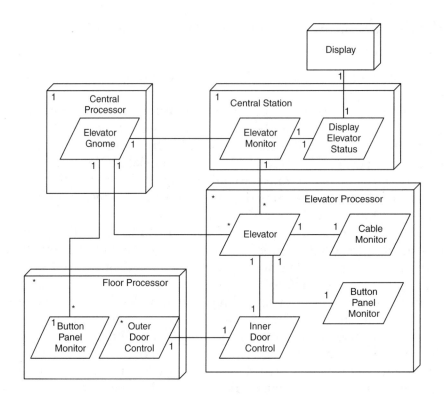

Figure 5-10: *Elevator Task Diagram*

objects generally arises by aggregation—that is, a composite object is composed of component objects, some of which may execute in separate threads. In this case, a single state of the composite object may be composed of multiple states of these components.

«active» objects respond to events and dispatch them to their aggregate parts. This process can be modeled as a finite state machine. The other orthogonal component is due to the thread itself having a number of states. Because the active object represents the thread characteristics to the system, it is natural to make this an orthogonal component of the active object.

Figure 5-11 shows the two orthogonal components of a typical «active» object class. The dashed line separates the orthogonal components of the *Running* superstate. Each transition in the event processing component can take place only while the «active» object is in one of the

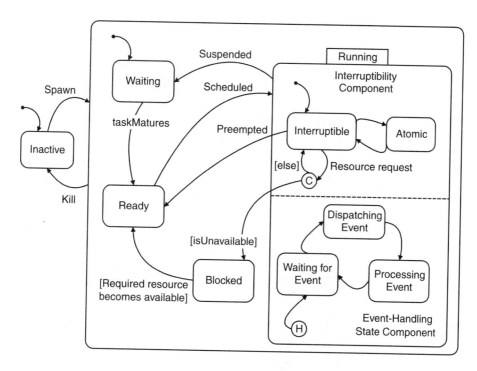

Figure 5-11: *Concurrency in Active Objects*

substates of the *Running* superstate of the thread component. After all, that is the only time it actually consumes CPU cycles. On the other hand, if the running thread becomes preempted or suspended, the event processing component will resume where if left off, as indicated by the history connector.

Table 5-4 provides a brief description of the states.

Table 5-4: *States of the Active Object Thread Component*

State	Description
Inactive	The thread is not yet created.
Waiting	The thread is not ready to run, but is waiting for some event to put it in the *Ready* state.
	(continued)

Table 5-4 (*cont.*)

State	Description
Ready	The thread is ready to run and is waiting to execute. It is usually stored in a priority FIFO queue.
Running	The thread is running and chewing up CPU cycles. This superstate contains two orthogonal, concurrent components.
Interruptible	The thread is running and may be preempted. This is a substate of the *Interruptibility Component* of the *Running* state.
Atomic	The thread is running but may not be preempted. Specifically, task switching has been disabled. This is a substate of the *Interruptibility Component* of the *Running* state.
Blocked	The thread is waiting for a required resource to become available so that it may continue its processing.
Waiting for event	The thread is waiting for an event to handle. This is a substate of the *Event-Handling State Component* of the *Running* state.
Dispatching Event	The object is handling an incoming event and deciding which aggregates should process it. This is a substate of the *Event-Handling State Component* of the *Running* state.
Processing Event	The designated aggregate of the active object composite is responding to the event. This is a substate of the *Event-Handling State Component* of the *Running* state.

5.7 Defining Threads

During analysis, classes and objects were identified and characterized and their associations defined. In a multitasking system, the objects must be placed into threads for actual execution. This process of task-thread definition is two-fold:

- Identify the threads.
- Populate the threads with classes and objects from the analysis and design process.

There are several strategies that can help you define the threads based on the external events and the system context. They fall into the general approach of grouping events in the system so that a thread handles one or more events and each event is handled by a single thread.

There are conditions under which an event may be handled by more than one thread. One event may generate other *propagated* events, which may be handled by other threads. For example, the appearance of waveform data may itself generate an event to signal another thread to scale the incoming data asynchronously. Occasionally, events may be multicast to more than one thread. This may happen when a number of threads are waiting on a shared resource or are waiting for a common event that permits them all to move forward independently.

5.7.1 Identifying Threads

Internal and external events can be grouped together into threads in a variety of ways. Some common event grouping strategies are:

- Single event groups
  In a simple system, it may be possible to create a separate thread for each external and internal event. This is usually not feasible in complex systems with dozens or even hundreds of possible events or when thread switch time is significant relative to the event-response timing.

- Sequential processing
  When it is clear that a series of steps must be performed in a sequential fashion, this may be grouped within a single thread.

- Event source
  This strategy groups together events from a common source. For example, group all the events related to ECG numerics into one thread (such as HR Available, ECG Alarms, and so forth), all the NIBP (noninvasive blood pressure) data in another, the ventilator data in another, the anesthetic agent in another, and the gas-mixing data in yet another. In an automobile, sources of events might be the ignition, braking, and engine-control systems. In systems with clearly defined subsystems producing events that have roughly the same period, this may be the simplest approach.

- Interface device (a.k.a. port)
  This grouping strategy encapsulates control of a specific interface within a single thread. For example, the (periodic) SDLC data can be handled in one thread, the (episodic) RS232 data to the external models in another, and the (episodic) user buttons and knobs in another. This strategy is a specialization of the event source grouping strategy.

- Related information
  Consider grouping all waveforms to be handled by a single thread, and all measured numeric parameters within another thread. Or all information related to airfoil control surfaces in each wing and tail section might be manipulated by separate threads. This grouping may be appropriate when related data is used together in the user problem domain. Another name used for this grouping is *functional cohesion*.

- Arrival pattern
  If data arrives at a given rate, a single periodic thread could receive all the relevant data and dispatch it to different objects as necessary. Aperiodic events might be handled by a single interrupt handler and, similarly, dispatch control to appropriate objects. Generally, this grouping may be most useful with internal events, such as timer interrupts, or when the periods of events naturally cluster around a small set of periods. *Note that this is the primary strategy used to identify threads that have deadlines—use of other policies with time-constrained event responses can lead to priority inversion unless the designers are especially careful.*

- Target object/Computationally intense processing
  One of the purposes of rendezvous objects is to encapsulate and provide access to data. As such, they are targets for events, both to insert and remove data. A waveform queue object server might have its own thread for background scaling and manipulation, while at the same time, participating in threads depositing data within the queue object and removing data for display.

- Purpose
  Alarms serves one purpose—to notify the user of the system of anomalies so that he or she can take corrective action or vacate the premises, whichever seems more appropriate. This might form one event group. Grouping safety checks within a watchdog thread,

such as checking for stack overflow or code corruption, might form another. This purpose might map well to a use case.

- Safety concerns
  The system hazard analysis may suggest threads. One common rule of thumb in safety-critical systems is to separate monitoring from actuation. In terms of thread identification, this means that a thread that controls a safety-relevant process should be checked by an independent thread. From a safety perspective, it is preferable to run safety checks on a separate processor so that common-mode hardware and software faults do not affect both the primary and the safety processing simultaneously.

During concurrency design, you must add events to groups for which it appears appropriate so that each event is represented in at least one group. Any events remaining after the initial grouping can be considered independently. As mentioned earlier, it is recommended that thread actions that have hard deadlines use the Arrival Pattern strategy to ensure a schedulable set of threads. Create a task diagram in which the processing of each group is represented by a separate thread. Most events will only occur within a single thread, but sometimes events must be dispatched to multiple threads.

Frequently, one or more of these groupings will emerge as the primary decomposition strategy of the event space, but it is also common to mix grouping strategies. When the grouping seems complete and stable, you have identified an initial set of threads that handle all events in your system. As the product development evolves, events may be added to or removed from groups, new groups may suggest themselves, or alternative grouping strategies may present themselves. This should lead the astute designer to alternative designs worth consideration.

5.8 Assigning Objects to Threads

Once a good set of threads is identified, you may start populating the groups with objects. Note that the previous sentence referred to *objects*, not *classes*. Objects are specific instances of classes, which may appear in different threads or as an interface between threads. There are classes that create only a single instance in an application (singletons), and there are classes that instantiate to multiple objects that all reside within a single thread. But in the general case, classes instantiate a number of objects that may appear in any number of threads. For example, there may be queues of threads, queues of waveform data, queues of numeric data, queues of network messages, command queues, error queues, alarm queues, and so forth. These might appear in a great many threads, even though they are instances of the same class (queue).

5.9 Defining Thread Rendezvous

So far in this chapter, we have looked at what constitutes a thread, some strategies to select a set of threads, and how to populate threads with objects. The remainder of this chapter provides ways to define how the threads communicate with each other.

There are a number of strategies for intertask communication. The simplest by far is to use the OS to send messages from one thread to another. While this approach maintains encapsulation and limits coupling among threads, it is expensive in terms of compute cycles and is relatively slow. Lightweight, expeditious communication is required in many real-time systems in order for the threads to meet their performance requirements. In this chapter, we will consider some methods for intertask communication that are both lightweight and robust.

The two main reasons for thread communication are to share information and to synchronize control. The acquisition, manipulation, and display of information may all occur in different thread threads with different periods and may not even take place on the same processor, necessitating some means to share the information among these threads. Synchronization of control is also very common in real-time systems. In asynchronous threads that control physical processes, one thread's completion (such as emptying a chemical vat) may form a precondition for another process (such as adding a new volatile chemical to the vat). The thread synchronization strategy must ensure that such preconditions are satisfied.

When threads communicate, the rendezvous itself has attributes and behavior, which make it reasonable to model it as an associative class. The important questions to ask about thread synchronization are:

- Are there any preconditions for the threads to communicate? A precondition is generally a data value that must be set, or some object must be in a particular state. If a precondition for thread synchronization exists, it should be checked by a guarding condition before the rendezvous is allowed to continue.

- What should happen if the preconditions are not met, as when the collaborating thread is not available? The rendezvous can:

  ▾ Wait indefinitely until the other thread is ready (a *waiting rendezvous*)

  ▾ Wait until either the required thread is ready or a specified period has elapsed (*timed rendezvous*)

  ▾ Return immediately (*balking rendezvous*) and ignore the attempt at thread communication

  ▾ Raise an exception and handle the thread communication failure as an error (*protected rendezvous*)

- If data is to be shared via the rendezvous class, what is the relationship of the rendezvous object with the object containing the required information? Options include:

  ▾ The rendezvous object contains the information directly.

  ▾ The rendezvous object holds a reference to the object containing the information, or a reference to an object serving as an interface for the information.

  ▾ The rendezvous object can temporarily hold the information until it is passed to the target thread.

Remember that objects must ensure the integrity of their internal data. If the possibility exists that shared data can be simultaneously *write* or *write-read* accessed by more than a single thread, then it must be protected by some mechanism, such as a mutual-exclusion semaphore. In general, synchronization objects must handle:

- Preconditions
- Access control
- Data access

5.9.1 Sharing Resources

Rendezvous objects control access to resources, and classical methods exist to handle resource usage in a multitasking environment. In the simplest case, resources can be simultaneously accessed—that is, access is nonatomic. Many devices use predetermined configuration tables burned into FLASH or EPROM memory. Because processes can only read the configuration table, many threads can access the resource simultaneously without bad effects.

When data access involves writing, it requires some form of access control to ensure data integrity. Clearly, if multiple internal attributes must be simultaneously updated, another reader thread cannot be permitted to read these values while only some of them are updated.

In large collections of objects, it may be necessary to allow read accesses in one or more portions of the database even while other sections are being updated. Large airline reservation databases must function in this fashion, for example. Algorithms to control these processes are well-defined and available in texts on relational and object databases.

5.9.2 Assigning Priorities

Thread *priority* is distinct from the importance of the actions executed by the thread. Priority in a preemptive priority scheme determines the *required timeliness* of the response to the event or precondition. For example, in an ECG monitor, in order to have smoothly drawn waveforms, waveform threads must have a high priority to ensure that they run often enough to avoid a jerky appearance. ECG waveforms have tight timeliness requirements. On the other hand, a jerky waveform is not as important to patient outcome as alarming when the patient is at risk. An asystole alarm is activated when the monitor detects that the heart is no longer beating. Clearly, bringing this to the attention of the physician is very important, but if the alarm took an extra second to be annunciated, it would not affect patient outcome. Such an alarm is very important, but does not have a very high priority.

In *rate monotonic scheduling* (RMS), the assignment of priorities is simple—the priority of all threads is inversely proportional to their periods. The shorter the period, the higher the priority. The original RMS scheme assumed that the deadline is equal to the period. When this is not true, the priority should be assigned based on the deadline rather than the period. In general, the RMS scheduling makes intuitive sense—threads with short deadlines must be dealt with more promptly than those with longer deadlines. It is not uncommon to find a few exceptions to the rule, however. RMS scheduling and the associated mathematics of proving schedulability are beyond the scope of this book. For a more detailed look, see [7] and [8].

5.10 Looking Ahead

Analysis is all about the development of a consistent logical model that describes all possible acceptable solutions to a problem. Design is about *optimization*—selecting a particular solution that optimizes some set of design criteria in a way that is consistent with the analysis model.

Architectural design consists of the specification of the kind and quantity of devices, the media and rules they use to communicate, and the large-scale software components mapping to the physical architecture. The units of software architecture are subsystems and threads. Subsystems are typically layered sets of packages arranged in a hierarchical fashion. Threads cut through all layers, although they are rooted in a single active object.

The software architecture must map to the set of physical devices. The UML shows this mapping with the deployment diagram. This diagram shows not only nodes and communication paths, but it can also show the large-scale software components.

The iterative refinement implementation strategy builds these layered subsystems using vertical slices passing through all layers, as well. Each vertical slice constitutes an iterative prototype. Prototypes build upon the services defined in the previous prototypes. The order of prototypes is determined by the required services, as well as by the level of risk. By elaborating high-risk prototypes early, overall project risk is lowered as early as possible with a minimum of rework.

The specification of the concurrency model is very important to performance in real-time systems. This concurrency model identifies a relatively small number of threads and populates these threads with the objects identified in the analysis model. Intertask communication allows threads to share information and to synchronize control. This is often accomplished by using a Rendezvous Pattern to ensure robust exchange of information.

The next step is to specify the middle layer of design, known as mechanistic design. This level of design focuses on the collaboration of small groups of classes and objects. In the process of mechanistic design, we will add classes to optimize information or control flow and to specify details that have been so far ignored.

5.11 References

[1] *UML Semantics Appendix M1-UML Glossary Version 1.3 Beta R6.* Santa Clara, CA.: Rational Corporation, 1999.

[2] Rumbaugh, James, Michael Blaha, William Premerlani, Frederick Eddy, and William Lorensen, *Object-Oriented Modeling and Design.* Englewood Cliffs, NJ: Prentice Hall, 1991.

[3] Buschmann, Frank, Regine Meunier, Hans Rohnert, Peter Sommerlad, Michael Stal, *A System of Patterns: Pattern-Oriented Software Architecture.* Chichester: John Wiley & Sons, 1996.

[4] Alexander, C., S. Ishikawa, and M. Silverstain, *A Pattern Language.* New York: Oxford University Press, 1977.

[5] Gamma, Erich, Richard Helm, Ralph Johnson, and John Vlissides, *Design Patterns: Elements of Reusable Software.* Reading, MA: Addison Wesley Longman, 1994.

[6] Douglass, Bruce Powel, *Statistical Analysis of Simulated Multinerve Networks: Use of Factor Analytical Methods.* Ph.D. Dissertation. Vermillion, SD: USD Medical School, 1984.

[7] Douglass, Bruce Powel, *Doing Hard Time: Developing Real-Time Systems with UML, Objects, Frameworks, and Patterns.* Reading, MA: Addison Wesley Longman, 1995.

[8] Klein, Mark, Thomas Ralya, Bill Pollak, Ray Obenza, and Michael Gonzalez Harbour, *A Practitioner's Handbook for Real-Time Analysis: Guide to Rate Monotonic Analysis for Real-Time Systems.* Boston: Kluwer Academic Publishers, 1993.

Chapter 6

Mechanistic Design

This chapter explains the middle level of design, called mechanistic design, which deals with how collaborations (small sets of classes and objects that collaborate to achieve common goals) can be optimized. Mechanistic design is primarily organized around the discovery and use of patterns of object collaboration. These design patterns are reified solutions to structurally similar problems. Some architectural patterns are given in the previous chapter, but this chapter will identify several smaller-scale patterns useful in real-time embedded systems.

Notation and Concepts Discussed

Mechanistic design patterns	Smart Pointer Pattern	Rendezvous Pattern
Observer Pattern	Container Pattern	State Pattern
MVC Pattern	Interface Pattern	State Table Pattern
Transaction Pattern	Policy Pattern	

6.1 What Is Mechanistic Design?

Mechanistic design is concerned with adding and organizing classes to support a particular implementation strategy. The mechanistic design process elaborates the analysis model and iterates it by adding objects to facilitate a particular design. As mentioned earlier, a set of classes and objects working together is called a *collaboration.* A collaboration is defined in terms of specific classes playing named roles (called *classifier roles*). When the collaborators may be replaced with others that can fulfill those roles, the collaboration is called a *pattern.* The roles define, in an abstract sense, the formal parameter list for the pattern. When bound with an actual parameter list (the classes whose instances will play the part of those roles at run-time), the pattern may be instantiated into a collaboration. A *mechanism* [1] is a type of pattern that is limited in scope to a few classes (that is, it does not have architectural scope), but it is generally applicable in many circumstances.[1]

A typical real-time system may have dozens or even hundreds of mechanisms operating concurrently. While the analysis model identifies the classes and objects fundamental to the problem domain, mechanistic design reorganizes these entities and adds objects to facilitate their collaboration. A common example is the addition of container classes to handle multi-valued roles[2] in associations.

In the analysis model, many associations will have multi-valued roles. For example,

- A customer can have many bank accounts.
- An autopilot can use many sensors and actuators.
- A physiological parameter can be shown in different views simultaneously.

The most common implementation of a 1 to 1 association is a pointer or reference in the client that allows the client to send messages

---

[1] One of my favorite mechanisms is *Crazy Ed's Original Cave Creek Chili Beer,* in which beer collaborates with a jalepeno chili (Black Mountain Brewing Company, Cold Spring, MN, and Cave Creek, AZ). I find it a keen programming-skill enhancer and a good general solution to a wide variety of problems.

[2] A *multi-valued role* of an association is defined as an association role with a nonunity multiplicity, such as (0,1) or *.

to the server (for example, call one of the server's member functions),
such as:

```
class Actuator {
    int value;
public:
    int gimme(void) { return value; };
    void set(int v) { value = v; };
};

class Autopilot {
    Actuator *s;
public:
    void AutoPilot(Server *YourActuator): s(YourActuator) { };
    // send msg to Server object s
    void setIt(int a) { s->set(a); }
    void IncIt(void) {
        int a = s->gimme();
        s->set(++a);
    };
};
```

The class *Autopilot* uses pointer *s* to locate its *Actuator* object. It can
then send the object messages like *s->set(a)* and *s->gimme()*. The use of a
simple pointer is appropriate because the multiplicity of the association is 1 to 1. But what if the association is 1 to *?

It is entirely possible to build the ability to manage collections of
Actuator objects directly into the *Autopilot* class. A strategy could be
used, such as using a vector, linked-list, or binary tree to manage the
collection by adding operations into the class *Autopilot* for adding, finding, sorting, and deleting these objects in the collection.

This simple approach has a number of drawbacks. First of all, the
machinery to manage the collection is entirely unrelated to the primary
purpose of the class *Autopilot*. Inserting such methods would obscure
this purpose. Second, depending on the nature of the collection itself,
the management of the collection may be quite complex, such as balancing AVL or Red-Black trees. Adding this behavior would make the
class large and complex, as well. Further, managing collections is a subject
domain of its own and such collection class packages may be purchased.
Building the behavior directly into the *Autopilot* class makes reuse of these
libraries impossible. If the system has 20 classes with multi-valued roles,
this behavior must be rewritten for each class. Building the behavior

directly into each class that uses it makes changing to a different kind of collection much more difficult.

The more common approach is to introduce a new class during mechanistic design, one to handle the vagaries of managing the contained objects. Such a class is called a *collection* or *container* class. This allows third-party libraries to be used, separates out unrelated concerns of container management, and allows the type of collection to be changed fairly easily. The analysis model identified the association and its multiplicity, but the use of a container class is a design decision, because it is a specific way to implement the analysis model. The use of collection classes is so common that it can be reified into a design pattern:

> When a class must manage a number of objects of the same class, a useful design approach is to add a container class between the primary class and the set of multiple objects.

So it is with all of mechanistic design. Classes are added to facilitate the implementation of the analysis model. This is the classic elaborative, or iterative, development method—repeated refinement of the model via reorganization and addition.

In the following section, we'll present a number of design patterns that can be profitably applied in the design of real-time systems. The use of these patterns simplifies the system's design and allows reuse on a grander scale than the reuse of individual objects and classes.

6.2 Mechanistic Design Patterns

As discussed in the previous chapter, design patterns consist of:

- A common problem, including common problem context
- A general approach to a solution
- Consequences of the pattern

The problem statement describes the general characteristics of the problem at hand. This description may include context and preconditions. For example,

Problem: When exception handling is used, raw pointers can lead to memory leaks when exceptions are thrown. The use of temporary pointers within normal C++ functions or class member functions may not be properly cleaned up if an exception is thrown, because the inline delete operator may be bypassed. This does not apply to objects, because when objects go out of scope, their destructors are called. Raw pointers do not have destructors.

This problem statement identifies a problem common to designs within many domains. The context is broad—programs using C++ with exception handling. Because a generally applicable solution to this problem is available, it can be reified into a design pattern:

Solution: Rather than use a raw pointer, a smart pointer object can be used when a temporary pointer is needed. The smart pointer is responsible for identifying if it must deallocate memory when the pointer is destroyed.[3] This requires an internal mechanism, such as reference counting, to determine whether other smart pointers are referring to the same object in memory.

Naturally, design patterns have pros and cons. The following are the consequences of the design pattern:

Consequences: The smart pointer makes the design more robust in the presence of thrown exceptions, but it increases the code complexity somewhat and requires an additional level of indirection for each pointer reference. Although this can be made syntactically invisible to the user, it involves a small run-time overhead. Enforcement of the smart pointer policy cannot be automated, but must be ensured by consensus and review. Further, if smart and raw pointers are both applied against the same object, reference counting should be disabled.

Mechanistic design patterns are medium scale, involving as few as two or as many as a dozen classes. Several patterns are provided in this

---

[3] There may be other pointers to the memory, so it is not obvious in general whether the memory being pointed to can be safely deleted when the pointer itself is destroyed.

chapter, but this is a rich area of active research. The interested reader should look into the references for more patterns.[4]

As specified, you may find these patterns too specific or too general. Feel free to adapt them to the particular needs of your system.

Table 6-1 shows the patterns covered in this chapter.

6.2.1 Simple Patterns

This section lists some simple patterns in common use.

Table 6-1: *Mechanistic Patterns*

Category	Pattern Name	Purpose
Simple patterns	Observer	Allow multiple clients to effectively share a server and be autonomously updated
	Model-view-controller	Separate concerns of user input, data maintenance and manipulation, and display
	Transaction	Control communication between objects with various levels of reliability
	Smart pointer	Avoid problems associated with dumb pointers
Reuse	Container	Abstract away data structuring concepts from application domain classes to simply model and facilitate reuse
	Interface	Abstract away the type of an object from its implementation to support multiple implementations of a given type and to support multiple types with a common internal structure
	Policy	Provide the ability to easily change algorithms and procedures dynamically
	Rendezvous	Provide a flexible mechanism for lightweight inter-task communication

---

[4] Another good source of patterns is the Patterns Home Page at *http://hillside.net/patterns/patterns.html*. Other interesting Web pages can be found by looking for "design patterns" on your favorite Web search engine.

6.2.1.1 Observer Pattern[5]

It is common that a single source of information acts as a server for multiple clients that must be autonomously updated when the data value changes. This is particularly true with real-time data acquired through sensors. The problem is how to design an efficient means for all clients to be notified.

The Observer Pattern (a.k.a. *Publish-Subscribe*) is one design solution (see Figure 6-1). A single object, called the *Server*, provides the data automatically to its clients, called *Observers.* These are abstract classes that may be subclassed (into *Concrete Server* and *Concrete Observer*) to add the specialized behavior to deal with the specific information being served up.

The observers register with the server by calling the server's Subscribe() method and deregister by calling the Detach() method. When the server receives a subscribe message, it creates a *Notification Handle* object, which includes the address of the object. This address may be a pointer if the object is in the same data address space, or it may be a logical address or identifier to be resolved by a separate communications subsystem or object broker if the target object is in a remote address space.

The *Notification Handle* class is subclassed to distinguish its update policy. The update policy defines the criteria for when data is sent to the observer. Typically, this is periodic, episodic, or epi-periodic (both). In some cases, it may be sufficient to use the same policy universally, but using a policy makes the design pattern more general. It is common for an episodic policy to be used exclusively, but this is insufficient for many applications. In safety-critical systems, for example, a lost message could result in an unsafe system. By periodically sending the data to the observers, the system is hardened against random message loss.

Notification of the observers is straightforward. When the server acquires data via the Acquire() method, it scans its notification list looking for *Notification Handles* referring to objects with an episodic update policy. The AcceptTick() method is called on a timer event. When this method is called, the notification list is scanned for *Notification Handles* that are due for an update. When data is sent, the time of the next update for that target object is computed and stored in the *TimeOfNextUpdate* attribute.

---

[5] This rendition of the Observer Pattern is somewhat different from that found in most pattern references, but I've found it particularly useful in hard real-time environments.

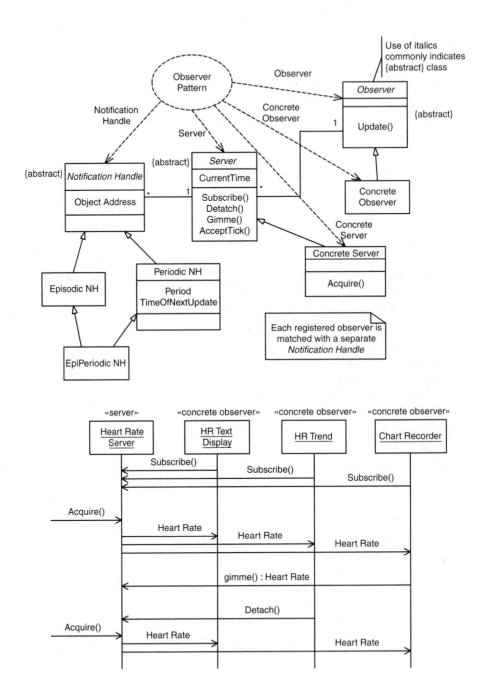

Figure 6-1: *Observer Pattern*

To manage the notification list, this pattern is usually combined with the Collection Pattern. For distributed or multiprocessor systems, this pattern is often elaborated into the Proxy or Broker Patterns, described in the previous chapter.

The Observer Pattern is useful when many clients need to access a single object. The pattern simplifies the creation of these clients because once they register, they will be automatically notified of the data based on their selected policy. This continues until they detach from the server.

The following entities participate in the pattern:

- *Server*

  The *Server* is an abstract class that defines the interface to which the abstract observer class adheres. It uses the Update() method of the Observer to pass the value to the Observer. The methods of interest are:

  ▾ *Subscribe(target address, policy)*

  This method adds the object indicated by target address to the notification list by creating a *Notification Handle* object. The particular subclass created depends on the policy parameter. The policy parameter is of an enumerated type updatePolicy that consists of values [episodic, periodic, epiPeriodic]. Address may be a pointer value if the object is within the local address space, or an object identifier that a broker or communications system can resolve into a pointer in its target address space.

  ▾ Detach(target address)

  This method undoes the action of the Subscribe() method by deleting the *Notification Handle* object corresponding to the target address.

  ▾ Gimme()

  This method allows a direct query of the data value. It is not uncommon to have the return value for this method be a parameterized value that requires template instantiation of the *Server* class.

  ▾ AcceptTick()

  This method is called by a timing object (such as OS-provided timers) to indicate either the passage of time or the counting of an event sequence. This increments the CurrentTime attribute. When this method is called, the server scans its notification list for *Periodic Notification Handle* objects that are due for an update.

- *Concrete Server*
  This is a subclass of the *Server*. This class extends the *Server* class with the data attributes of interest and the Acquire() method. This may either be a passive class with an active object calling the Acquire() method, or it may itself be active. It has the method:

  ▼ *Acquire()*
  This method gets the data for the server. When this method is called, data messages are sent to all objects with *Episodic Notification Handles.*

- *Observer*
  The abstract *Observer* class calls the Subscribe() method of the *Server* so that it will be updated automatically and Detach() when it no longer wishes to be updated. It has the method

  ▼ Update(value)
  This method is called by the *Server* to pass the value. It is logically a callback function.

- *Concrete Observer*
  This class subclasses the *Observer* and adds local storage for the attribute needed, as well as methods required to perform its client function.

- *Notification Handle*
  This is a local reference to a registered *Observer* owned and managed by the *Server*. It is created when an *Observer* calls Subscribe() and is destroyed when it calls Detach(). It contains the attribute *Object Address*, which is the reference to the Update() function of the *Observer*. The set of all *Notification Handles* is referred to here as the notification list. The notification list is maintained by the *Server* so that it can call the Update() method of registered *Observers* when appropriate.

- *Episodic Notification Handle*
  This is a subclass of *Notification Handle*. It adds no attributes or methods, but it helps define the *Notification Handle* class hierarchy. *Observers* registered with this update policy are updated only when the data changes.

- *Periodic Notification Handle*
  This is a subclass of *Notification Handle* and is used to notify *Observers* on a periodic basis. This hardens the *Observer* in the event

of message loss or corruption. The subclass adds the attributes of *Period* and *TimeOfNextUpdate*. The *Server* scans the *Periodic Notification Handles* periodically. When the notification time has elapsed, the referenced *Observer* is updated and the *TimeOfNextUpdate* is recomputed.

6.2.1.2 Model-View-Controller (MVC) Pattern

Many objects have orthogonal components that accept and respond to user-generated events, maintain the model data, and display this data to the user. If these components are combined into a single monolithic object, they are artificially tightly coupled, which results in more work to maintain these objects and limits the reusability of the components. A very common set of orthogonal components of objects is

- Model—the data component of the object
- View—how the data values are displayed
- Controller—receives and processes events from the view

This is captured in the classic design pattern Model-View-Controller, popularized by Smalltalk many years ago. For example, an ECG monitor senses and determines heart rate. Heart rate can be viewed in many ways:

- As an icon—perhaps using different symbols to represent normal rates, bradycardia, and tachycardia, varying the size or color if desired
- As a number—it can be shown as a single string of numeric characters or as a textual array of the last *n* values or as a computed average
- As a graphic—pie charts, histograms, rulers can all be used
- As an alarm—used to indicate potential life-threatening conditions
- As a sound—a computer-generated voice can announce the heart rate periodically

How it is displayed has little consequence on how the data is acquired or manipulated. By separating these concerns, a small set of collaborating objects work together. Each of these objects is concerned with a different subject matter as it applies to the model. This pattern is applicable in real-time systems that have displays, particularly when data must be both controlled and displayed.

The MVC pattern is a simplified and specialized form of the Observer Pattern. This pattern can be implemented using pointers or the publish-subscribe method as in the more general Observer Pattern. If the objects participating in the pattern are relatively static, then using pointers is the easier implementation. If the objects will dynamically change or if the *Controller* or *View* objects may not be known to the *Model* at compile-time, then the subscription approach is preferable.

The following objects participate in this pattern:

- *Model*
  The *Model* object holds the data of interest. It is also known as the *application object*. It updates the *view* and the *controller* as necessary, usually using an episodic update policy.

- *View*
  The *View* object represents a view of the data to the user. The *View* registers with the *Model* so that it can be automatically updated when the data changes or periodically, or both. The *View* also creates the *Controller* object because the *Controller* must handle events specific to the kind of view that is currently active.

- *Controller*
  This object receives and responds to events related to the view of the model. It may receive knob turns, mouse moves, key presses, or button clicks. It responds to these events appropriate to the semantics of the model.

The scenario shown in Figure 6-2 shows a valve that is controlled by a knob with a numeric view of the aperture size on the screen. In this case, the knob sends the events to the model, which changes the position. As a result of the position being changed, the view is updated. This allows the display to track the actual position of the knob in the event that knob messages are lost or corrupted. The knob, receiving the updated aperture value, knows that its message has been received, so it need not be resent.

6.2.1.3 Transaction Pattern

Real-time systems use communications protocols to send and receive critical information among internal processors and with external actors in the environment. Within the same system, messages may have different levels of criticality, and therefore may have different requirements for the reliability of message transfer. Furthermore, various media have different reliability, as do environments.

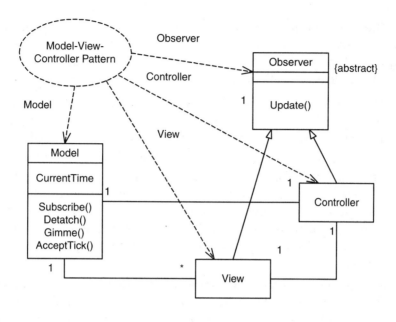

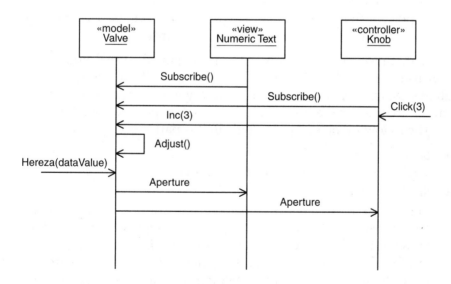

Figure 6-2: *Model-View-Controller Pattern*

The Transaction Pattern is used when reliable communications is required over unreliable media, or when extraordinary reliability is required. For example, suppose the system needs three distinct levels of communications reliability:

1. At most once (AMO)—a message is transmitted only once. If the message is lost or corrupted, it is lost. This is used when lightweight transfer is required and the reliability of message transfer is high, compared with the probability of message loss.

2. At least once (ALO)—a message is transmitted repeatedly until either an explicit acknowledgment is received by the sender or a maximum retry count is exceeded. This is used when the reliability of message transfer is relatively low, compared with the probability of message loss, but receipt of the same message multiple times is okay.

3. Exactly once (EO)—a message is treated as an ALO transaction except that should a message be received more than once due to retries, only the first message instance will be acted upon. This is used when message transfer reliability is relatively low but it is important that a message is acted on only once. *Increment* or *toggle* messages, for example, must be acted on only once.

The Transaction Pattern is particularly suited to real-time systems that use a general communications protocol with a rich grammar. It allows the application designers flexibility in their choice of communications method so that they may optimize for speed or reliability.

The following objects participate in this pattern:

*   *Source*
    The source is the originator of the message.

*   *Sender*
    The *Sender* is the communications protocol engine that marshals and transmits the message. It parses enough of the message to know if it must create a *Sender Transaction* (*Transaction Type* is ALO or EO). The *Sender* also accepts Acknowledgments and searches its list of *Send Transactions* for matching transactions. If one is found, the *Send Transaction* is destroyed. Sometimes, an explicit receipt is requested by the *Source*, in which case the *Source* is notified. If the acknowledgment does not match any existing *Send Transactions*, it is quietly discarded.

- *Sender Transaction*
  This is the transaction created (and destroyed) by the *Sender*. Each transaction corresponds to a single ALO or EO message. It tracks the number of times the message has been transmitted, as well as its retry period. If an acknowledgement specifiying the original *MsgID* is not received within the retry period, the message is retransmitted and the transmit count is incremented. If the count exceeds *Max Retries*, the *Source* is notified.

- *Message*
  The *Message* contains the data of interest to the *Source* and *Target*, but it also contains metadata[6] as well, such as a *MsgID* and *Transaction Type*. The *MsgID* must be unique within the lifespan of the transaction object so that it uniquely identifies the message. The *Transaction Type* tells the *Sender* and *Receiver* whether transaction objects are required for this message.

- *Receiver*
  This is the communications protocol engine on the receiving side that accepts messages over the communications media, demarshals them, and passes them off to the target objects. If necessary (Transmission Type for the incoming message is EO), the *Receiver* creates a *Receive Transaction*. Before creating a new *Receive Transaction*, the current transaction list is searched for a match. If one is found, it means that the message is a duplicate, therefore it may be discarded after resetting the transaction's *TimeToLive* attribute. Periodically, the *TimeToLive* attribute is decremented. Once it decrements to zero, the *Receive Transaction* is discarded.

- *Receive Transaction*
  This object tracks the receipt of messages using EO semantics. It is created when the *Receiver* gets a message with the EO transaction type. It has a *TimeToLive* attribute that is periodically decremented. If another message is received with a matching *MsgID*, the *TimeToLive* is reset to its original value and the duplicate message is quietly discarded. Finally, when the *TimeToLive* attribute decrements to 0, the *Receiver* destroys the *Receiver Transaction* object.

- *Target*
  This is the ultimate destination of the message sent from the *Source*.

---

[6] Metadata is information that is self-describing.

The AMO semantics are the simplest to implement. To implement AMO semantics, no transaction objects are required. The reliability of the communications medium and protocol are sufficiently high, and the consequences of a lost message are sufficiently low so that no extra measures are required. Transferring messages using AMO semantics is fast and requires the least computation resources.

ALO semantics require that the *Sender* object maintain a transaction object until an explicit acknowledgment is received back from the *Receiver*. If an acknowledgment is received, the transaction object is destroyed. If no acknowledgment is received within the retry period, then the *Sender* automatically retransmits the message to the *Receiver*. If the *Sender* fails to successfully get the message to the receiver (that is, the *Max Retries* count is exceeded), the *Sender* originator is notified so that corrective measures can be initiated.

The *Sender* cannot distinguish between a loss of the message and a loss of the acknowledgment, so it can happen that the *Receiver* object receives the message more than once. This is generally not a problem for operations such as set() when setting an absolute value, but it becomes problematic when the operation is something like increment(). ALO semantics are incompatible with incremental operations.

EO semantics require transaction objects on both sides. The *Sender* and *Send Transaction* objects function exactly as they do to support ALO semantics. What is different is that the *Receiver* object must now manage *Receive Transactions*. When the *Receiver* receives a message with an EO transaction type, it creates a *Receive Transaction* object and sets its *TimeToLive, TriggerPeriod,* and *MsgID*. Once the *TimeToLive* attribute decrements down to zero, the *Receive Transaction* object is destroyed. If a duplicate message is received before that occurs, the *TimeToLive* is reset back to its *TriggerPeriod*. The scenario in Figure 6-3 shows an EO transaction.

6.2.1.4 Smart Pointer Pattern

The problems with pointers are well-known to C and C++ programmers. They fall into several categories:

- Pointers may be used before they are initialized.
- Pointers may be used after the memory they point to has been released (dangling pointer).
- Memory may not be released (memory leak).

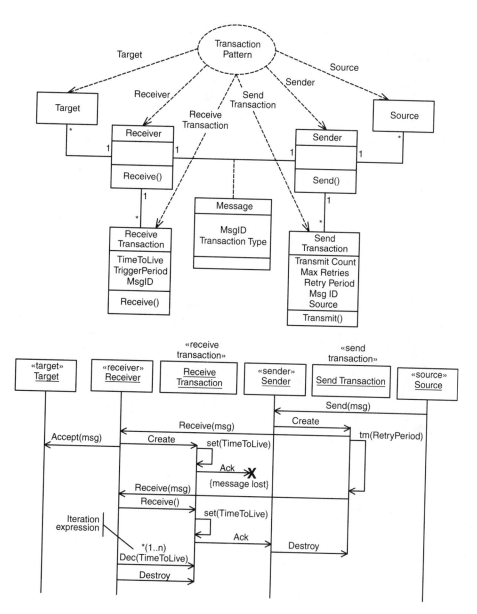

Figure 6-3: *Transaction Pattern*

- Pointer arithmetic may result in erroneous addresses being used.
- Target objects may be in different memory addresses.

All experienced C and C++ programmers have not only seen these problems—they have also committed these offenses against Truth, Justice, and the Object Way. These languages make it so easy to misuse pointers and so hard to find these errors. Even programs that appear to be robust can lead to subtle pointer problems. Just to prove how easy it is, we'll provide some simple examples of memory leaks.

The first example is a procedure that accepts and uses a pointer.

```
void test(int* p) {
    int* a = p;    // line 1
    *p = 17;    // line 2
    delete a;    // line 3
    *p = 99;    // line 4
};
```

What if the parameter p is not initialized? Then lines 2 and 4 will wreak havoc. This is a very common problem in C and C++ programs. What about when line 3 is executed? Then line 4 is in error, because p now points to memory that is released. Further, does the caller of *test* know that the memory that p points to has been released? What further use of this pointer is made in the remainder of the program?

Many pointer problems are more subtle. For example, can you identify the problem in the code below?

```
class myClass {
    int a;
public:
    int get(void) { return a; }
    void put(int temp) { a = temp; }
};

class usesMC {
public:
    void test(void) {
        myClass *pMC = new myClass;
        pMC->put(75);
        //
        myTestFunction(); // function defined outside class
        //
        delete pMC;
    };
};
```

The problem is that if myTestFunction() throws an exception, the *myClass* object pointed to by *pMC* will not be deleted. Using raw pointers in C++ for local function objects is always an error whenever the compiler puts in exception-handling code. By default, all ANSI-compliant C++ compilers must put in exception-handling code because 1) they're required to, and 2) the standard C++ libraries throw exceptions. Thus, this ostensibly correct code can lead to memory leaks.

The Smart Pointer is a common pattern meant to eliminate, or at least mitigate, the myriad problems that stem from the manual use of raw pointers:

- While raw pointers have no constructor to leave them in a valid initial state, smart pointers can use their constructors to initialize them to NULL or force the precondition that they are constructed pointing to a valid target object.

- While raw pointers have no destructor and so may not deallocate memory if they suddenly go out of scope, smart pointers determine whether it is appropriate to deallocate memory when they go out of scope and call the delete operator.

- While a raw pointer to a deleted object still holds the address of the memory at which the object used to be (and hence can be used to reference that memory illegally), smart pointers can automatically detect that condition and refuse access.

The simplicity of the Smart Pointer Pattern shown in Figure 6-4 belies its usefulness. Although the mechanism is simple, significant functionality is hidden within the detailed design of the smart pointer class. The next chapter will discuss several detailed designs for smart pointers meant to optimize various uses.

6.2.2 Reuse Patterns

The patterns in this section use encapsulation and abstraction to improve reuse of classes. They may provide other advantages, as well, but their primary purpose is to separate and encapsulate different areas of concern within an object into separate objects.

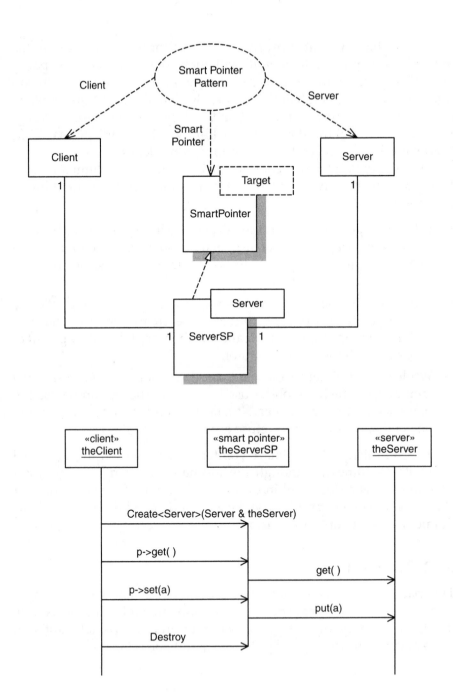

Figure 6-4: *Smart Pointer Pattern*

6.2.2.1 Container Pattern

Analysis models the "what" of a system—what it is; what are the fundamental concepts involved; and what are the important relations and associations among them. Design specifies the "how" of all the unspecified portions of the system. One important "how" of design is how message transport for each message will be implemented; is it a function call, an OS mail message, a bus message, an RPC, or something even more exotic? Another important how is the resolution of associations with multivalued roles.

When one object has a 1-to-many association, the question arises as to the exact mechanism the "1" class will use to access the "many" objects. One solution is to build features into the "1" class to manage the set of contained objects. These facilities typically manifest themselves as operations, such as add(), remove(), first(), next(), last(), and find(). Often, the semantics of the associate dictates elaborate operations, such as maintaining the set of objects in a specific order, or balancing the tree. Building these features into every class that must maintain a 1-to-many association is repugnant for several reasons outlined in Section 6.1. The common solution to these problems is to insert a container object (a.k.a. *collection object*) between the "1" and the "many."

Adding a container object to manage the aggregated objects doesn't entirely solve the problem, because often the container must be accessed by several clients. If the container itself keeps track of the client position, it will become confused in a multiclient environment. To get around this, *iterators* are used in conjunction with the containers. An iterator keeps track of where the client is in the container. Various clients use different iterators so that the separate concerns of managing the collection and tracking position within the container are abstracted away from each other. A single client may use several different iterators. The Standard Template Library (STL), a part of the ANSI C++ standard, provides many containers, with a variety of iterators, such as *first*, *last*, and so on.

Like the previous pattern, the Container Pattern is very simple, although the container itself may be quite complex internally (see Figure 6-5). This pattern will be elaborated more in the next pattern.

The following objects participate in the Container Pattern:

- *Container*
  The *Container* manages the collection and provides accessor operations.

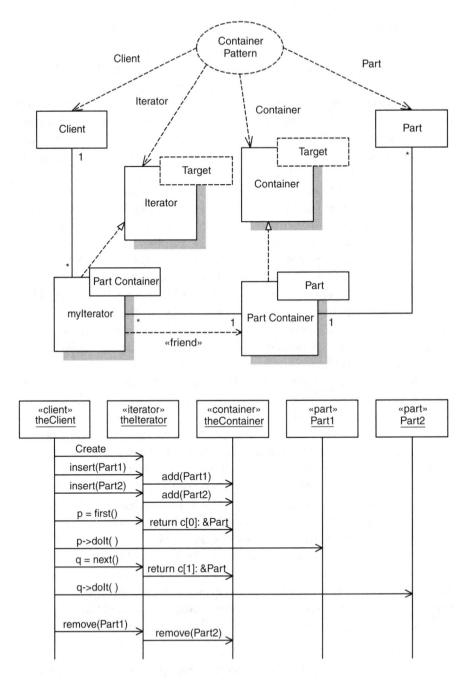

Figure 6-5: *Container Pattern*

- *Iterator*

  The *Iterator* acts like a smart pointer and mediates access to the parts for the *Client*. An iterator query access, such as first() or next(), typically returns a pointer to a *Part* object. Insertion and deletion may also be mediated through the iterator.

- *Client*

  The *Client* is the object needing access to the *Part* objects managed by the *Container*.

- *Part*

  The *Part* objects are the objects managed by the *Container*. In a system managing bank accounts, this might be individual accounts or transactions within those accounts.

6.2.2.2 Interface Pattern[7]

In languages like C++, the interface provided by a class is bound tightly to its implementation. As discussed earlier, strictly speaking the interface of an object is its *type* and the implementation specification is its *class*. C++ mixes these metaphors so that most of the time the difference is unnoticeable. Unfortunately, binding the type and class together limits the reusability of a class. There are a number of cases in which explicit separation of interface and implementation is useful.

First, a common implementation may be appropriate for a variety of uses. If a class could provide different interfaces, a single underlying implementation could meet several needs. For example, many common computer science structures, such as trees, queues, and stacks can actually use a single underlying implementation, such as a linked list. The relatively complex innards of the common implementation can be used in different ways to implement the desired behavior, even though the ultimate clients are clueless about what happens behind the scenes.

Second, by separating an interface, it becomes easier to change an implementation or add a new and different interface. As in our container example in the previous paragraph, it becomes a simple matter to add a new container (for example, an extensible vector) by creating an interface

---

[7] This pattern uses classes to represent interfaces; this is not the same as a UML interface. A UML interface is a collection of operations of a *Classifier* and is not instantiable. This pattern is useful when the implementation language does not support UML notion of interfaces directly

that provides the correct services to the client but implements those services in terms of primitive operations of existing containers.

Last, it happens sometimes that you want different levels of access into the internals of an object. Interfaces can be constructed to provide different levels of access for various client objects and environments. For example, you might want classes that provide services to users to be able to use only a subset of all operations, while a different set is provided in "service mode," and a much different set is provided in "remote debugging mode."

The Interface Pattern (a.k.a., the Adapter Pattern) solves all of these problems. It is a very simple pattern and is so common that the UML actually provides the stereotype «interface» in the language specification.

The scenario shown in Figure 6-6 illustrates how the Interface Pattern separates the interface from its implementation. The *Client* object needs a stack-like container and so associates to the *myStack* object. The *myStack* object itself does not directly manage the collection. Instead, *myStack* associates to a linked list object that actually manages the collection. *myStack* provides the proper interface to the *Client* (such as push() and pop()) but implements this interface by using the operations provided by the linked list class (such as insertAtEnd(), getLast(), and deleteLast()). Thus, given a linked list, it is a simple matter to provide a stack or queue.

6.2.2.3 Policy Pattern

Classes are often structurally similar or even identical, but they may differ in terms of how they operate internally. For example, it is possible that a class looks the same but makes different time/space/complexity/safety/reliability optimization choices. The selection of different algorithms to implement the same black-box behavior is called a *policy.* Policies can be abstracted away from the main class to simplify the interface, improve reuse, and even allow dynamic choices of policies based on operating condition or state.

The objects participating in the Policy Pattern are:

- *Client*
  Uses the services and operations of the *Context* object.

- *Context*
  Provides services to the *Client* and a context for the *Policy* object. It will invoke the services of the *Policy* object necessary to implement the policy within its context.

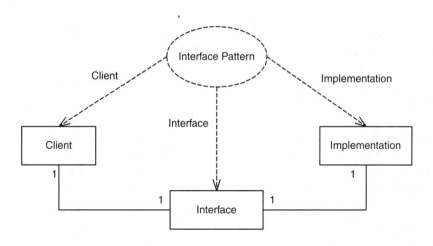

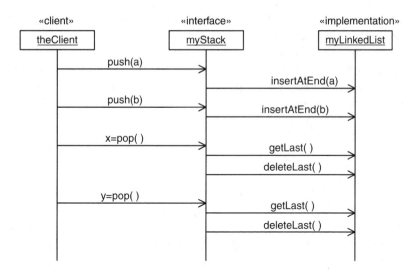

Figure 6-6: *Interface Pattern*

- *Abstract Policy*
  Provides a virtual interface to the *Concrete Policy* object for the *Context Object*.
- *Concrete Policy*
  Implements the algorithm and services for the selected policy.

The scenario in Figure 6-7 shows a typical use of a Policy Pattern in safety-critical applications. A *Client* associates with the *Heart Rate Server* to get patient information. If this information is corrupted (and EMI in an operating room can be extremely high), then patient safety may be compromised. To improve safety, the *Heart Rate Server* uses a safety policy to detect corruption. Such a policy may use feedback error detection schemes, such as checksums, cyclic redundancy checks, and one's complement storage or feedforward error correction, such as triple redundancy or Hamming codes. A CRC error detection policy is used in the scenario in Figure 6-7.

This particular scenario shows a *Heart Rate Source* object updating the *Heart Rate Proxy*. When new data is received from the *Heart Rate Source*, the *Heart Rate Proxy* requests the *CRC Policy* object to compute a CRC on the data. *theClient* object gets the heart rate from the *Heart Rate Proxy* via its get() operation. The *Heart Rate Proxy's* get() operation checks the data against the CRC stored in the *CRC Policy* object via the latter's check() member function. If it returns OK, then the heart rate is returned to the *Client*. If it returns BAD, then the *Heart Rate Proxy* requests a new value from the *Heart Rate Source*, recomputes the CRC, and then checks the CRC. If this now works, then the heart rate is returned. If it still fails (not shown in the scenario), the *Heart Rate Proxy* could retry or throw an exception to *theClient*.

6.2.2.4 Rendezvous Pattern

Rendezvous refers to the synchronization of concurrent tasks. In fact, the use of a mutual exclusion semaphore is also called a *unilateral rendezvous*. The more common use of the term *rendezvous* refers to the synchronization of more than one task. For example, the rendezvous of more than two tasks is referred to as a bilateral rendezvous.

The problem of task synchronization occurs in many real-time systems. Formally, a rendezvous is a means of enforcing the preconditional invariants of both participant tasks. Consider the state model in Figure 6-8.

The figure shows a trilateral rendezvous in which three threads (shown as orthogonal state components) must synchronize. One thread is involved in the preparation of the vat to be used to mix the reagents for the desired reaction. The other two threads prepare the reagents—one of which must be heated and one of which must be cooled. Only

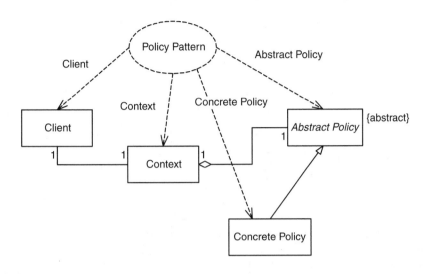

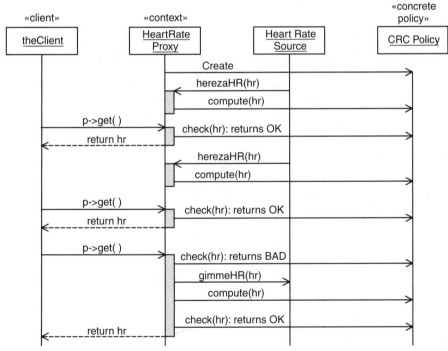

Figure 6-7: *Policy Pattern*

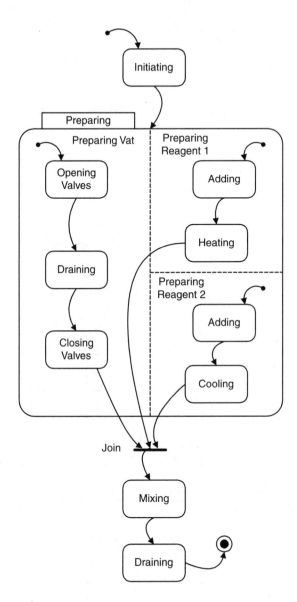

Figure 6-8: *Trilateral Rendezvous Problem*

when all three orthogonal state components have completed their preparatory activities are the components allowed to be mixed together (mixing details are not shown).

Synchronization of threads can be solved with the Rendezvous Pattern, shown in Figure 6-9.

This pattern consists of a coordinating passive object (called the *Rendezvous* object), clients that must synchronize, and mutex blocking semaphores. Blocking semaphores are used to force the threads to wait until all preconditions are met. More-elaborate behavior can be implemented using timed or balking semaphores, if desired.

The following objects participate in this pattern:

- *Rendezvous* object

  The *Rendezvous* object coordinates the synchronization process and glues the mutex semaphores to client thread objects. Each *Rendezvous* object typically handles a single synchronization point. Each participant client thread has an association with the *Rendezvous* so that it can call its wait() operation. The *Rendezvous* handles the coordination of the *Lock* objects and identifies when all *Locks* are in their locked state. When this is true, all *Locks* are signaled that they may release their captured threads and enter their unlocked state. This object implements a standard *monitor* used to coordinate the participating threads.

- *Lock*

  The *Lock* objects have two states—locked and unlocked (the default initial state). When a client thread calls the wait() operation on the *Rendezvous*, it uses the *ObjectID* to select the appropriate *Lock* and change its state. Each client has its own *Lock,* created when the *Rendezvous* is initially created. *Locks* may be implemented in several ways. The most common are the busy wait and the sleep wait. In the busy wait approach, the lock( ) operation loops until the synchronizing condition (all required threads are waiting) is met. Care must be taken with this approach that the OS allows the other threads to run while the current client thread loops. The sleep-wait solution puts the client thread to sleep, pending an OS event. This OS event is issued by the *Rendezvous* object when the preconditions are satisfied.

- *Thread*

  The *Thread* object in the pattern is a normal object that operates within an asynchronous thread. It calls the *Rendezvous* object's wait() method and remains blocked until the *Lock* allows its lock() call to complete and returns control back to the *Thread* object.

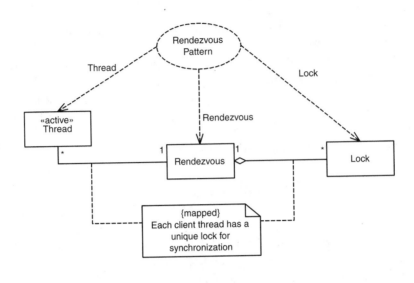

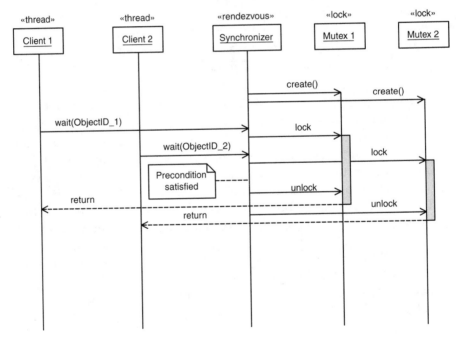

Figure 6-9: *Rendezvous Pattern*

The scenario shows a typical bilateral rendezvous. The *Rendezvous* object is created knowing the number of objects required to meet the precondition and their *ObjectIDs*. The *Thread* objects are some objects executing within separate OS threads that associate with the (passive) *Rendezvous* object. As each client thread becomes ready to synchronize, it sends a wait() message to the *Rendezvous* object, identifying itself with its *ObjectID*. The *Rendezvous* object registers each pending client in a separate *Lock* created for this purpose. Once all clients have registered with the *Rendezvous* object, the precondition is satisfied and the threads may now continue.

This pattern is a very effective way to coordinate a set of threads that need to share a resource or reach a common state. If the participating threads have timeliness requirements, then analysis should be done to determine the schedulability of the pattern (see [6] and [7] for the analytic methods).

One of the issues with the naïve realization of this pattern is that it does not bound *priority inversion*, which is the execution of a lower-priority task when a higher-priority thread is ready to run. In the presence of mutual exclusion protection on resources, if a higher-priority thread becomes ready to run but cannot because a lower-priority thread owns a required resource, then the lower-priority thread must continue to run at least until it releases the required resource. In this case, the higher-priority thread is said to be *blocked*. Whenever resources must be shared among the threads and the resources require mutual exclusion to ensure their integrity, such a system *always* presents some level of priority inversion.

Dealing with a single level of priority inversion is relatively simple. However, what happens if an intermediate-priority thread becomes ready to run while the lower-priority thread is blocking the higher-priority thread? If it preempts the lower-priority thread, the higher-priority thread is now blocked by two lower-priority threads (the lower-priority thread owning the required resource and the intermediate-priority thread). Such a scheme is said to have *unbounded priority inversion,* because in principle any number of intermediate-priority threads can preempt the lower-priority task and prevent it (and thereby the higher-priority thread) from completing. Such systems are very difficult to schedule effectively.

The solutions used in real-time systems center around bounding the priority inversion. This can be done in a number of ways. For example, the resource can be given a *priority ceiling* attribute. This is the priority of the highest-priority thread that will ever access it. Whenever a thread locks the resource, its current priority can then be temporarily elevated to the resource's priority ceiling (until it releases the resource). This prevents intermediate-priority threads from preempting the thread as long as it owns the resource. See [6] and [7] for more details on these algorithms.

6.3 Looking Ahead

Mechanistic design is concerned with specifying the details of inter-object collaboration. Parameterized patterns for small groups of objects acting together within collaborations are referred to as *mechanisms*. Mechanistic design takes the collaborative groups of objects identified in analysis and adds design-level objects to facilitate and optimize their implementation. For example, containers and iterators are added to manage associations consisting of multiple objects. Smart pointer objects glue associations together in such a way as to eliminate memory leaks and inappropriate pointer dereferencing. Policy objects abstract away strategies and algorithms from their context so that they can be easily modified or replaced, even while the system executes.

Many objects added during mechanistic design reappear in other designs because they solve problems common to many systems. These collaborations are reified into mechanistic design patterns. These patterns are templates of object interaction that consist of a problem, a context, and a structural solution. The reification of the patterns allows them to be cataloged and studied systematically, which allows them, in turn, to be reused in future projects. This chapter presented a number of patterns useful in mechanistic design. The interested reader is invited to explore the references for more patterns.

The final chapter in this book discusses the detailed design of object-oriented systems in a real-time context. Detailed design is concerned with the implementation of data structures and algorithms within the scope of a single class. Space and time complexity trade-offs are made during detailed design in order to achieve the performance requirements specified for your system.

6.4 References

[1] Booch, Grady, James Rumbaugh, and Ivar Jacobson, *The Unified Modeling Language User's Guide*. Reading, MA: Addison Wesley Longman, 1999.

[2] Gamma, Erich, Richard Helm, Ralph Johnson, and John Vlissides, *Design Patterns: Elements of Reusable Software*. Reading, MA: Addison Wesley Longman, 1995.

[3] Buschmann, Frank, Regine Meunier, Hans Rohnert, Peter Sommerlad, and Michael Stal, *A System of Patterns: Pattern-Oriented Software Architecture*. Chichester: John Wiley & Sons, 1996.

[4] Coplien, James, and Douglas Schmidt, ed., *Pattern Languages of Program Design*. Reading, MA: Addison Wesley Longman, 1995.

[5] Vlissides, John, James Coplien, and Norman Kerth, ed., *Pattern Languages of Program Design 2*. Reading, MA: Addison Wesley Longman, 1996.

[6] Douglass, Bruce Powel, *Doing Hard Time: Developing Real-Time Systems with UML, Objects, Frameworks, and Patterns*. Reading, MA: Addison Wesley Longman, 1999.

[7] Klein, Mark, Thomas Ralya, Bill Pollak, Ray Obenza, and Michael Gonzalez Harbour, *A Practitioner's Handbook for Real-Time Analysis: Guide to Rate Monotonic Analysis for Real-Time Systems*. Boston: Kluwer Academic Publishers, 1993.

Chapter 7

Detailed Design

In the preceding chapters, we've seen how architectural design defines the largest-scale strategic design decisions and how mechanistic design specifies exactly how groups of objects collaborate. Now it is time to peer inside the objects themselves and design their internal structure. Detailed design specifies details such as the storage format used for attributes, the implementation of associations, the set of operations the object provides, the selection of internal algorithms, and the specification of exception handling within the object.

Notation and Concepts Discussed

Geekosphere	Data collections	Visibility
Data structure	Realizing associations	Algorithms
Derived attributes	Operations	Exceptions

7.1 What Is Detailed Design?

You're just about at the point at which you can actually run code on that pile of wires and chips cluttering up your geekosphere,[1] so if you're like me, you're getting pretty excited (see [6] for a detailed explanation of the

---

[1] Geekosphere (n): the area surrounding one's computer (*Jargon Watch*, Hardwired, 1997).

phenomenon). If architectural design is deciding which planet to fly to and mechanistic design is the flight path to the selected planet, then detailed design is deciding on which rock you want to eat your tube of salami sandwich once you arrive.[2] It is the smallest level of decomposition before you start pounding code.

The fundamental unit of decomposition in object-oriented systems is the *object*. As we have seen, it is a natural unit from which systems can be specified and implemented. We have also seen that it is necessary, but insufficient, for large-scale design. Mechanistic design deals with mechanisms (groups of collaborating objects), and architectural design is concerned with an even larger scale—domains, tasks, and subsystems. At the root of it all remains the object itself, the atom from which the complex chemistry of systems is built.

Although most objects are structurally and behaviorally simple, this is certainly not universal. Every nontrivial system contains a significant proportional of "interesting" objects that require further examination and specification. The detailed design of these objects allows the objects to be correctly implemented, of course, but also permits designers to make trade-off decisions to optimize the system.

One definition of an object is "data tightly bound to its operations, forming a cohesive entity." Detailed design must consider both the structure of information and its manipulation. In general, the decisions made in detailed design will be:

- Data structure
- Implementation of associations
- Set of operations defined on the data
- Visibility of data and operations
- Algorithms used to implement those operations
- Exceptions handled and thrown

7.2 Data Structure

Data format in objects is generally simple, because if it were not, a separate object would be constructed to hold just the data. However, not

---

[2] My personal choice would be the Yogi rock on Mars (see http://www.jpl.nasa.gov, a public mirror site for the Mars Pathfinder mission).

only must the structure of the data be defined, the valid ranges of data, accuracy, preconditions, and initial values must also be specified during detailed design. This is true of "simple" numeric data just as much as of user-defined data types. After all, aircraft, spacecraft, and missile systems must perform significant numeric computation without introducing round-off and accuracy errors, or bad things are likely to happen.[3] Consider a simple complex number class. Complex numbers may be stored in polar coordinates, but let's stick to rectilinear coordinates for now. Most applications that use complex numbers require fractional values, so using ints for the real and imaginary parts wouldn't meet the need. What about using floats, as in:

```
class complex_1 {
public:
    float iPart, rPart;
   // operations omitted
};
```

That looks like a reasonable start. Is the range sufficient? Most floating point implementations have a range of 10^{-40} to 10^{+40} or more, so that is probably okay. What about round-off error? Because the infinite continuous set of possible values is stored and manipulated as a finite set of machine numbers, just representing a continuous value using floating point format incurs some error. Numerical analysis identifies two forms of numerical error—absolute error and relative error [1]. For example, consider adding two numbers, 123456 and 4.567891 using 6-digit, precision floating point arithmetic:

123456.000000

+000004.567891

123460.567891 = $0.123460567891 \times 10^6$

Because this must be stored in 6-digit precision, the value will be stored as 0.123460×10^6, which is an absolute error of 0.567891. Relative error is computed as

$$\frac{(A\text{-}B) - [m(A) - m(B)]}{A - B}$$

---

[3] Having one's F-16 flip upside down when crossing the equator is an example of such a bad thing.

where m(x) is the machine number representation of the value x. This gives us a relative error of 4.59977×10^{-8} for this calculation. Although this error is tiny, errors can propagate and build during repeated calculation to the point at which it makes your computations meaningless.

Subtraction of two values is a common source of significant error. For example,

$$0.991012312$$
$$-0.991009987$$
$$\overline{0.000002325 = 0.2325 \times 10^{-5}}$$

But truncating these numbers to six digits of precision yields:

$$0.991012$$
$$-0.991010$$
$$\overline{0.000002 = 0.20 \times 10^{-5}}$$

which is an absolute error of 0.325×10^{-5} and a relative error of 14%. This means that we may have to change our format to include more significant digits, change our format entirely to use infinite precision arithmetic,[4] or change our algorithms to equivalent forms when a loss of precision is likely. For example, when computing 1-cos(x) when the angle close to zero can result in the loss of precision. You can use the trigonometric relation:

$$1 - \cos(\phi) = 2 \sin(\tfrac{\phi}{2})$$

to avoid round-off error.[5]

Data is often constrained beyond its representation limit by the problem domain. Planes shouldn't pull a 7g acceleration curve, array indices shouldn't be negative, ECG patients rarely weigh 500 Kg, and automobiles don't go 300 miles per hour.[6] Attributes have a range of

---

[4] Infinite precision arithmetic is available in some LISP-based symbolic mathematics systems, such as Derive and MacSyma.

[5] Widely different computational results of algebraically equivalent formulations can lead to hazardous situations (see [5]).

[6] Normally, that is. The Darwin award, given to the person who finds the most ingenious way to kill him- or herself each year, was awarded to the guy who strapped a JATO (jet-assisted take off) pack to his 1967 Chevy Impala and hit a rocky cliff several

valid values and when they are set unreasonably, these faults must be detected and corrective actions must be taken. Mutator operations (operations that set attribute values) should ensure that the values are within range. These constraints on the data can be specified on class diagrams using the standard UML constraint syntax, such as "{range 0..15}."

Subclasses may constrain their data ranges differently than their superclasses. Many designers feel that data constraints should be monotonically decreasing with subclass depth—that is, that a subclass may constrain a data range further than its superclass. Although systems can be built this way, this violates the Liskov Substitution Principle (LSP):

> An instance of a subclass must be freely substitutable for an instance of its superclass.

If a superclass declares a color attribute with a range of {white, yellow, blue, green, red, black} and a subclass restricts it to {white, black}, then what happens if the client has a superclass pointer and sets the color to red, as in:

```
enum color {white, yellow, blue, green, red, black};
class super {
protected:
    color c;
public:
    virtual void setColor(color temp); // all colors valid
};

class sub: public super {
public:
    virtual void setColor(color temp);
    // only white and black now valid
};
```

Increasing constraints down the superclass hierarchy is a dangerous policy if the subclass is used in a polymorphic fashion.

Aside from normal attributes identified in the analysis model, detailed design may add *derived* attributes, as well. Derived attributes

---

miles away going well over 350 miles per hour. (To his credit, he tried to stop—the brake pads melted away before he became airborne for 1.4 miles and left a blackened 3-foot-deep crater in the rock wall 125 feet above the roadway).

are values that can in principle be reconstructed from other attributes within the class, but are added to optimize performance. They can be indicated on class diagrams with a «derived» stereotype, and defining the derivation formula within an associated constraint, such as "{age = currentDate—startDate}."

For example, a sensor class may provide a 10-sample history, with a get(index) accessor method. If the clients want to know the average measurement value often, they can compute this from the history, but it is more convenient to add an average( ) operation, like so:

```
class sensor {
    float value[10];
    int nMeasurements, currentMeasurment;
public:
    sensor(void): nMeasurements(0), currentMeasurement(0) {
        for (int j = 0; j<10; j++) value[10] = 0;
};

    void accept(float tValue) {
        value[currentMeasurement] = tValue;
        currentMeasurement = (++currentMeasurement) \ 10;
        if (nMeasurements < 10) ++nMeasurements;
        };

    float get(int index=0) {
        int cIndex;
        if (nMeasurements > index) {cIndex =
            currentMeasurement-index-1; // last valid one
            if (cIndex < 0) cIndex += 10;
            return value[cIndex];
        else
            throw "No valid measurement at that index";
        };

    float average(void) {
        float sum = 0.0;
        if (nMeasurements > 0) {
            for (int j=0; j < nMeasurements-1; j++)
                sum += value[j];
            return sum / nMeasurements;
            }
        else
            throw "No measurements to average";
        };
```

```
    };
```

The average() operation exists only to optimize the computational path. If the average value were needed more frequently than the data was monitored, the average could be computed as the data is read:

```
class sensor {
    float value[10];
    float averageValue;
    int nMeasurements, currentMeasurment;
public:
    sensor(void): averageValue(0), nMeasurements(0),
            currentMeasurement(0) {
        for (int j = 0; j<10; j++) value[10] = 0;
    };

    void accept(float tValue) {
        value[currentMeasurement] = tValue;
        currentMeasurement = (++currentMeasurement) \ 10;
        if (nMeasurements < 10) ++nMeasurements;
            // compute average
        averageValue = 0;
        for (int j=0; j < nMeasurements-1; j++)
            averageValue += value[j];
            averageValue /= nMeasurements;
        };

    float get(int index=0) {
    int cIndex;
        if (nMeasurements > index) {
            cIndex = currentMeasurement-index-1; // last valid one
            if (cIndex < 0) cIndex += 10;
            return value[ cIndex];
        else
            throw "No valid measurement at that index";
        };

    float average(void) {
        if (nMeasurements > 0)
            return averageValue;
        else
            throw "No measurements to average";
    };
};
```

In this case, the derived attribute *averageValue* is added to minimize the required computation when the average value is needed frequently.

7.2.1 Data Collection Structure

Collections of primitive data attributes may be structured in myriad ways, including stacks, queues, lists, vectors, and a forest of trees. The layout of data collections is the subject of hundreds of volumes of research and practical applications. The UML provides a role constraint notation to indicate different kinds of collections that may be inherent in the analysis model. Common role constraints for multivalued roles include:

{ordered}	Collection is maintained in a sorted manner.
{bag}	Collection may have multiple copies of a single item.
{set}	Collection may have, at most, a single copy of a given item.
{hashed}	Collection is referenced via a keyed hash.

Some constraints may be combined, such as {ordered set}. Another common design scheme is to use a key value to retrieve an item from a collection. This is called a *qualified association*, and the key value is called a *qualifier*.

Figure 7-1 shows examples of constraints and qualified associations. The association between *Patron* and *Airline* is qualified with *Frequent Flyer Num*. This qualifier will be ultimately implemented as an attribute within the *Patron* class and will be used to identify the patron to the *Airline* class. Similarly, the *Patron* has a qualified association with *Library* using the qualifier *Library Card Num*. The associations between *Airline* and *Flight* and between *Library* and *Book* have constrained multivalued roles. The former set must be maintained as an ordered set, while the latter is a hashed bag. Note also the use of a text note to constrain the *Patron's age* attribute. The stereotype indicates that it is a derived attribute, and the constraint shows how it is computed. Other constraints can be added as necessary to indicate valid ranges of data and other representational invariants.

Selection of a collection structure depends on what characteristics should be optimized. Balanced trees, for example are very fast to search, but inserting new elements is complex and costly because of the need to rotate the tree to maintain balance. Linked lists are simple to maintain, but searching takes relatively long.

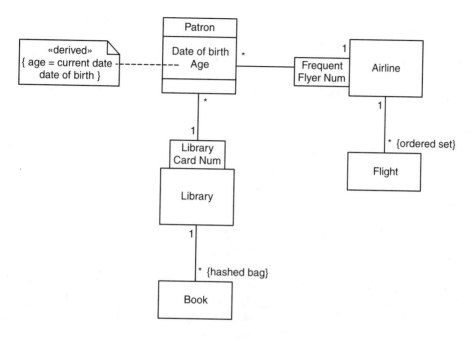

Figure 7-1: *Role Constraints and Qualified Associations*

7.3 Associations

Associations among objects allow client objects to invoke the operations provided by server objects. There are many ways to implement associations, depending on the nature and locality of the objects and their association. Implementations appropriate for objects within the same thread fail when used across thread or processor boundaries. Accessing objects with multivalued roles must be done differently than with a 1-to-1 association. Some implementation strategies that work for composition don't work for client-server associations. One purpose of detailed design is to resolve the management of associations within the objects.

The simplest cases are the 1 to 1 or 1 to (0,1) associations between objects within the same thread. The 1 to (0,1) is best done with a pointer to the server object, because there are times when the role multiplicity is zero (that is, the pointer is null). A 1 to 1 association may also be implemented with a reference (in the C++ sense), because the association link is always valid.[7] A 1 to 1 composition association may also use an inline class declaration, which would be inappropriate for the more loosely coupled client-server association. Normal aggregation is implemented in exactly the same way as an association. The class below shows these simple approaches:

```
class testAssoc {
    T myT; // appropriate only for 1 to 1 composition
    // ok for 1 to 1 or 1 to (0,1) association or composition
    T* myT2;
    T& myT3; // ok for 1 to 1 association or composition
};
```

As discussed in the previous chapter, multivalued roles are most often resolved using the Container Pattern. This involves inserting a container class between the two classes with the multivalued role, and possibly iterators, as well, as shown in Figure 7-2. The reader is referred to the previous chapter for more detail on the Container Pattern.

Crossing thread boundaries complicates the resolution of associations somewhat. Simply calling an operation across a thread boundary is not generally a good idea because of mutual exclusion and reentrancy problems. It can be done if sufficient care is taken. The target operation can be implemented using mutual exclusion guards, and both sides must agree on the appropriate behavior if access cannot be immediately granted. Should the caller be blocked? Should the caller be returned to immediately, with an indication of failure? Should the caller be blocked, but only for a maximum specified period of time? All of these kinds of rendezvous are possible and appropriate in different circumstances.

Although directly calling an operation across a thread boundary is lightweight, it is not always the best way. If the underlying operating system or hardware enforces segmented address spaces for threads, it may not even be possible. Operating systems provide additional means for intertask communication, such as OS message queues and OS pipes.

An OS message queue is the most dominant approach for requesting services across a thread boundary. The receiver thread's active

---

[7] C++ requires that references always be valid—that is, a NULL reference is semantically illegal.

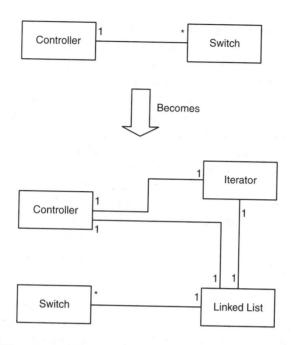

Figure 7-2: *Detailed Design of Multivalued Roles*

object reads the message queue and dispatches the message to the appropriate component object. This approach has a fairly heavy run-time cost, but it maintains the inherent asynchronicity of the threads.

OS pipes are an alternative to message queues. They are opened by both client and server objects and are a slightly more direct approach for the client to invoke the services of the server.

When the service request must cross processor boundaries, the objects must be more decoupled. Common operating services to meet intra-processor communications include sockets and remote procedure calls (RPCs). Sockets usually implement a specified TCP/IP protocol across a network. The common protocols are the Transmission Control Protocol (TCP) and User Datagram Protocol (UDP). The TCP/IP protocol suite does not make any guarantees about timing, but it can be placed on top of a data link layer, which does. TCP supports reliable transmission using acknowledgments; it also supports what are called stream sockets. UDP is simpler and makes no guarantees about reliable transmission.

Finally, some systems use RPCs. Usually, RPCs are implemented using a blocking protocol so that the client is blocked until the remote procedure completes. This maintains the function-call-like semantics of the RPC, but it may be inappropriate in some cases.

Using any of these approaches that cross the thread boundary (with the exception of the direct guarded call), requires a different implementation in the client class. The client must now know the thread ID and a logical object ID to invoke the services. So rather than a C++ pointer or reference, *ad hoc* operating-system-dependent means must be used.

These methods can be implemented using the Broker Pattern from Chapter 5 or the Observer Pattern in Chapter 6. The Observer Pattern allows the server to be remote from the client, but requires that the client know the location of the server. The Broker Pattern adds one more level of indirection, requiring only that the client know a logical name for the target object, which allows the Broker to identify and locate the server.

Note that this discussion has been independent of the underlying physical medium of interprocessor communication. It can be implemented using shared memory, Ethernet networks, or various kinds of buses, as appropriate. Reusable protocols are built using the Layered Architecture Pattern so that the data link layer can be replaced by one suitable for the physical medium, with a minimum of fuss.

7.4 Operations

The operations defined by a class specify how the data may be manipulated. Generally, a complete set of primitive operations maximizes reusability. A *set* class template typically provides operators, such as add item or set, remove item or subset, and test for item or subset membership. Even if the current application doesn't use all these operations, adding the complete list of primitives makes it more likely to meet the needs of the next system.

Analysis models abstract class operations into object messages (class, object, sequence, and collaboration diagrams), state event acceptors (statecharts), and state actions (statecharts). The great majority of the time, these messages are directly implemented as operations in the server class using the implementation strategy for the association that supports the message passing (see the previous section).

Analysis and early design models only specify the public operations. Detailed design often adds operations that are only used internally. These operations are due to the functional decomposition of the public operations. For example, a queue might provide the following set of public operations:

```
template <class T, int size>
class queue {
protected:
    T q[size];
    int head, tail;
public:
    queue(void): head(0), tail(0);
    virtual void put(T myT);
    virtual T get(void);
};
```

A cached queue caches data locally but stores most of it on a more remote, but larger, data store, such as a hard disk. Operations can be added to implement the caching so that it is invisible to the client, maintaining LSP:

```
template <class T, int size>
class cachedQueue : public queue<T, size> {
protected:
    void writeToDisk(void);
    void readFromDisk(void);
public:
    cachedQueue(void): head(0), tail(0);
    virtual void put(T myT);      // new version uses writeToDisk
                                  // when cache fills
    virtual T get(void);          // new version uses readFromDisk
                                  // when data is not cached
};
```

These operations are added to support the additional functionality of the *cachedQueue* subclass.

Functional decomposition of operations is shown in structured methods using structure charts. Because the UML does not provide any means for showing structural functional decomposition within classes, I recommend using structure charts when this view is necessary.

7.5 Visibility

Visibility in the UML refers to *accessibility* of internal object elements by other objects. Visibility is always a design concern. The general guidelines of visibility are:

If clients need it, make it visible, otherwise make it inaccessible.
This first guideline is pretty obvious. Once you are down in the depths of detailed design, you should have a pretty good idea about which messages are being sent to an object. If other clients depend on the service, then they must be able to call it. This is none other than the old "data-hiding" principle in vogue since the '70s.

Make only semantically appropriate operations visible.
This guideline seeks to avoid pathological coupling among classes. For example, suppose a class is using a container class. Should the operations be GetLeft() and GetRight() or Prev() and Next()? The first pair makes the implementation visible (binary tree), while the latter pair captures the essential semantics (ordered list).

Attributes should never be directly visible to clients.
This guideline is similar to the previous one in that it wants to avoid tight coupling whenever possible. If clients have direct access to attributes, they fundamentally depend on the structure of that attribute. Should the structure change, the clients all become instantly broken and must be modified, as well. In adition, accessor and mutator operations applied to that attribute can ensure that preconditions are met, such as valid ranges or consistency with other class attributes. Direct access to the attribute circumvents these safeguards.

When different levels of visibility are required to support various levels of coupling, use the Interface Pattern to provide the different sets of interfaces.
Sometimes, a class must present different levels of access to different clients. When this is true, the Interface Pattern described in the previous chapter is an obvious solution. A class can have many different interfaces, each providing the semantically appropriate interface to its clients.

The UML provides a simple, if peculiar, syntax for specifying visibility on the class diagram: A visibility attribute is prepended to the class member. The UML defines the following visibility attributes:

Private—accessible only within the class itself
- Protected—accessible only by the class and its sub-classes
+ Public—generally accessible by other classes

Some theorists are adamant that attributes should be private (as opposed to protected) and that even subclasses should go through accessor methods to manipulate them. Personally, I find that view somewhat draconian, because subclasses are already tightly coupled with their superclasses, but to each his or her own.

Another approach to providing different levels of access is through the use of friend classes.[8] Friends are often used as iterators in the Container Pattern, discussed in Chapter 6. Another use is the facilitation of unit testing by making unit-testing objects friends of the class under test.

7.6 Algorithms

An algorithm is a step-by-step procedure for computing a desired result. The complexity of algorithms may be defined in many ways, but the most common is *time complexity,* the amount of execution time required to compute the desired result. Algorithmic complexity is expressed using the "order of" notation. Common algorithmic complexities are:

- $O(c)$
- $O(\log_2 n)$
- $O(n)$
- $O(n \log_2 n)$
- $O(n^2)$
- $O(n^3)$

where c is a constant and n is the number of elements participating in the algorithmic computation.

---

[8] The use of friend classes results in a kind of "clothing-optional" design, which, although it can be fun, may make some designers nervous.

All algorithms with the same complexity differ from each other only by a multiplicative and additive constant. Thus, it is possible for one O(n) algorithm to perform 100 times faster than another O(n) algorithm and be considered of equal time complexity. It is even possible for an O(n^2) algorithm to outperform an O(c) algorithm for sufficiently small n. The algorithmic complexity is most useful when the number of entities being manipulated is large (as in "asymptotically approaching infinity") because then these constants become insignificant and the complexity order dictates performance. For small n, they can only be given as rules of thumb.

Execution time is not the only optimization criterion applied to systems. Objects may be designed to optimize:

- Run-time performance
  - ▾ Average performance
  - ▾ Worst-case performance
  - ▾ Deterministic (predictable) performance
- Run-time memory requirements
- Simplicity and correctness
- Development time and effort
- Reusability
- Extensibility
- Reliability
- Safety
- Security

Of course, to some degree these are conflicting goals (which is why they are called *trade-offs*). For example, some objects must maintain their elements in sorted order. A Bubble sort is very simple, so it requires a minimum of development time. Although it has a worst-case run-time performance of O(n^2), it can actually have better performance than more-efficient algorithms if n is small. Quicksort is generally much faster (O($\log_2 n$) in the normal case; O(n^2) in the worst case), but it is more complicated to implement. It is not always best to use a Quicksort, and it is not always worst to use a Bubble sort, even if the Quicksort is demonstrably faster for the data set. Systems spend most of their time executing a small portion of the code. If the sorting effort is tiny compared with other system functions, the additional time necessary to correctly implement the Quicksort might be more profitably spent elsewhere (such as trying to find some other use for that JATO pack in the garage).

Some algorithms have good average performance, but their worst case performance may be unacceptable. In real-time systems, raw performance is usually not an appropriate criterion—deterministic performance is more crucial. Often, embedded systems must run on a minimum of memory, so efficient use of existing resources may be very important. The job of the designer is to make the set of design choices that results in the best overall system, and this includes its overall characteristics.

Classes with rich behavior must not only perform correctly, they must also be optimal in some sense. Most often, average execution speed is the criterion used for algorithm selection, but as we saw in Section 7.1, many other criteria may be used. Once the appropriate algorithm is selected, the operations and attributes of the class must be designed to implement the algorithm. This will often result in new attributes and operations that assist in the execution of the algorithm.

For example, suppose you are using the Container Pattern and decide that a balanced AVL tree container is best.[9] An AVL tree is named after its inventors, Adelson, Velskii, and Landis. It takes advantage of the fact that the search performance of a balanced tree is $O(\log_2 n)$. A balanced binary tree is one in which all subtrees are the same height ±1 node. Each node in an AVL tree has a balance attribute,[10] which must be in the range [-1, 0, +1] for the tree to be balanced. The problem with simple trees is that their balance depends on the order in which elements are added. In fact, adding items in a sorted order to an ordinary binary tree results in a linked list, with search properties of $O(n)$. By balancing the tree during the addition and removal of items, we can improve its balance and optimize its search performance.

Let's assume that we want an inorder tree—that is, a tree in which a node is always greater than its left child and less than its right child,

---

[9] An AVL tree is not a specifically real-time example, but the algorithm is well-known and straightforward, so we will use it here for discussion.

[10] This is a derived attribute. It can be explicitly stored and maintained during addition and deletion, or it can be recomputed as necessary.

such as the one in Figure 7-3. Note that node 10 is greater than its left child (6) and less than its right child (12). If we now add a 9 to the tree, we could make it the left child of node 10 and the parent of node 6, but this would unbalance the tree, as shown in Figure 7-4. If we then balance the tree, we might end of up a tree, as in Figure 7-5.

AVL trees remain balanced because whenever a node that unbalances the tree is inserted or removed, nodes are moved around using techniques called *tree rotations* to regain balance. The algorithm for adding a node to an AVL tree looks like this:

1. Create the new node with NULL child pointers, and set the attribute *Balance* to 0.
2. If the tree is empty, set the root to point to this new node and return.
3. Locate the proper place for the node insertion and insert.
4. Recompute the balance attribute for each node from the root to the newly inserted node.
5. Locate an unbalanced node (balance factor is ±2). This is called the pivot node. If there is no unbalanced node, then return.
6. Rebalance the tree so that it is now balanced. There are several different situations:

   a. *Pivot* has a balance of +2. Rotate the subtree based at the *Pivot* left.

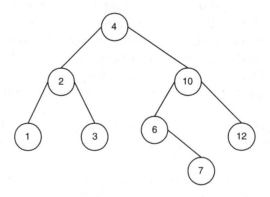

Figure 7-3: *Balanced Inorder Tree*

   b. *Pivot* has a balance of –2. Rotate the subtree based at the *Pivot* right.

7. Continue balancing subtrees on the search path until they are all in the set [-1, 0 +1].

   Rotating left means to replace the right child of the *Pivot* as the root of the subtree, as shown in Figure 7-6. Right rotations work similarly

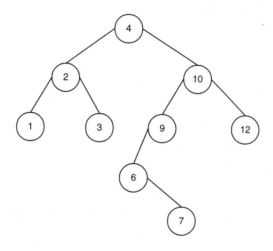

Figure 7-4: *Unbalanced Tree after Adding Node 9*

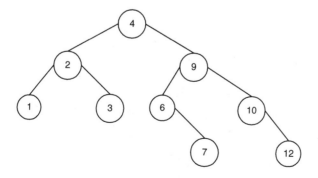

Figure 7-5: *Rebalanced Tree*

and are applied when the balance of the *Pivot* is −2. Often, double rotations are required to achieve a balanced tree, such as a left-right or a right-left rotation set.

The set of operations necessary to meet this algorithm are:

```
typedef class node {
public:
    data d; // whatever data is held in the tree nodes
    int balance; // valid values are -1, 0 , 1
    node* leftPtr;
    node* rightPtr;
} * nodePtr;

class avlTree {
    nodePtr root;
    void rotateLeft(nodePtr n);
```

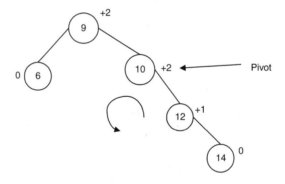

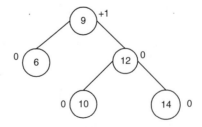

Figure 7-6: *Left Rotation*

```
        void rotateRight(nodePtr n);
    public:
        void add(data a);
        void delete(data a);
        nodePtr find(data a);
    };
```

Structured English and pseudocode, as shown, work perfectly well in most circumstances to capture the essential semantics of algorithms. The UML does define a special kind of state diagram, called an *activity diagram*, which may be helpful in some cases.

Activity diagrams depict systems that may be decomposed into activities—roughly corresponding to states that mostly terminate upon completion of the activity rather than as a result of an externally generated event. Activity diagrams may be thought of as a kind of flowchart in which diagrammatic elements are member function calls. Figure 7-7 shows the activity diagram for the add operation of our AVL tree class.

The full syntax of Activity Diagrams is shown in Figure 7-8.

Activity diagrams have several elements in common with statecharts, including starting and ending activities, forks, joins, guards, and states (called *action states*). What is different is the decision points, the use of the states, and swim lanes. Decision points show branch points, based on guards, of program flow. The states mostly represent function invocations that have a single exit transition taken when the function completes. Unlike statecharts, there is no requirement that the action states be all within the same object. Swim lanes visually group the action states. They have no semantics but are often used to show concurrent threads of execution. Two stereotyped action states can be shown on the activity diagram in Figure 7-8, one for explicitly sending an event and one for explicitly receiving an event.

Sequence diagrams, shown in detail elsewhere in this book, can also be used to show algorithms within individual objects. Sequence diagrams usually show multiple objects collaborating by sending messages. These messages can be explicit function calls to show detailed algorithms. Sequence diagrams are weaker than activity diagrams in the sense that they don't show concurrency well.

Action states can themselves be decomposed into more-detailed activity diagrams or can use a different notation entirely. Again, pseudocode, text, or a mathematical formulation can be used as alternative representations.

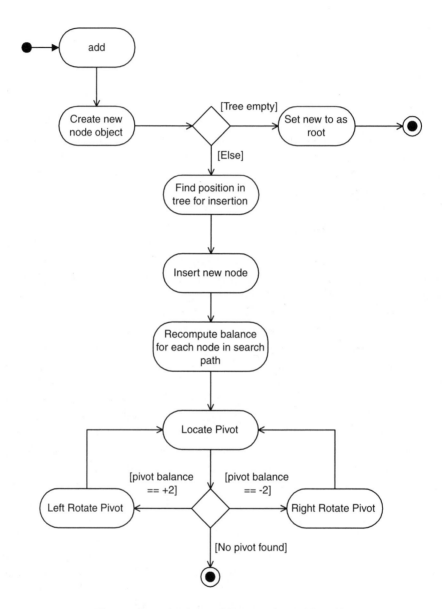

Figure 7-7: *Activity Diagram for Add Node*

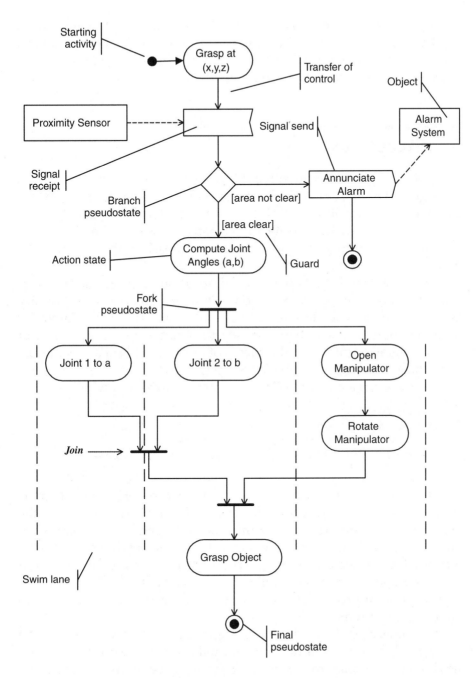

Figure 7-8: *Activity Diagram Notation*

Algorithms prescribe the activities that constitute a desired process [3]. That is, algorithms are, in their very essence, the decomposition of a function into smaller functions. This does not obviate the power of the object-oriented approach; it enhances it.

7.7 Exceptions

In reactive classes, exception handling is straightforward—exceptions are signals (associated with events) specified in the class state model that result in transitions being taken and actions being executed. In nonreactive classes, the specification means is less clear. The minimum requirements are to identify the exceptions raised by the class and the exceptions handled by the class.

Exception handling is a powerful addition to programming languages. Language-based exception handling provides two primary benefits. The first is that exceptions cannot be ignored. The C idiom for exception handling is to pass back a return value from a function, but this is generally ignored by the clients of the service. When was the last time you saw the return value for printf checked?

The correct usage for the C fopen function is the following:

```
FILE *fp;
if ( (fp = fopen("filename," "w")) == NULL) {
    /* do some corrective action */
    exit(1); /* pass error indicator up a level */
    };
```

Many programmers, to their credit, do just that. However, there is no enforcement that the errors be identified or handled. It is up to the good graces of the programmer and the code peer review process to ensure this is done. With exceptions, the error condition cannot be ignored. Unhandled exceptions are passed to each preceding caller until they are handled—a process called *unwinding the stack.* The terminate-on-exception approach has been successfully applied to programs in Ada and C++ for many years.

The other benefit of exception handling is that it separates the exception handling itself from the normal execution path. This simplifies both the normal processing code and the exception-handling code. For example, consider the following standard C code segment:

```
if ( (fp = ftest1(x,y,z))) == NULL) {
    /* do some corrective action */
    printf("Failure on ftest1");
    exit(1); /* pass error indicator up a level */
    };

if (!ftest2()) {
    /* do some corrective action */
    printf("failure on ftest2");
    exit(1);
    };

if (ftest3() == 0) {
    /* do some corrective action */
    printf("failure on ftest3");
    exit(1);
    };
```

This is arguably more difficult to understand than the following code:

```
// main code is simplified
try {
    ftest1(x,y,z);
    ftest2();
    ftest3();
}

// exception handling code is simplified
catch (test1Failure& t1) {
    cout <<"Failure on test1";
    throw; // rethrow same exception as in code above
}
catch (test2Failure& t2) {
    cout << "Failure on test2";
    throw;
};
catch (test3Failure& t3) {
    cout << "Failure on test3";
    throw;
};
```

The second code segment separates the normal code processing from the exception processing, making both clearer.

Each operation should define the exceptions that it throws, as well as the exceptions that it handles. There are reasons to avoid using formal C++ exceptions specifications [2], but the information should be captured nonetheless. Exceptions should never be used as an alternative way to terminate a function, in much the same way that a crowbar should not be used as an alternative key for your front door. Exceptions indicate that a serious fault requiring explicit handling has occurred.

Throwing exceptions is computationally expensive, because the stack must be unwound and objects destroyed. The presence of exception handling in your code adds a small overhead to your executing code (usually around 3%), even when exceptions are not thrown. Most compiler vendors offer nonstandard library versions that don't throw exceptions, and therefore this overhead can be avoided if exceptions are not used. Destructors should *never* throw exceptions or call operations that can throw exceptions, nor should the constructors of exception classes throw exceptions.[11]

Exception handling applies to operations (that is, functions) and is a complicating factor in the design of algorithms. In my experience, writing *correct* programs (that is, those that include complete and proper exception handling) is two to three times more difficult than writing code that merely "is supposed to work."[12]

Capturing the exception handling is fundamentally a part of the algorithm design and therefore can be represented along with the normal aspects of the algorithms. Exceptions can be explicitly shown as events on either statecharts or activity diagrams.

That still leaves two unanswered questions:

- What exceptions should I catch?
- What exceptions should I throw?

The general answer to the first question is that an operation should catch all exceptions that it has enough context to handle or that will make no sense to the current operation's caller.

The answer to the second is "all others." If an object does not have enough context to decide how to handle an exception, its caller might.

---

[11] In C++, if an exception is thrown while an unhandled exception is active, the program calls the internal function terminate() to exit the program. As the stack is unwound during exception-handling, local objects are destroyed by calling their destructors. Thus, destructors are called as part of the exception handling process. If a destructor is called because its object is being destroyed due to an exception, any exception it throws will terminate the program immediately.

[12] In contrast to prevailing opinion, I don't *think* this is solely due to my recently turning 40 and the associated loss of neural cells.

Perhaps the caller can retry a set of operations or execute an alternative algorithm.

At some point, exception handling runs out of stack to unwind, so at some global level, an exception policy must be implemented. The actions at this level depend on the severity of the exception, its impact on system safety, and the context of the system. In some cases, a severe error with safety ramifications should result in a system shutdown, because the system has a fail-safe state. Drill presses or robotic assembly systems typically deenergize in the presence of faults, because that is their fail-safe state. Other systems, such as medical monitoring systems, may continue by providing diminished functionality or reset and retry, because that is their safest course of action. Of course, some systems have no fail-safe state. For such systems, architectural means must be provided as an alternative to inline fault correction.

7.8 Summary

One definition of an object is "a set of tightly coupled attributes and the operations that act on them." Detailed design takes this microscopic view to fully specify the characteristics of objects than have been hitherto abstracted away and ignored. These characteristics include the structuring of the attributes and identification of their representational invariants, resolution of abstract message passing into object operations, and selection and definition of algorithms, including the handling of exceptional conditions.

Attributes are the data values subsumed within the objects. They must be represented in some fashion supported by the implementation language, but that is not enough. Most often, the underlying representation is larger than the valid ranges of the attribute, so the valid set of values of the attributes must be defined. Operations can then include checking the representational invariants to ensure that the object remains in a valid state.

Analysis models use the concept of message passing to represent the myriad ways that objects can communicate. Detailed design must decide upon the exact implementation of each message. Most often, messages are isomorphic with operations, but that is only true when the message source is always in the same thread of execution. When this is not true, other means, such as OS message queues, must be employed to provide interobject communication.

Many objects are themselves algorithmically trivial and do not require a detailed specification of the interaction of the operations and attributes. However, in every system, a significant proportion of objects have "rich" behavior. Although this requires additional work, it also provides the designer with an opportunity to optimize the system performance along some set of criteria. Algorithms include the handling of exceptions, and this is usually at least as complex as the primary algorithm itself. Algorithms can be expressed using state charts or activity diagrams. Other representations, such as mathematical equations, pseudocode, or text can be used, as well.

7.9 References

[1] Douglas, Bruce Powel, *Numerical Basic*. Indianapolis: Howard Sams, 1983.
[2] Meyers, Scott, *More-Effective C++: 35 New Ways to Improve Your Programs and Designs*. Reading, MA: Addison Wesley Longman, 1996.
[3] Harel, David, *Algorithmics*. Reading, MA: Addison Wesley Longman, 1993.
[4] Barry, Dave, *Dave Barry's Complete Guide to Guys*. New York: Fawcett Columbine Books, 1995.
[5] Neumann, Peter, *Computer-Related Risks*. Reading, MA: Addison Wesley Longman, 1995.

Appendix A

Notational Summary

This appendix provides a summary of the UML notation discussed in this book. It is organized by diagram type to facilitate its use as a reference during development.

Class Diagram

Shows the existence of classes and
relationships in a logical view of a system

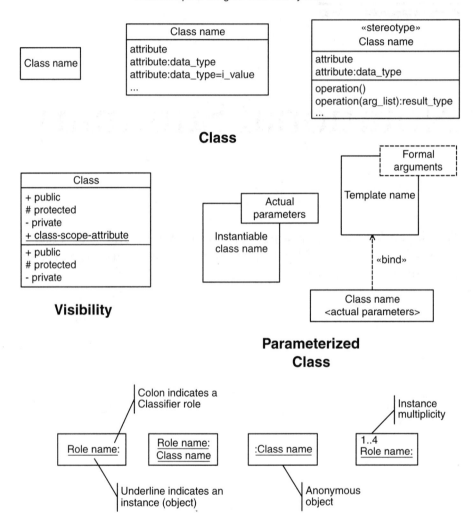

Class

Visibility

**Parameterized
Class**

Object

Class Diagram

Shows the existence of classes and
relationships in a logical view of a system

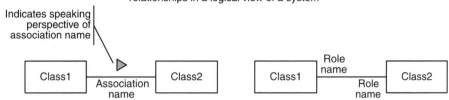

Multiplicity Symbol	Meaning
1	Exactly 1
0,1	Optionally 1
x..y	From x to y inclusive
a,b,c	Only specific values of a, b, and c
1..n	One or greater
*	0 or more

Role multiplicity

Associations may be labelled using any
combination of names, role names, and multiplicity

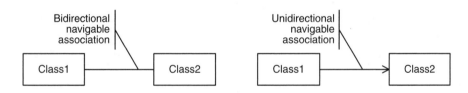

Association

Class Diagram

Shows the existence of classes and
relationships in a logical view of a system

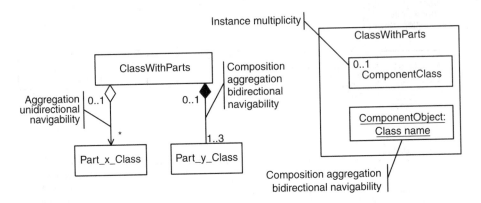

Aggregation and Composition

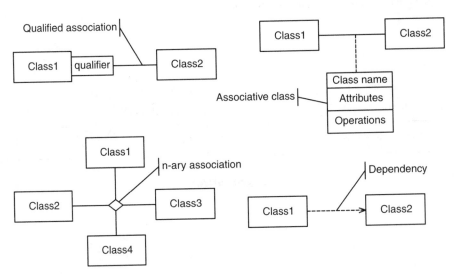

Advanced Associations

Class Diagram

Shows the existence of classes and
relationships in a logical view of a system

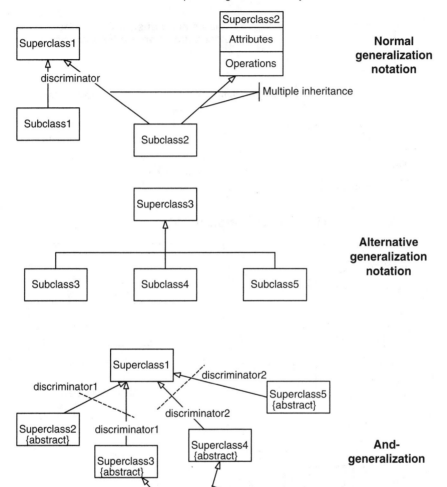

**Normal
generalization
notation**

**Alternative
generalization
notation**

**And-
generalization**

Generalization and Specialization

Class Diagram

Shows the existence of classes and
relationships in a logical view of a system.

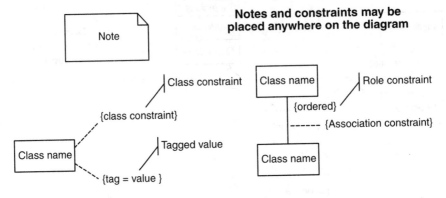

**Notes and constraints may be
placed anywhere on the diagram**

Notes and Constraints

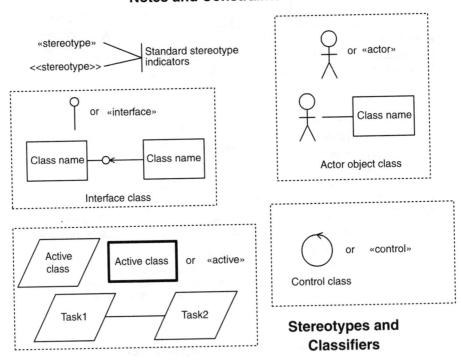

Stereotypes and
Classifiers

Collaboration Diagram

Shows a sequenced set of messages illustrating a specific
example of object interaction.

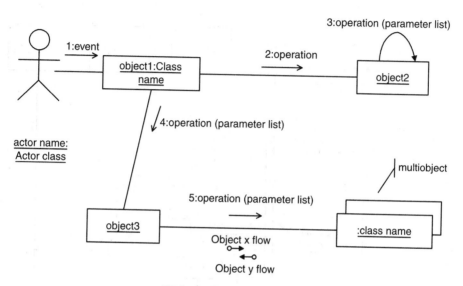

Object Collaboration

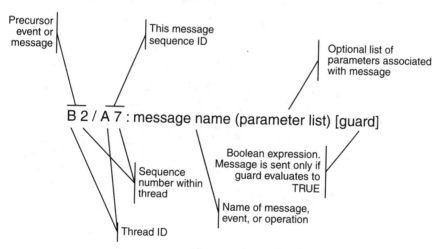

Message Syntax

Sequence Diagram

Shows a sequenced set of messages illustrating a specific example of object interaction.

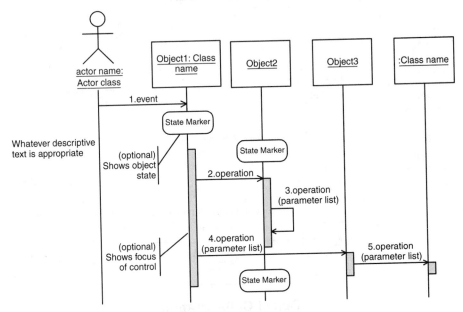

Sequence diagrams have two dimensions. The vertical dimension usually represents time, the horizontal represents different objects. These dimensions may be reversed.

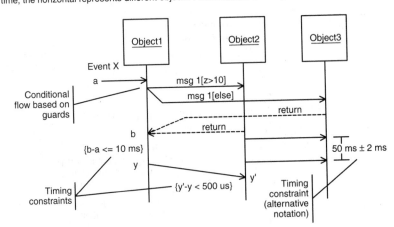

Advanced Sequence Diagrams

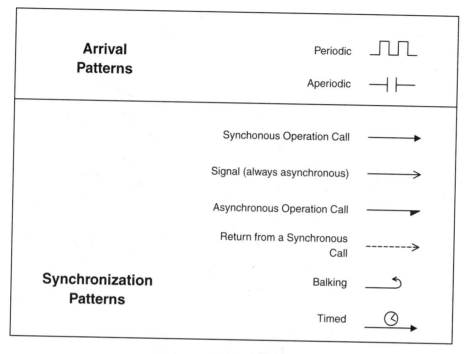

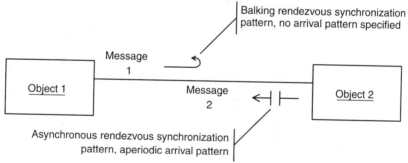

Message Stereotypes

Use Cases

Use cases show primary areas of collaboration between the system and the actors in its environment. Use cases are isomorphic with function points.

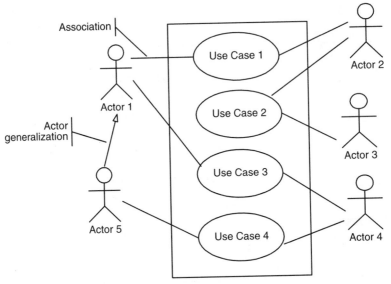

Use Case Diagram

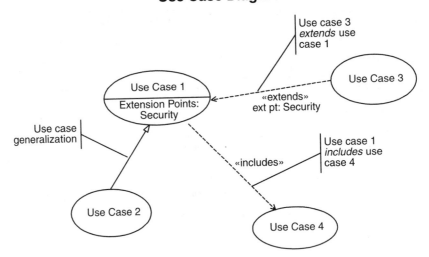

Use Case Relationships

Implementation Diagrams

Implementation diagrams show the run-time dependencies and packaging structure of the deployed system.

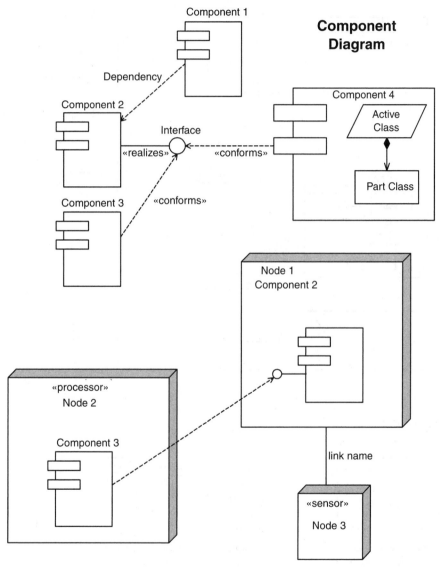

Component Diagram

Deployment Diagram

Package Diagram

Shows a grouping of model elements. Packages may also appear within class and object diagrams.

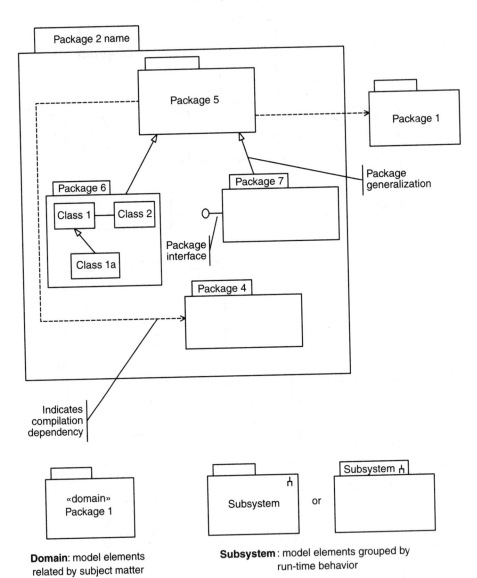

Package 2 name

Package 5

Package 1

Package generalization

Package 6

Class 1 — Class 2

Class 1a

Package 7

Package interface

Package 4

Indicates compilation dependency

«domain»
Package 1

Domain: model elements related by subject matter

Subsystem   or   Subsystem

Subsystem: model elements grouped by run-time behavior

Statechart

Shows the sequences of states for a reactive class or interaction during its life in response to stimuli, together with its responses and actions.

State name

entry / action-list
event-name:action-list
do / activity-list
defer/ event-list
...
exit /action-list

State icon

Name of the event triggering the transition

List of actions to be executed when transition taken

event-name '['guard-condition']' '/' action-list

Boolean condition must evalutate to TRUE for the transition to be taken

Transitions

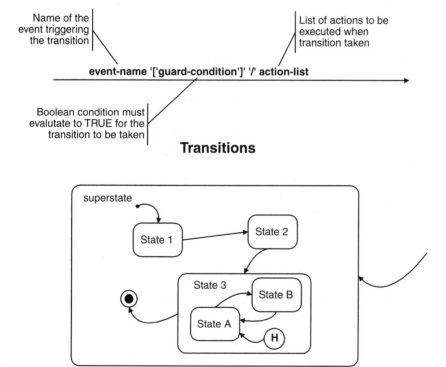

Nested States

Statechart

Shows the sequences of states for a reactive class or interaction during its life
in response to stimuli, together with its responses and actions.

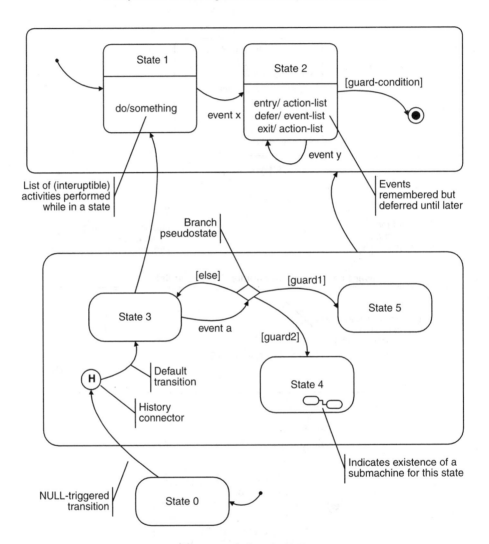

Sequential substates

Statechart

Shows the sequences of states for a reactive class or interaction during its life
in response to stimuli, together with its responses and actions.

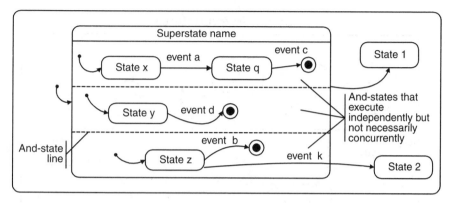

Orthogonal Substates (and-states)

Symbol	Symbol Name	Symbol	Symbol Name
C or ◇	Branch Pseudostate *(type of junction pseudostate)*	H	(Shallow) History Pseudostate
T or ◉	Terminal, or Final, Pseudostate	H*	(Deep) History Pseudostate
* or n	Synch Pseudostate		Initial, or Default, Pseudostate
	Fork Pseudostate		
	Join Pseudostate		Junction Pseudostate
[g] [g]	Choice Point Pseudostate		Merge Junction Pseudostate *(type of junction pseudostate)*
		label	Stub Pseudostate

Pseudostates

Statechart

Shows the sequences of states for a reactive class or interaction during its life in response to stimuli, together with its responses and actions.

Synch Pseudostates

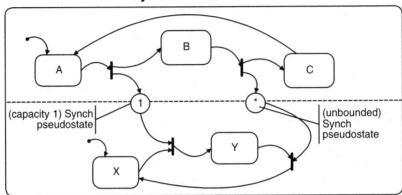

(capacity 1) Synch pseudostate

(unbounded) Synch pseudostate

Submachines

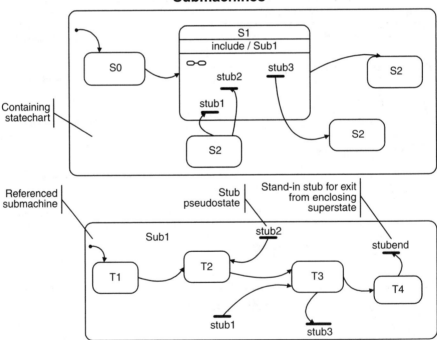

Containing statechart

Referenced submachine

Stub pseudostate

Stand-in stub for exit from enclosing superstate

Activity Diagrams

Activity Diagrams are a specialized form of state diagrams in which most or all transitions are taken when the state activity is completed.

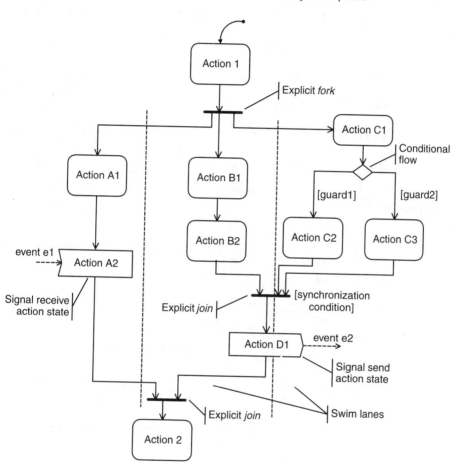

Timing Diagrams

Timing diagrams show the explicit change of state along a linear time axis.
(Timing diagrams are not in the UML standard.)

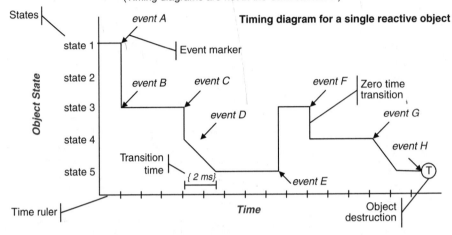

Timing diagram for a single reactive object

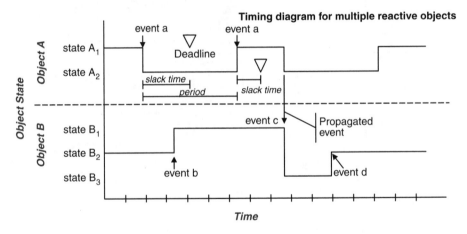

Timing diagram for multiple reactive objects

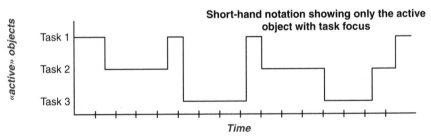

Short-hand notation showing only the active object with task focus

Timing Diagrams

Shading can be used to show execution state for «active» objects.
(Timing Diagrams are not in the UML standard.)

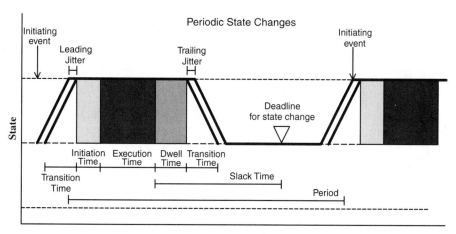

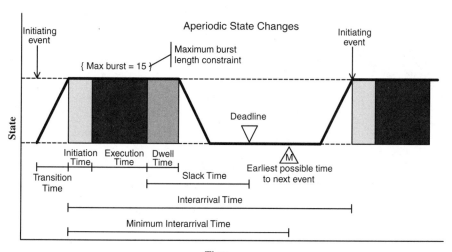

Appendix B

The Future of the UML for Real-Time

B.1 Standardization in the Object Management Group

The Object Management Group (OMG) contains more than 800 companies joined together for a common purpose—to promote standardization within the object community. Its primary efforts are focused on two complementary technologies—Common Object Request Broker Architecture (CORBA) and the Unified Modeling Language (UML). The process of standardization is not controlled by a single member company but rather is controlled by a process of technical evaluation and member consensus and voting. It is, in fact, the OMG that owns the UML and controls when and how it will be updated and modified.

A standard in the OMG typically follows a well-defined process. First, a Request for Proposal (RFP) is issued to address some identified need. RFPs contain mandatory and optional requirements that the technical aspects of the submissions must address. Member companies then band together[1] to create technical submissions that address the

---

[1] The OMG allows different levels of membership. Only voting members can submit against an RFP.

mandatory and optional requirements of the RFP. Sometimes, there are multiple submissions, and, sometimes, all the interested members form a single submissions group. Once the submissions deadline on the RFP has expired, a relevant task force (TF) of the OMG evaluates the submissions, usually for a period of 120 days. Following that, the submitters may have to modify their submission to address identified weaknesses or errors. This usually takes several more months. Once the TF believes the submissions are ready for a vote, the OMG votes on acceptance of the submissions, either selecting one of the submissions or rejecting all. Finally, a revision task force (RTF) is created to work out any technical errors or omissions in the submission and integrate it with the preexisting standards, possibly replacing or updating the original standards in the process.

Standards bodies are political, as well as technical, entities. The entire RFP-submission-revision process takes a couple of years or more to occur. It is unlikely that an RFP issued in January 2000 will result in an updated standard before 2002. This is because of the sheer amount of work involved, as well as the politicking, voting, evaluation, and approvals required.

The important point here is that this is *never* driven by a single company, so if you ever here a tool vendor say, "We're submitting this as a proposal to the OMG, and because we're <insert Big Name Vendor here>, it will, of course, become a standard," you should treat whatever they have to say as so much marketing hyperbole.

As one of the co-chairs of the Real-Time Analysis and Design Working Group (RTAD-WG) of the OMG (representing I-Logix, one of the core developers of the original UML submission and its subsequent revision), I am aware of the content and timeframes for RFPs that relate to the real-time and embedded development community, as well as being an active participant in their creation and in their technical content. Currently, there are a number of RFPs either issued or waiting to be issued that are especially relevant to the readers of this text. The purpose of this appendix is to let the readers know what kinds of changes to expect in the UML over the next few years.

At this time, four RFPs are particularly relevant: the Action Semantics RFP; the Scheduling, Performance, and Time RFP; the Non-Time-Related Quality of Service RFP; and the Complex Systems Modeling RFP. Of these, only the first two are issued at the time of this writing. They are available to the public at the OMG Web site *www.omg.org*. One of the important evaluation criteria for each of these RFPs is that minimalist submissions will be favored. Ideally, a submission would demonstrate the adequacy of the existing UML to address the RFP requirements. Failing that, submissions that introduce a minimal number of changes to the existing standard will be preferred.

It should be noted that each of these RFPs is more of a set of tweaks than a substantial change to the existing UML metamodel. They are relatively minor enhancements meant to address perceived shortcomings.

B.2 Action Semantics

This RFP came about because the 1.1 revision of the UML standard (the first released standard) had only a vague notion of what actions were. For the most part, they were relegated to "uninterpreted text." This is a problem for a couple of reasons. First, in order for tools, such as the I-Logix tool Rhapsody to automatically generate code from UML models, it needs to understand the precise semantics of actions and their execution. In Rhapsody's case, I-Logix made very reasonable assumptions about what those were based on their extensive theoretical knowledge[2] and practical experience in building executable models. The assumptions are very much within the spirit of the UML and are compliant with the specification. However, other tools are likely to make different assumptions. One of the major benefits of the UML is the potential for *model interchange* among tools. If the vendors do not support a common detailed action semantics metamodel, the possibility of exchanging models and having them execute in exactly the same way is small.

The name of this RFP is *Precise Action Semantics for the UML: Request for Proposal.* It is available on the OMG Web site as document ad/98-08-05. This RFP requires submissions to make minimal changes to the UML specification and even then represents *optional* features to be added to the UML.

---

[2] David Harel, inventor of statecharts, is one of the founders of I-Logix. He, Eran Gery, and I all contributed to the original development of the UML. Eran Gery was also a principal participant in the UML1.1 RTF, heading up the statechart semantics subgroup.

The author is part of a group (of mostly tool vendors) constructing a precise action semantics metamodel as part of the submission against this RFP. We expect this submission to be made in the spring of 2000, which, if all proceeds smoothly, could result in a modification to the existing UML standard by 2001 or 2002.

B.3 Scheduling, Performance, and Time

This RFP came about because of the need to analyze UML models (in a portable way) for schedulability and performance. This has a number of aspects, some semantic, others purely notational. The semantic issues have to do with the ability to represent different kinds of time in the metamodel and somehow link these times with various relevant existing metaclasses, such as operations, active classes, and state machines.

The requirements of this RFP may be grouped into several categories:

- Models of time and clocks
  The submission must provide means to model time and its passage, as well as sources of time, such as timers and clocks.

- Models of resources
  Because resources lie at the heart of much of what makes schedulability analysis difficult, the submission must model different kinds of resources, including physical resources (such as CPUs and buses) and logical resources (such as shared data, message queues, locks, and so forth).

- Models of concurrency
  The submission must provide a means to model different kinds of schedulers, tasks, and how these things map to resources.

The RFP is called *UML Profile for Scheduling, Performance, and Time: Request for Proposal* and is OMG document number ad/99-03-13. By RFP standards, this one is large and relatively complex, containing many requirements that submissions must address. Nevertheless, we anticipate very little change to the existing UML metamodel and its semantics.

I am currently heading up a team that is working on a submission against this RFP. Our goal is to have a submission finalized by spring 2000. If all goes well, the RTF can begin work in late 2000, resulting in a modification to the UML standard by as early as 2002. Incidentally, I intend that timing diagrams, as presented in this book, will be an important part of the notation added in this submission.

B.4 Non-Time-Related Quality of Service

At the time of this writing, this RFP is not yet written. However, there is a consensus within the RTAD-WG that the UML must be able to model issues such as reliability and safety in order to be used in mission-critical and safety-relevant applications. Many of the quality of service requirements for application systems are time-related. As such, the requirements of the previous RFP should handle them. This RFP is targeted at the quality of service requirements unrelated to time or schedulability. The writing of this RFP is expected to be starting in late 1999.

B.5 Complex Systems Modeling RFP

This RFP is also not yet written. There is a feeling among some, but not all, members of the RTAD-WG that the UML's support for modeling large and complex systems is inadequate. This is a controversial view in light of the UML's support for packaging, components, and subsystems and is likely to be the most contentious and, potentially, the most drawn out RFP mentioned in this chapter. The writing of this RFP is expected to begin in early to mid 2000.

Index

317

Object Solutions
Managing the Object-Oriented Project
Grady Booch
Addison-Wesley Object Technology Series

Object Solutions is a direct outgrowth of Grady Booch's experience with object-oriented projects in development around the world. This book focuses on the development process, and is the perfect resource for developers and managers who want to implement object technologies for the first time or refine their existing object-oriented development practice. Drawing upon his knowledge of strategies used in both successful and unsuccessful projects, the author offers pragmatic advice for applying object technologies and controlling projects effectively.

0-8053-0594-7 • Paperback • 336 pages • ©1996

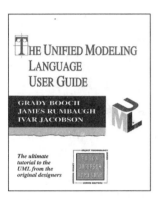

The Unified Modeling Language User Guide
Grady Booch, James Rumbaugh, and Ivar Jacobson
Addison-Wesley Object Technology Series

The Unified Modeling Language User Guide is a two-color introduction to the core eighty percent of the Unified Modeling Language, approaching it in a layered fashion and showing the application of the UML to modeling problems across a wide variety of application domains. This landmark book is suitable for developers unfamiliar with the UML or modeling in general, and will also be useful to experienced developers who wish to learn how to apply the UML to advanced problems.

0-201-57168-4 • Hardcover • 512 pages • ©1999

Surviving Object-Oriented Projects
A Manager's Guide
Alistair Cockburn
Addison-Wesley Object Technology Series

This book allows you to survive and ultimately succeed with an object-oriented project. Alistair Cockburn draws on his personal experience and extensive knowledge to provide the information that managers need to combat the unforeseen challenges that await them during project implementation. Independent of language or programming environment, the book supports its key points through short case studies taken from real object-oriented projects, and an appendix collects these guidelines and solutions into brief "crib sheets"—ideal for handy reference.

0-201-49834-0 • Paperback • 272 pages • ©1998

Doing Hard Time
Developing Real-Time Systems with UML, Objects, Frameworks, and Patterns
Bruce Powel Douglass
Addison-Wesley Object Technology Series

Doing Hard Time is written to facilitate the daunting process of developing real-time systems. The author presents an embedded systems programming methodology that has been proven successful in practice. The process outlined in this book allows application developers to apply practical techniques—garnered from the mainstream areas of object-oriented software development—to meet the demanding qualifications of real-time programming.

0-201-49837-5 • Hardcover with CD-ROM • 800 pages • ©1999

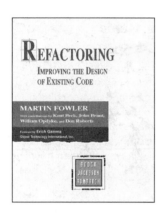

Refactoring
Improving the Design of Existing Code
Martin Fowler, with contributions by Kent Beck, John Brant, William Opdyke, and Don Roberts
Addison-Wesley Object Technology Series

Refactoring is the process of changing a software system in such a way that it does not alter the external behavior of the code, yet improves its external structure. In this book, Martin Fowler, Kent Beck, John Brant, William Opdyke, and Don Roberts show you where opportunities for refactoring can typically be found, and how to go about reworking a bad design into a good one. In addition to discussing the various techniques of refactoring, the authors a detailed catalog of more than seventy proven refactorings.

0-201-48567-2 • Hardcover • 464 pages • ©1999

Real-Time Programming
A Guide to 32-bit Embedded Development
Rick Grehan, Robert Moote, and Ingo Cyliax

This book teaches you how to write software for real-time embedded systems—software that meets unforgiving objectives under numerous constraints. The authors present the key topics that are relevant to all forms of real-time embedded development and offer complete coverage of the embedded development cycle, from design through implementation. A practical, hands-on approach is emphasized, allowing you to start building real-time embedded systems immediately using commercial, off-the-shelf hardware and software.

0-201-48540-0 • Paperback with CD-ROM • 720 pages • ©1999

Software Reuse
Architecture, Process and Organization for Business Success
Ivar Jacobson, Martin Griss, and Patrik Jonsson
Addison-Wesley Object Technology Series

This book brings software engineers, designers, programmers, and their managers a giant step closer to a future in which object-oriented component-based software engineering is the norm. Jacobson, Griss, and Jonsson develop a coherent model and set of guidelines for ensuring success with large-scale, systematic, object-oriented reuse. Their framework, referred to as "Reuse-Driven Software Engineering Business" (Reuse Business), deals systematically with the key business process, architecture, and organization issues that hinder success with reuse.

0-201-92476-5 • Hardcover • 528 pages • ©1997

The Unified Software Development Process
Ivar Jacobson, Grady Booch, and James Rumbaugh
Addison-Wesley Object Technology Series

The Unified Software Development Process goes beyond other object-oriented analysis and design methods by detailing a family of processes that incorporate the complete lifecycle of software development. This new book, representing the collaboration of Ivar Jacobson, Grady Booch, and James Rumbaugh, clearly describes the different higher-level constructs—notation as well as semantics—used in the models. Thus, stereotypes such as use cases and actors, packages, classes, interfaces, active classes, processes and threads, nodes, and most relations are described intuitively in the context of a model.

0-201-57169-2 • Hardcover • 512 pages • ©1999

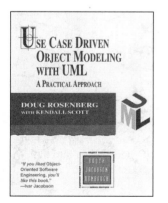

Use Case Driven Object Modeling with UML
A Practical Approach
Doug Rosenberg, with Kendall Scott
Addison-Wesley Object Technology Series

This book presents a streamlined approach to UML modeling that includes a minimal but sufficient set of diagrams and techniques you can use to get from use cases to code quickly and efficiently. *Use Case Driven Object Modeling with UML* provides practical guidance that will allow software developers to produce UML models quickly and efficiently, while maintaining traceability from user requirements through detailed design and coding. The authors draw upon their extensive industry experience to present proven methods for driving the object modeling process forward from use cases in a simple and straightforward manner.

0-201-43289-7 • Paperback • 192 pages • ©1999

Software Project Management

A Unified Framework

Walker Royce

Addison-Wesley Object Technology Series

This book presents a new management framework uniquely suited to the complexities of modern software development. Walker Royce's pragmatic perspective exposes the shortcomings of many well-accepted management priorities and equips software professionals with state-of-the-art knowledge derived from his twenty years of successful from-the-trenches management experience. In short, the book provides the software industry with field-proven benchmarks for making tactical decisions and strategic choices that will enhance an organization's probability of success.

0-201-30958-0 • Hardcover • 448 pages • ©1998

The Unified Modeling Language Reference Manual

James Rumbaugh, Ivar Jacobson, and Grady Booch

Addison-Wesley Object Technology Series

James Rumbaugh, Ivar Jacobson, and Grady Booch have created the definitive reference to the UML. This two-color book covers every aspect and detail of the UML and presents the modeling language in a useful reference format that serious software architects or programmers should have on their bookshelf. The book is organized by topic and designed for quick access. The authors also provide the necessary information to enable existing OMT, Booch, and OOSE notation users to make the transition to UML. The book provides an overview of the semantic foundation of the UML through a concise appendix.

0-201-30998-X • Hardcover with CD-ROM • 576 pages • ©1999

Applying Use Cases

A Practical Guide

Geri Schneider and Jason P. Winters

Addison-Wesley Object Technology Series

Applying Use Cases provides a practical and clear introduction to developing use cases, demonstrating their use via a continuing case study. Using the Unified Software Development Process as a framework and the Unified Modeling Language as a notation, the authors step the reader through applying use cases in the different phases of the process, focusing on where and how use cases are best applied. The book also offers insight into the common mistakes and pitfalls that can plague an object-oriented project.

0-201-30981-5 • Paperback • 208 pages • ©1998

An Embedded Software Primer

David E. Simon

This book is an accessible introduction for any programmer who wants to make the transition from more traditional software development to embedded systems. David Simon introduces the broad range of applications for embedded software and then reviews each major issue facing developers. *An Embedded Software Primer* describes the implications of limited memory and processor resources and shows how embedded software handles external events without human intervention. This book explores the role of real-time operating systems, and shows how developers can reduce time to market without compromising quality.

0-201-61569-X • Paperback with CD-ROM • 448 pages • ©1999

Addison-Wesley Computer and Engineering Publishing Group

How to Interact with Us

1. Visit our Web site

http://www.awl.com/cseng

When you think you've read enough, there's always more content for you at Addison-Wesley's web site. Our web site contains a directory of complete product information including:

- Chapters
- Exclusive author interviews
- Links to authors' pages
- Tables of contents
- Source code

You can also discover what tradeshows and conferences Addison-Wesley will be attending, read what others are saying about our titles, and find out where and when you can meet our authors and have them sign your book.

2. Subscribe to Our Email Mailing Lists

Subscribe to our electronic mailing lists and be the first to know when new books are publishing. Here's how it works: Sign up for our electronic mailing at **http://www.awl.com/cseng/mailinglists.html**. Just select the subject areas that interest you and you will receive notification via email when we publish a book in that area.

3. Contact Us via Em

cepubprof@awl.c

Ask general questions about our bo
Sign up for our electronic mailing l
Submit corrections for our web

bexpress@awl.c

Request an Addison-Wesley cata
Get answers to questions regarc
your order or our produ

innovations@awl.c

Request a current Innovations Newslet

webmaster@awl.c

Send comments about our web

jcs@awl.c

Submit a book propc
Send errata for an Addison-Wesley bc

cepubpublicity@awl.c

Request a review copy for a member of the me
interested in reviewing new Addison-Wesley ti

We encourage you to patronize the many fine retailers who stock Addison-Wesley titles. Visit our online directory to find stores near you or visit our online store: **http.//store.awl.com/** or call **800-824-7799**.

Addison Wesley Longman
Computer and Engineering Publishing Group
One Jacob Way, Reading, Massachusetts 01867 USA
TEL 781-944-3700 • FAX 781-942-3076